CREATING
the covenant

Participant Guide

Episodes 1–8

 Abingdon Press

COVENANT BIBLE STUDY
PARTICIPANT GUIDES (CREATING, LIVING, TRUSTING)

Covenant Bible Study resources include:

Creating, Living, and Trusting Participant Guides, ISBN 978-1-5018-4015-9
Creating the Covenant: Participant Guide, ISBN 978-1-4267-7216-0 (large print ISBN 978-1-63088-625-7)
Living the Covenant: Participant Guide, ISBN 978-1-4267-7217-7 (large print ISBN 978-1-63088-626-4)
Trusting the Covenant: Participant Guide, ISBN 978-1-4267-7218-4 (large print ISBN 978-1-63088-627-1)

Covenant Bible Study: Covenant Meditations, ISBN 978-1-4267-7220-7
Covenant Bible Study: Covenant Meditations ePub, ISBN 978-1-4267-7221-4

Covenant Bible Study: Leader Guide, ISBN 978-1-4267-7223-8
Covenant Bible Study: Leader Guide ePub, ISBN 978-1-4267-7225-2

Covenant Bible Study: DVD Video (set of three), ISBN 978-1-4267-8678-5
Covenant Bible Study: MP4 Video Episodes (download individually from CovenantBibleStudy.com)

CEB Study Bible, hardcover ISBN 978-1-6092-6028-6, decotone ISBN 978-1-6092-6040-8
CEB Study Bible: Large Print Edition, hardcover ISBN 978-1-60926-176-4

To order resources or to obtain additional information for participants, Covenant groups, and leaders, go to www.CovenantBibleStudy.com or to www.cokesbury.com. All print resources are available exclusively from these online sites, from Cokesbury reps, or by calling Cokesbury (800-672-1789).

Contents

Creating the Covenant

Other Covenant Modules

Living the Covenant

Trusting the Covenant

CREATING
the covenant

Covenant Group Participants and Leader

Name	Phone	E-mail

Covenant Group Meeting Location _____

Covenant Group Meeting Day and Time _____

CovenantBibleStudy.com username _____ password _____

Bible Readings at a Glance

Sign up with your group at CovenantBibleStudy.com to get daily readings by e-mail from your group leader.

Episode 2

Day 1	Genesis 1–3	Creation and the human role within it	❑
Day 2	Genesis 6:5–9:17; 11:1-9	End of the old world—beginning of the new world	❑
Day 3	Genesis 12; 15; 17; 22	Abraham and nationhood	❑
Day 4	Genesis 27–28; 32–33	Jacob and the biblical family	❑
Day 5	Genesis 37; 41; 43; 45; 50	Joseph and his brothers in Egypt	❑
Day 6	Covenant Meditation on Genesis 1:26-31	Who are we?	❑
Day 7	Group Meeting Experience with Genesis 9:7-17	The Bible's first covenant	❑

Episode 3

Day 1	Exodus 1–4	Oppression, survival, and the charge of a leader	❑
Day 2	Exodus 13:17–15:21	Crossing boundaries for freedom	❑
Day 3	Exodus 20–24	Sinai covenant	❑
Day 4	Leviticus 19–22	Holiness Code	❑
Day 5	Numbers 11–14	In the wilderness	❑
Day 6	Covenant Meditation on Leviticus 19:1-2	You must be holy because God is holy.	❑
Day 7	Group Meeting Experience with Exodus 20:1-17	Ten Commandments	❑

Episode 4

☐ Day 1	Mark 1–4	God's kingdom is near.
☐ Day 2	Mark 12–14	God's kingdom is not here yet.
☐ Day 3	Matthew 4–7	New instruction for a new kingdom
☐ Day 4	Matthew 11–13	New way of life
☐ Day 5	Matthew 18–22	Jesus is the new Teacher.
☐ Day 6	Covenant Meditation on Mark 10:13-16	God's kingdom belongs to people like these.
☐ Day 7	Group Meeting Experience with Matthew 9:18-33	Jesus as deliverer

Episode 5

☐ Day 1	Romans 1–3	God's solution for the human condition
☐ Day 2	Galatians 1:1–3:5; 5:2-12	The sufficiency of Christ's sacrifice for salvation
☐ Day 3	Galatians 3:6–4:7; Romans 4	Righteousness: Abraham's trust in God's promise
☐ Day 4	Romans 5–8; Galatians 5:13-25	Reconciliation with God; freedom in the Spirit
☐ Day 5	Romans 9–11	God's faithfulness to Israel
☐ Day 6	Covenant Meditation on Galatians 3:23-29	All are one in Christ Jesus.
☐ Day 7	Group Meeting Experience with Romans 14:1–15:2	Practicing grace

Episode 6

☐ Day 1	Hebrews 1–2; Psalm 8	Praise for God's Son
☐ Day 2	Hebrews 3–4; Numbers 14	Faithfulness and loyalty
☐ Day 3	Hebrews 4:14–7:28; Psalm 110	Jesus is our covenant mediator.
☐ Day 4	Hebrews 8:1–10:18; Leviticus 16	Jesus grants us entrance to the most holy place.
☐ Day 5	Hebrews 10:19–13:25	Faith hall of fame
☐ Day 6	Covenant Meditation on Hebrews 6:10-11	Grateful love serves.
☐ Day 7	Group Meeting Experience with Hebrews 5:11–6:12	Honor

Episode 7

Day 1	1 Corinthians 1–4	Immature boasting	❏
Day 2	1 Corinthians 7–10	My freedom is good, but it's not always good for others.	❏
Day 3	1 Corinthians 11–14	No person is better than another.	❏
Day 4	1 Corinthians 15; 2 Corinthians 1:1-11; 4–6	Our faith is pointless without Christ's resurrection.	❏
Day 5	1 Corinthians 16; 2 Corinthians 7–9	Cheerful generosity	❏
Day 6	Covenant Meditation on 2 Corinthians 4:7-12	God will rescue us.	❏
Day 7	Group Meeting Experience with 1 Corinthians 13:4-8	Love never fails.	❏

Episode 8

Day 1	Deuteronomy 5–9	The Ten Commandments and the greatest commandment	❏
Day 2	Deuteronomy 29–32	Old and new covenants	❏
Day 3	Joshua 1–2; 23–24	Moses reinvented	❏
Day 4	Judges 1–2; 19–21	Downward spiral	❏
Day 5	1 Samuel 13–15; 28:3-25	Tragedy of King Saul	❏
Day 6	Covenant Meditation on Deuteronomy 6:4-9	Renewing the covenant	❏
Day 7	Group Meeting Experience with Deuteronomy 6:1-19	A portrait of the covenant	❏

Old Testament

Book of the Bible	Abbreviation	Episode	Participant Guide Page
Genesis	Gen	2	Creating, 21
Exodus	Exod	3	Creating, 31
Leviticus	Lev	3	Creating, 31
Numbers	Num	3	Creating, 31
Deuteronomy	Deut	8	Creating, 83
Joshua	Josh	8	Creating, 83
Judges	Judg	8	Creating, 83
Ruth	Ruth	9	Living, 9
1 Samuel	1 Sam	8	Creating, 83
2 Samuel	2 Sam	11	Living, 33
1 Kings	1 Kgs	11	Living, 33
2 Kings	2 Kgs	11	Living, 33
1 Chronicles	1 Chron	22	Trusting, 65
2 Chronicles	2 Chron	22	Trusting, 65
Ezra	Ezra	22	Trusting, 65
Nehemiah	Neh	22	Trusting, 65
Esther	Esth	9	Living, 9
Job	Job	19	Trusting, 31
Psalms	Ps	18	Trusting, 21
Proverbs	Prov	13	Living, 55
Ecclesiastes	Eccl	13	Living, 55
Song of Songs	Song	9	Living, 9
Isaiah	Isa	16 21	Living, 85 Trusting, 53
Jeremiah	Jer	20	Trusting, 41
Lamentations	Lam	20	Trusting, 41
Ezekiel	Ezek	20	Trusting, 41
Daniel	Dan	23	Trusting, 75
Hosea	Hos	16	Living, 85
Joel	Joel	16	Living, 85
Amos	Amos	16	Living, 85
Obadiah	Obad	16	Living, 85
Jonah	Jon	16	Living, 85
Micah	Mic	16	Living, 85
Nahum	Nah	16	Living, 85
Habakkuk	Hab	16	Living, 85
Zephaniah	Zeph	16	Living, 85
Haggai	Hag	16	Living, 85
Zechariah	Zech	16	Living, 85
Malachi	Mal	16	Living, 85

New Testament

Book of the Bible	Abbreviation	Episode	Participant Guide Page
Matthew	Matt	4	Creating, 41
Mark	Mark	4	Creating, 41
Luke	Luke	10	Living, 21
John	John	17	Trusting, 9
Acts	Acts	10	Living, 21
Romans	Rom	5	Creating, 51
1 Corinthians	1 Cor	7	Creating, 71
2 Corinthians	2 Cor	7	Creating, 71
Galatians	Gal	5	Creating, 51
Ephesians	Eph	14	Living, 65
Philippians	Phil	14	Living, 65
Colossians	Col	14	Living, 65
1 Thessalonians	1 Thess	12	Living, 43
2 Thessalonians	2 Thess	12	Living, 43
1 Timothy	1 Tim	12	Living, 43
2 Timothy	2 Tim	12	Living, 43
Titus	Titus	12	Living, 43
Philemon	Phlm	14	Living, 65
Hebrews	Heb	6	Creating, 63
James	Jas	15	Living, 75
1 Peter	1 Pet	15	Living, 75
2 Peter	2 Pet	15	Living, 75
1 John	1 John	17	Trusting, 9
2 John	2 John	17	Trusting, 9
3 John	3 John	17	Trusting, 9
Jude	Jude	15	Living, 75
Revelation	Rev	24	Trusting, 85

Covenant Creative Team

Editorial

Theodore Hiebert, Old Testament Editor
Jaime Clark-Soles, New Testament Editor
Magrey deVega, Leadership Editor
Pam Hawkins, Meditations Editor
David Teel, Project Manager
Paul Franklyn, General Editor and Associate Publisher
Neil M. Alexander, Publisher

Video Cohosts

Christine Chakoian, Senior Pastor,
    First Presbyterian Church, Lake Forest, IL
Shane Stanford, Senior Pastor,
    Christ United Methodist Church, Memphis, TN

Writers: Creating the Covenant

Episode 2	Theodore Hiebert, Francis A. McGaw Professor of Old Testament, McCormick Theological Seminary, Chicago, IL
Episode 3	Alejandro F. Botta, Associate Professor of Hebrew Bible, Boston University, Boston, MA
Episode 4	Stephanie B. Crowder, Adjunct Professor of Biblical Studies, McCormick Theological Seminary, Chicago, IL
Episode 5	Diane Grace Chen, Associate Professor of New Testament, Palmer Theological Seminary, King of Prussia, PA
Episode 6	David A. deSilva, Trustees' Distinguished Professor of New Testament and Greek, Ashland Theological Seminary, Ashland, OH
Episode 7	Monya A. Stubbs, Former Associate Professor of New Testament, Austin Presbyterian Theological Seminary, Austin, TX
Episode 8	Brent A. Strawn, Professor of Old Testament, Candler School of Theology, Atlanta, GA

Production and Design

Christy Lynch, Production Editor
Jeff Moore, Packaging and Interior Design
Emily Keafer Lambright, Interior Design
PerfecType, Typesetting

CovenantBibleStudy.com

Christie Durand, Analyst
Gregory Davis, Developer
David Burns, Designer
Dan Heile, Database Analyst

Video Production: Revolution Pictures, Inc.

Randy Brewer, Executive Producer
Michelle Abnet, Producer
Ry Cox, Codirector
Jeff Venable, Codirector
Chris Adams, Photography Director
Brandon Eller, Prop Master
Dave Donnelly, Post Editor
Perry Trest, Colorist

Creating the Covenant

RELATIONSHIPS
Reading the Bible to live and love well

Covenant Prayer

For those who want to learn how to love God and others

They read aloud from the scroll, the Instruction from God, explaining and interpreting it so the people could understand what they heard. (Nehemiah 8:8)

For those whom God makes new

This day is holy to our LORD. Don't be sad, because the joy from the LORD is your strength! (Nehemiah 8:10)

OUR LONGING FOR RELATIONSHIP

Covenant names our yearning to live and belong in loving relationships with self, God, and others.

LIFE THAT FITS AND CONNECTS

We probably have seen scrapbooks or family photo albums (in binders, books, or online). What kind of pictures or mementos do you find in books like this? Did your family keep a scrapbook or photo album from your childhood?

Covenant Bible Study promises new life that fits and connects with God and others. Life that makes sense. Life that finds its source in God. Life lived together.

The Bible is a book like no other, and reading it is a rewarding experience. The assumption is that reading the Bible will improve our lives. But in spite of this assumption, many of us try to read this book and give up—usually after trying to read it from cover to cover. We often become confused by the strange names, places, and events that seem so distant from our daily lives. It can make us feel defeated, and so we throw in the towel and trust that someone else (pastor, scholar, or teacher) will make sense of this book and pass on the "high points" to the rest of us.

But our anxiety about reading the Bible may be connected to a deeper frustration and longing—a longing to connect with and come alive to something real, something lasting that promises to help us live well. Awash in a world of flickering words and images on glowing screens, we thirst for depth, for something that faithfully delivers on a promise to make a difference where we learn, work, and play. We want more than a superficial faith. Yet for many, the Bible seems like the last place for this kind of reality check.

Covenant Bible Study is one way to dispel this anxiety and reconnect with the deepest realities of our faith. Its goal is to cultivate lifelong trust in God and help participants discover the Bible as a friend for life. Covenant is based on the simple idea that we live well when we love well. When we read it together, we remember and retell the deepest story we know. This is the story of who we are, where we come from, and where we go wrong. And the story ends well because faithful love is at work in everything to restore hope, freedom, and wholeness to our lives.

The Bible follows the sometimes faithful and sometimes faithless responses of Israel and the church, tracking changes in the lives of key people and the community itself as they respond to God's call. We find ourselves in tales of rivalry and rebellion, and in stories of corruption, catastrophe, and crisis. We see our own anxious desire for security expressed in its narratives of idolatry and rigid tribal boundaries. But we also see our misplaced loyalties graced by God's restoring love. These grace-filled stories give us hope that God will make beautiful things out of the fragments and dust of our fallen lives.

The Bible speaks in more than one voice. It contains many conversations and perspectives, inviting us to join a discussion that began with creation in Genesis and extends to our street corners, coffee shops, offices, schools, and dinner tables. Covenant Bible Study is one way to continue that conversation. When we ask questions, share stories, and wrestle with some of the biggest issues facing us as human beings, this living conversation is woven into our lives. Reading the Bible together helps us deal with questions like, "How—or even—*Is* God with us? Is any of this real or true?" Real experiences and real questions come together in our search for something we can trust—a scripture reliable enough to be called a friend for life.

In the process, we discover that God is not anxious about this ongoing discussion, but that God actually shows up in some powerful ways, in loyal relationship, when we open ourselves and risk joining the conversation. Covenant Bible Study is an opportunity to belong to a group of friends discovering how the Bible is a companion for life.

Do your parents or grandparents ever tell competing versions of the same events? Do you have any "memories" that turned out to be the story you've always been told? Does that make them more or less reliable?

A Covenant Bible Study consists of:

1. A **small group** of adults who pledge to read and study the Bible individually and together for an extended period of time. The group's purpose is to deepen commitment to live as faithful followers of Jesus Christ.

2. An **experience** that trains participants in disciplined daily Bible reading, prayer, and holy conversation. Participants learn these skills by responding to participant guides, study Bibles, videos, and devotional meditations. The experience becomes accountable at weekly meetings in a group setting for fellowship, learning, and the shared practice of interpreting scripture. This setting is where scripture meets everyday experience within and beyond your church life.

3. A **promise** to cultivate practical wisdom, so that the knowledge of the participant and the group is enlarged when interpreting the Bible and conversing about life. What results is a covenant relationship with God that will redeem a broken world in need of transformation.

The Bible is a conversation partner for life. Reading it recalls and even rewrites our deepest stories, helping us recognize and respond to the true God who saves a suffering, shattered world.

The Covenant Bible experience helps participants:

1. **learn** by dispelling anxiety about understanding the Bible;

2. **grow** by practicing conversation about scripture and relationships in a group;

3. **change** by improving skills for reading the Bible and living faithfully;

4. **discover** by naming your unique identity and purpose through the scriptural witness;

5. **share** by belonging to a group of friends in faith;

6. **experience** by invoking God's power and presence through spiritual reading and listening practices; and

7. **serve** by responding to what you learn and bringing covenant love to others.

Living well depends primarily on the attachments that we form. These bonds can be described in terms of who and what we love. Who and what we love expresses who we are (our identity) and also shows what matters most to each of us (our purpose).

In the Old Testament, Deuteronomy insists that the basic human yearning for healthy relationship is based in faithful love: "Israel, listen! Our God is the LORD! Only the LORD! Love the LORD your God with all your heart, all your being, and all your strength" (Deut 6:4-5). In the New Testament, Jesus acknowledges Deuteronomy ("love the Lord your God") as the greatest expectation in the scriptures, and then he preaches: "You must love your neighbor as you love yourself" (Matt 22:39). Jesus confirms that you will find it hard to love a neighbor if your well-being (your whole heart and mind) is fragmented or distracted by substitutes for loyal love or by selfish desires.

Love has a learning curve. When we better understand God's faithful love expressed through scripture in the stories, songs, instructions, prophecies, and prayers for help, we find that living well together is always about our relationships.

Covenant as an organizing pattern for studying the whole scripture

"Covenant" is the solemn and enduring commitment made between God and human beings to be in a fruitful and creative relationship. When Christians speak about a relationship with God, we invoke the language and images of covenant. To express the relationship, we might say, "God is my father," or "Jesus is my friend," or "I am God's child." These expressions invoke commitment and loyalty.

This emphasis on covenant in the Bible is one way to get the big picture. It helps make sense of a long, ancient book that seems very strange and overwhelming. The Christian Bible is actually a library of sixty-six interrelated books. Think of the Bible as a quilt with sixty-six squares. Covenant is a dominant pattern that runs through this quilt because:

1. In the Torah (Genesis through Deuteronomy), God's relationship with God's people is grounded in a series of covenants. Torah is the Instruction (or Teaching; also called "the Law" in the King James Version) that maintains the relationship between God's word (the expectations established by God) and God's faithful or loyal people. The Torah shows that what we put in our mouths and consume with our minds will affect our well-being, the health of our relationship with God, and our relationships with others. As you will learn in Episode 2 on the Torah and Genesis, covenant in the Bible is based on the relationships formed by the first human families. Our best (and sometimes most painful) experiences in life come from learning how to love each other in a family.

2. Sometimes covenant is also understood in contractual and legal terms. We use the word *covenant* when describing how a group of neighbors might agree to get along with each other for mutual benefit. This sort of "neighborhood agreement" goes back to ancient times, when a tribal leader or ruler would "cut a covenant" with a neighboring tribe. These legal analogies can stimulate useful conversation about the responsibilities that are embedded in contemporary relationships with our families, friends, and government. However, the legal sanctions

The Christian Bible is actually a library of sixty-six interrelated books. Think of the Bible as a quilt with sixty-six squares. Covenant is a dominant pattern that runs through this quilt.

and retributions that were prescribed for violating a covenant in ancient societies can raise difficult issues that require thoughtful Christian reflection. A Covenant Bible Study group is a safe place to discuss the expectations we have for each other in our homes and communities.

3. Covenant is the dominant theme of the core stories (about the leading personalities) in the Bible, including the five major covenants that are based in promises and fulfilled through Noah, Abraham, Moses, David, and Jesus. A story is a great way to show us (rather than simply tell us) what faithful love looks like. The books of Esther and Ruth, for example, are models of faithful covenant love. The history writings from Deuteronomy through 2 Kings are also based in covenants that show how the well-being of God's people is determined by their loyalty to God and their commitment to this relationship.

4. Many of the prophets, but especially Hosea and Jeremiah, are schooled by covenant theology as they confront leaders who have responsibilities toward God and their communities. A breached covenant is how the prophets eventually explain the exile and the near extermination or scattering of Israelites by Babylon and Assyria. Jeremiah, in the "Book of the Covenant" (Jer 30–33), yearns for a new covenant that is cut into our hearts.

5. We look back at that expectation and yearning for a covenant inscribed on our hearts, and we as Christians realize that this new life is possible through Jesus, the one who reconciles us to God through his faithfulness on the cross. In the Gospels, God's kingdom is a vision of a better future for the new community of Christ-followers.

6. When the early Christians were "born again" and referred to each other as "sister" or "brother," they established their kinship through a family. Covenant life was the context for the letters to the Christian communities (for example, at Corinth or Ephesus) as they grappled with the ethical implications of living in relationships. This kind of covenant community is apparent when referring to Jesus as the head and the church as the body. This is also why Paul often refers to himself as the father of his parishioners. When we think of the most intimate relationships known to human beings—mother, father, sister, brother, lover, child, partner, spouse, friend—each of these identities was and is used by Christians to describe the covenant relationships between the people, their Lord, and their community.

Many Christians make a promise to read the whole Bible in a year. That is really hard to do, especially alone. Most people stall before Leviticus. To gain an in-depth understanding of the whole Bible, Covenant offers patient and flexible guidance. The three participant guides encourage your group to meet in eight-week segments:

1. *Creating the Covenant*

2. *Living the Covenant*

3. *Trusting the Covenant*

It feels great each time your group finishes working through one of the participant guides, because it means you've also finished working through about a third of the Bible. The books of the Bible are arranged to cover the whole scripture while emphasizing the themes that are drawn from the covenants in the Bible.

The initial eight weeks feature how the covenant community is created and established. The next eight weeks feature how the community wisely lives out their covenant in faithful love. The final eight weeks feature how the community and individuals are restored to hope—to trust God when troubling things happen.

Because the Christian Bible is fixed in a certain order from Genesis to Revelation, people often try to study scripture in that order. Typically Christians end up neglecting the unfamiliar Old Testament books and sticking to the New Testament (and perhaps some of the Psalms). While it might seem surprising to mix the books of the Old Testament and the New Testament, this Bible study's three-part covenant pattern will help us see that the New Testament writers were in conversation with the covenant themes of the Old Testament books.

Loving others in your group

Holy conversation about the Bible is vital to your spiritual health. You are part of a Covenant group. In a group, the participants get more than knowledge about the Bible. Knowledge isn't enough to sustain or deepen trust in God. Group participants actually form covenant relationships with each other as they examine and practice what it means to stay in love with God. As you learn to share and love and serve together, the members of the Covenant group make a commitment to each other. They learn to forgive each other if offended, and they make a commitment together to deepen their relationship with God.

Your leader will convene the Covenant group each week and help you develop a transforming conversation about the scriptures. This conversational approach is modeled for you in the weekly video episodes about the books you are studying. The Bible is most transformative when it is read and discussed together. Your understanding and life experience is shared, and as you listen to another's understanding of the story or hear about their practical experience, God's presence (the Holy Spirit) begins to turn and change hearts and minds. Amazing hope suddenly seems possible because God's love is discovered through these personal relationships.

Resources for the Covenant experience

1. *Participant Guides:* The three Covenant participant guides show you what to read and offer space to interact personally with the daily Bible readings, the prayers, and the weekly Covenant Meditations. The guides are available from Cokesbury as a print set (or individually).

2. *Covenant Meditations:* Many participants find great personal benefit and contentment in an intimate connection with God through praying scripture. In addition to the once-weekly meditation in the participant guides (on Day 6), a set of sixty-six additional Covenant meditations is available in print or as an eBook.

3. *CEB Study Bible:* Participants and leaders are encouraged to obtain and use this study Bible (published in 2013) to inform the daily readings and the group meeting experiences for Covenant. The *CEB Study Bible* is available in print.

4. *CovenantBibleStudy.com:* Encourage your leader to collect everyone's e-mail address and register your group online. In addition to meeting reminders, benefits include a daily e-mail of the assigned Bible reading to everyone in the group. At the website, participants can also download or stream the weekly video episodes (for a small fee), perhaps for a weekly meeting that was missed or to see what is ahead in the next weekly episode. Additional videos (including Bible stories retold) are mentioned occasionally in the text of the participant guides. These are also located at the website for personal or group viewing.

Guidelines for reading the Bible

Covenant is explained above as the key pattern throughout this in-depth Bible study. However, many participants will come to the Bible with further questions about how we got the Bible, when the stories or writing of the Bible took place, why we have an Old Testament and a New Testament, or who decided that we should read the Bible. These questions are answered in the articles of the *CEB Study Bible*. When you feel lost, get your bearings from the following articles, cited by page number and found toward the end of the *CEB Study Bible* (after the book of Revelation and before the phrase concordance):

You can find more Bible study resources at CovenantBibleStudy.com.

Next week in Episode 2, we will start with a fundamental human question: Who are we? In Genesis and the rest of the Torah, we learn about creating covenants with God and others. You will encounter God's covenant with all creation and then God's particular covenant with the people who descended from Abraham and Sarah.

SIGNS OF FAITHFUL LOVE

Covenant people read the Bible together to learn how to love God and others better.

Torah: Genesis

WHO ARE WE?
Creating covenants with God and others

Bible Readings

Day 1: Genesis 1–3

Day 2: Genesis 6:5–9:17; 11:1-9

Day 3: Genesis 12; 15; 17; 22

Day 4: Genesis 27–28; 32–33

Day 5: Genesis 37; 41; 43; 45; 50

Day 6: Covenant Meditation on Genesis 1:26-31

Day 7: Group Meeting Experience with Genesis 9:7-17

Covenant Prayer

For those who are suffering in chaos

Hear my prayer, LORD! Listen closely to my cry for help! (Psalm 39:12)

For those who celebrate new creation

Your word gives me new life. (Psalm 119:50)

OUR LONGING FOR RELATIONSHIP

We get into trouble—hurting ourselves, those we love, and the world—when we forget who we are and to whom we belong.

The Torah presents the instructions or teaching for worshipping God and living in a covenant community.

TORAH

The Christian and Jewish communities consider the first five books of the Bible as a separate portion of scripture. Christians call these books the Pentateuch, or "five books." The books tell stories about the earliest events in God's relationship with God's people. Jews call these books the Torah, which the Common English Bible translates as "Instruction." Beginning with the King James Version, however, *Torah* was often translated as "the Law." By calling these books the Torah, our attention is focused on the great covenant God made with the Israelites at Mount Sinai—described in Exodus, Leviticus, Numbers, and Deuteronomy. The Torah presents the instructions or teaching for worshipping God and living in a covenant community.

The aim of the Torah is to answer the question, "Who are we?" and the answer is vast and all-encompassing. Torah explains not only the unique character of the people of Israel and of God's relationship to the people, but also their role in the larger world. To do this, the Torah explains the nature of humanity in all of its cultural diversity. The Torah also explains God's relationship to Israel, and even more broadly, God's relationship to the created world in which Israel lived. The Torah's authors do all of this by telling the story of their own past, of how God brought nature, humanity, and Israel itself into being at the very beginning of time.

The Torah story is structured around crucial, community-shaping events. It begins with the creation of the natural world and the human role within it, followed by the first age of history, in which the human community fell into violence and perished in the great flood (Gen 1–8). In the new era of history following the flood, three great covenants redefine the human community and the role of the people of Israel within it.

> **Optional:** *An additional video on the tower of Babel and the unique role of Israel is available for download from* **CovenantBibleStudy.com**.

In the new era of history following the flood, three great covenants redefine the human community and the role of the people of Israel within it.

The first is God's covenant with Noah, humanity, and all living things (Gen 9:1-17). The second is God's covenant with Abraham and with his descendants, by which God selects a particular line of humanity for a particular role within it (Gen 15; 17). And the third is God's covenant with Israel itself, the descendants of Jacob's twelve sons, at Mount Sinai (Exod 19; 24; 31), where the great body of instructions that would define Israel as a community were collected and recorded.

The Torah, like many books in the Old Testament, and like the Old Testament as a whole, is the product of multiple voices from ancient Israel. Jewish and Christian traditions eventually came to regard the entire Pentateuch as transcribed by a single individual Moses, but biblical scholars in recent centuries have noticed evidence of multiple authors: double accounts of the same event, contrasting styles and theological perspectives, and knowledge of events later than Moses' time.

The liveliest stories in Genesis, Exodus, and Numbers come from the Torah's two earliest authors, who both lived during the Israelite monarchy: the Yahwist, so named because he used God's personal name, Yahweh (rendered "the Lord" in the CEB); and the Elohist, so named because he used the common word for "God," *Elohim*, in his narrative. The third contributor, a Priestly Writer, added his own traditions to the Yahwist's and Elohist's stories and organized them around God's three great covenants with Noah, Abraham, and Israel. He also contributed most of the expectations and instructions related to the Sinai covenant in Exodus, Leviticus, and Numbers. The fourth contributor's work, the book of Deuteronomy, was included in the Torah because it provided another record of the Sinai covenant. But based on style, theology, and vocabulary, we can tell that it was originally intended as the introduction to the Historical Books (Joshua through 2 Kings) that follow it. For this reason, it has been placed with the Historical Books in Episode 8.

GENESIS

The book of Genesis tells the first two parts of the larger Torah story: (1) how the world came into being and what role Israel's ancestors were given within it; and (2) how Israel itself emerged as a distinct community within the human race.

The first part of this story is described especially in the creation narratives at the beginning of Genesis (Gen 1–3). The authors of Genesis describe who they are in relation to the natural world, which they inhabit. In these creation stories they show themselves not merely as members of the Israelite community, or even of the human community, but also as members of the larger community of life in the entire creation, within which they are given clear roles and responsibilities. These roles and responsibilities reflect Israel's

The stories of Israel's origins and identity are family stories.

own understanding of its connection with nature and its place in the particular landscape and environment it inhabited.

In the second part of this Torah story in Genesis, when the new world is re-created after the flood, the authors of Genesis explain who they are in relation to the larger world of human cultures that they inhabit. To do this, they employ a complex web of genealogies with family stories to accompany them. These genealogies provide a comprehensive cultural map that documents how all of the peoples descended from the single family of Noah. This map shows how the different peoples are related to each other within the cultural world experienced by the authors of Genesis, and where exactly Israel fits into this larger human family.

In these genealogies and family stories, the main characters stand not only for themselves but for the people who descended from them and who made up the nations with which the authors of Genesis were familiar. Jacob and Esau, for example, in this week's reading for Day 4 (Gen 27–28; 32–33), represent the brothers in a family, but also the nations of Israel and Edom that descended from them.

In the stories of Genesis, community is conceived in terms of family and kinship systems. The stories of Israel's origins and identity are family stories, largely because the family is its basic unit. Its families are grouped into clans, its clans into tribes, and its tribes into a people, the nation of Israel. The authors thought carefully about their relationships in terms of the privileges and responsibilities of kinship. They examined Israel's relationship to God and its covenants with God, Israel's relationship to other cultures, and the family, clan, and tribal relationships within Israel itself. This kinship culture had consequences for entering into covenants and building community.

Day 1: Genesis 1–3
Creation and the human role within it

The Bible begins its account of who Israel was as God's people by describing who they were in relation to their environment, the world of nature that surrounded and sustained them. By starting their story at the creation of the world, the biblical authors affirm that the first and most basic community of life is the entire natural world.

Genesis actually preserves two traditions about the world's beginnings and Israel's place within it. Both of these traditions view the world from Israel's ancient understandings of the world and their particular geographical location within it—not from the new knowledge of the cosmos gained by modern science.

The first creation tradition (Gen 1:1–2:4*a*, probably from the Priestly Writer) describes creation in seven days. This description establishes the Sabbath on the seventh day as part of the world's own rhythms and orders. It's written in a very orderly style that may have been intended for reading in a worship setting. It gives humans a high role in creation: We are made in God's own image and commissioned to take charge of the animal world. The second creation tradition (Gen 2:4*b*–3:24, and probably from the Yahwist, who uses the divine name Yahweh) describes creation in a small, local garden. It's more earthy and is written in a more informal, story-like style. And it gives humans a much more modest role in creation: They are made out of the earth's topsoil and commissioned to farm (or "serve") the fertile land from which they were created.

As you read these two creation stories, note their similarities and differences and consider how more than one perspective provides a deeper understanding of the world and humanity than a single account could.

Day 2: Genesis 6:5–9:17; 11:1-9
End of the old world—beginning of the new world

Biblical writers shared the common ancient idea that a great flood brought an end to the first age of human history and introduced the new age of history in which they themselves lived. In these ancient stories, something went wrong in the first age that required starting over. Humanity had become violent and corrupt. So God selected Noah, the moral and exemplary man of his time, together with his family and a pair from each species of animal, to survive the flood and begin the world anew.

God begins the new world by establishing a covenant relationship with all living things. The covenant offers them life, protection, and a relationship with God for all time (Gen 9:1-17). Included in the Bible's

25

first covenant are the entire human race descended from Noah's family and all of the living things who survived the flood. The story of the city of Babel that follows (Gen 11:1-9) explains how the human members of God's first covenant became culturally diverse, even though they descended from a single family and wished to preserve a single culture. Because some readers have misread the story of Babel as a story of human pride and God's punishment for it, they have claimed that God rejected God's covenant relationship with the human race in order to make a covenant with Abraham alone. This biblical story, however, tells us that God's covenant with Abraham was a particular covenant within God's larger covenant with the human race as a whole.

What feelings do you have about cultural and racial differences in your neighborhood? In your church?

Day 3: Genesis 12; 15; 17; 22
Abraham and nationhood

God's covenant with Abraham is the Bible's second covenant, preserved by the Yahwist (Gen 15) and the Priestly Writer (Gen 17). It shows that within God's larger covenant with all of humanity and all living things (Gen 9:1-17), God established a particular kind of relationship with this line of Noah's descendants. This relationship is one that will define the people of Israel as a unique community within the human race as a whole. That community will be established as a nation among other ancient nations (Gen 12:2; 17:6), with a flourishing population (Gen 15:5; 17:2), and a land to sustain them (Gen 12:7; 15:18).

> **Optional:** *An additional video retelling the story of Abraham, Sarah, and the three visitors is available for download from* **CovenantBibleStudy.com**.

This model of a community in covenant relationship with God is based in kinship, culture, and politics. It mirrors the religious life and practices of its time and place, when culture, politics, and religion were a single integrated system. It contains a number of powerful ideas that sustained the lives of these people: the confidence in an enduring relationship with God, the belief that their lives and identities played an important part in God's world, a strong national and communal solidarity, and a close relationship to the land. At the same time, this model of community is packaged with specific cultural, ethnic, patriarchal, and political aspects that contemporary Christians may no longer wish to define in their own communities.

Both the Yahwist and the Priestly Writer have preserved records of the covenant with Abraham. Compare the Yahwist's style and theology of covenant in Genesis 15 with the style and theology of his creation story (Gen 2:4b–3:24). Compare the Priestly Writer's style and theology of covenant in Genesis 17 with the style and theology of his creation story (Gen 1:1–2:4a) and his record of the covenant with Noah (Gen 9:1-17).

Compare the covenant story in Genesis 15 with the covenant story in Genesis 17.

Day 4: Genesis 27–28; 32–33
Jacob and the biblical family

While Abraham is Israel's most typical ancestor to whom the promises of nationhood were first made, Jacob, his grandson, is the ancestor who received the nation's name, Israel, and whose twelve sons became ancestors of the twelve tribes that made up the nation (Gen 29–30). These stories about Jacob explain how he, rather than his older brother, Esau, became Isaac's primary heir, and they reveal traits of biblical characters and their families that puzzle and trouble modern readers. Jacob, Israel's namesake, and his mother, Rebekah, had to deceive Isaac and Esau to acquire the blessing that God gave to Jacob.

Community in ancient Israel, as in these stories of its ancestors, is grounded in family structures. These structures privilege the oldest male member of the family, the patriarch, and his oldest son, the family's legal heir. These same structures exclude women and secondary sons from the status and agency to participate in family decisions and to carry on the family's legacy. Rebekah and Jacob find ways to subvert traditional structures in order to claim their voices and their places in the family. Against convention and cultural expectations, God sides in each generation in the book of Genesis with those excluded from power and privilege within these kinship systems. The story of Rebekah and Jacob is one example of this (Gen 25:21-23; 28:13-15).

What puzzles or troubles you in the family stories about Jacob and Rebekah?

Day 5: Genesis 37; 41; 43; 45; 50
Joseph and his brothers in Egypt

The stories about Jacob's sons that conclude Genesis are some of the most colorful and emotional in the book. A key theme in them, as in every family story in Genesis, is sibling rivalry. As the first and most basic conflict in life, sibling rivalry in Genesis represents the conflicts that arise not just in the family, but also within the larger community of Israel, and even between Israel and its neighboring nations. The conflicts between Jacob's sons also represent the conflicts between the later tribes made up of their descendants, just as the conflict between Jacob and Esau also represents in a larger scope the conflict between their descendants, the Israelites and the Edomites.

In every family in Genesis but one, this deep and primal conflict that threatened to tear apart the fabric of the community was resolved through generosity and a great capacity for understanding. The one exception is the family who lived in the troubled age before the flood when Cain killed his brother, Abel (Gen 4:1-16). In all of the other family dramas, bloodshed was averted. In the stories of Jacob and Esau and of Joseph and his brothers, the wronged brother, with good reason and enough power to take revenge, instead forgave and restored the relationship that was broken.

The other key theme in these concluding stories in Genesis is God's protection of Jacob's family from death by famine. This protection extended beyond Jacob's family, however, to include all of Egypt and all of the known world that came to buy grain (Gen 41:57; 45:5). Before Egypt became a furnace of oppression in Exodus through Numbers, it was a refuge from hunger that shared its bounty with the world.

How did Jacob's troubled family resolve their conflicts?

Day 6: Genesis 1:26-31

Covenant Meditation: Who are we?

Each week on Day 6, we will approach and encounter scripture in a different way than in our study on Days 1–5. Through the following exercise, we will practice one form of spiritual reading that has been taught in the church for many generations—the practice of using our imagination. This practice is designed to deepen our ability to listen for what God is trying to reveal to us through scripture. It represents one way that we can learn to read the Bible devotionally, while also participating in study of the texts.

Read Genesis 1:26-31 again, but do so slowly, paying attention to each word, phrase, and action. In this passage, God addresses our question, "Who are we?" even before humanity is added to the scene of creation. Notice that what God says, God then does, and that we as human beings take form in God's imagination and words before we become part of the created order on earth.

Now read these verses of Genesis once more, using your imagination to place yourself nearby as God speaks and creates. What do you see? What colors, shapes, animals, and movements? What do you hear? What sounds come to mind as you read these words? Are there aromas or scents that you might associate with this scene as you take your time reading: the scent of the earth, of water, of animals? Can you imagine the feel of any textures, objects, or movements: breeze, rain, dirt? Allow all of your senses to bring your imagination to bear on this passage in Genesis, and notice what is stirred up for you. If you would like, write down your reflections as you follow this practice of spiritual reading, and then look back over how this way of reading may have opened the passage to you in a new way.

Group Meeting Experience

Genesis 9:7-17 | *The Bible's first covenant*

At the beginning of the new world following the flood, God makes the covenant that becomes the foundation for the Torah covenants that follow: the covenants with Abraham and with the people of Israel at Mount Sinai.

1. To gain an appreciation for the style of the Priestly Writer who structured the Torah around three great covenants, compare the language, vocabulary, and style of this covenant with the covenants with Abraham in Genesis 17 and with Israel in Exodus 31:12-18. Also compare to these the Priestly account of the world's creation in seven days in Genesis 1:1–2:4a. What are the key words, phrases, and features of Priestly style and thought?

2. With whom does God enter into relationship in this covenant?

3. What does this covenant claim about God's relationship to the world as a whole?

4. The Priestly Writer probably lived during the time of the exile (after 587 BCE), when his people's past had been destroyed and their future was in doubt. In this context, how might such a covenant provide hope for survival and a way forward?

5. In the Bible's first covenant, how might God's relation to the world, to all its forms of life, and to all its people inform our own understanding of our place and role in the world?

SIGNS OF FAITHFUL LOVE

God's covenant with us returns us to our true selves—
made in the image of God—and sends the Covenant
people out to be a blessing to the world God loves.

Exodus, Leviticus, Numbers

FREEDOM AND INSTRUCTION
Privileges and responsibilities of the covenant

Bible Readings

Day 1: Exodus 1–4

Day 2: Exodus 13:17–15:21

Day 3: Exodus 20–24

Day 4: Leviticus 19–22

Day 5: Numbers 11–14

Day 6: Covenant Meditation on Leviticus 19:1-2

Day 7: Group Meeting Experience with Exodus 20:1-17

Covenant Prayer

For children in refugee camps, war zones, sweatshops, and other oppressive circumstances where they are not free to receive a formal education

I will bless the LORD who advises me; even at night I am instructed in the depths of my mind. (Psalm 16:7)

For those who follow the call to teach, instruct, and share God's wisdom with children and youth

I will instruct you and teach you about the direction you should go. I'll advise you and keep my eye on you. (Psalm 32:8)

OUR LONGING FOR RELATIONSHIP

It's a privilege and a gift to experience a committed relationship, but a lasting relationship is always confirmed through responsibilities and expectations.

FREEDOM

Israel's liberation from oppression in Egypt, their journey through the wilderness, and their possession of the promised land is a story that echoes throughout the Old and the New Testaments.

Notice that God promises the land to Abraham (Gen 15:7), then to Isaac (Gen 26:3), and then to Jacob (Gen 28:13), without any of them ever receiving it. It's only after the Israelites cry out from their oppression that God notices and "remembers" the promise God made to Israel's ancestors (Exod 2:23-24). This triggers God's saving action. The first lesson from this liberation story is, therefore, that no liberation begins unless there is a strong outcry by the oppressed (compare Neh 5:1). No people can really be rescued unless they become aware of their need for help (compare Mark 2:17).

God's response to the people isn't timid. God states, "I am the LORD. I'll bring you out from Egyptian forced labor. I'll rescue you from your slavery to them. I'll set you free with great power and with momentous events of justice" (Exod 6:6). The same verbs are used in the New Testament to describe God's salvation (compare Luke 24:21; Matt 6:13; Col 1:13). This liberation of Israel was a very political act that became symbolic of how God can reverse human circumstances.

Several traditions are brought together in Exodus, Leviticus, and Numbers, resulting in the story of liberation as we have it in the Bible today (see the introduction to Genesis). The final editor was successful in combining all of them into a coherent narrative, but some inconsistencies and alternative versions of the same event still remain in the final form of the story. Examples of these different traditions can be found in the accounts of Moses and his father-in-law from Exodus 18 (Elohist) and Numbers 10:29-32 (Yahwist); the complaints of the Israelites in Exodus 16:1-12 (Priestly Writer) and Numbers 11:1-6 (Elohist); the manna from Exodus 16:13-35 (Priestly Writer) and Numbers 11:7-35 (Elohist); and the accounts of the crossing of the sea in Exodus 15.

The exodus tradition, hundreds of years later in Israelite history, served as a theological framework for the liberation from Babylon and return to Israel's homeland after the exile. God made proclamations to the exilic community full of images from the exodus:

The LORD your redeemer, the holy one of Israel, says,
For your sake, I have sent an army to Babylon,
and brought down all the bars,

turning the Chaldeans' singing into a lament.
I am the LORD, your holy one, Israel's creator, your king!
The LORD says—who makes a way in the sea
and a path in the mighty waters,
who brings out chariot and horse, army and battalion;
they will lie down together and will not rise;
they will be extinguished, extinguished like a wick.
Don't remember the prior things;
don't ponder ancient history.
Look! I'm doing a new thing;
now it sprouts up; don't you recognize it?
I'm making a way in the desert,
paths in the wilderness. (Isa 43:14-19)

Both acts of salvation, the liberation from Egypt and the liberation from Babylon, were fulfilled when the Israelites returned to live freely in the land of Israel.

The exodus tradition, hundreds of years later in Israelite history, served as a theological framework for the liberation from Babylon and return to Israel's homeland after the exile.

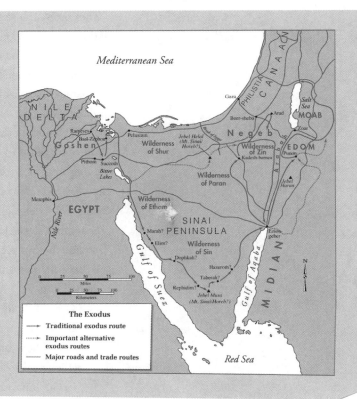

INSTRUCTION

The main purpose of the Torah is to teach the Israelites how to live a holy life in the midst of a just society. Such emphasis on the right behavior is also well represented in the New Testament, especially in the letter from James. Matthew (a very Jewish Gospel) also highlights this responsibility when Jesus states that "only those who do the will of my Father" will enter the kingdom of heaven (Matt 7:21).

Notice that the Instruction in the books of Exodus, Leviticus, and Numbers contains almost no statement or list of beliefs. Instead they include a long (perhaps today we would say too long) list of precepts, commandments, and ordinances for teaching Israel how to live an abundant, fulfilling, holy life (Lev 19:1-2; 26:1-13). Exodus, for example, contains two collections of instruction: the ethical Decalogue, or Ten Commandments (Exod 20:1-17), and the book of the covenant (Exod 20:18–23:33). These collections include prescriptions about the altar sacrifices (Exod 20:22-26), slaves (Exod 21:1-11), personal injuries (Exod 21:12-36), social and religious laws (Exod 22:18–23:9), and Israel's liturgical calendar (Exod 23:10-19).

The commandments are given to Israel in the context of their covenant relationship with God. They describe Israel's responsibilities as members of the covenant. The covenant tradition includes blessings (which result from Israel's obedience to the commandments) and curses (which result from Israel disregarding the commandments). Some of these curses are similar to ancient Near Eastern treaties between two kingdoms, one stronger than the other.

Leviticus aims to describe holy living. It develops a holiness spectrum, moving from the very holy, to the holy, to the clean, to the unclean, to the very unclean in the realms of space, people, rituals, and time. In space, for example, this spectrum moves from the most holy place in the temple, to the holy place, to the court, to the camp, and to the realm outside the camp. Such a spectrum of holiness was designed to prepare a place for the holy God among a people who didn't always practice holy living.

Other religions had a sense of holy space, but the sacredness of holy time came first in the biblical narrative. We see the establishment of holy time in the creation story in seven days at Genesis 1, which peaks with the seventh day, the Sabbath, which is for resting in God's presence.

Day 1: Exodus 1–4
Oppression, survival, and the charge of a leader

The storyteller sets the stage for the Israelites' escape and liberation by describing the arrival of all the descendants of Jacob in Egypt (Exod 1:1-7), their growth as a people and their oppression (Exod 1:8-22; 2:23-25), and the emergence of Moses (Exod 2:1-22). Moses is charged with leading the liberation (Exod 3:1–4:17) and returns to Egypt (Exod 4:18-31).

Moses' infancy story has a parallel in the Assyrian legend (dated to the seventh century BCE) about the Akkadian King Sargon (who reigned 2270–2215 BCE). Sargon is born secretly and left in a reed basket in a river, but he is rescued by a gardener to later become king. We don't know for sure that Moses' story is informed by this parallel, but it's not unusual for biblical writers (and even among writers today) to make use of the literary forms and themes common in their world to describe their own experiences.

The Egyptians' attempt to stop the growth of the people of Israel by killing their oldest male children is in clear opposition to God's promise to the patriarchs that they would have many descendants (Gen 15:4-6). Israel's oldest males, however, are saved by the tender hands of two midwives named Shiphrah and Puah, in what could be considered the first act of civil disobedience registered in the Bible. Disobeying the mighty Pharaoh and lying to him about it was the only way to save the lives of the infants and to secure the future of Israel (Exod 1:15-22).

> **Optional:** *An additional video on God's name and Moses is available for download from* **CovenantBibleStudy.com**.

Moses' reluctance to accept God's charge to lead Israel is echoed by other prophets in the Bible (compare Jer 1). God overcomes Moses' five objections and reveals his name: Yahweh, rendered "the LORD" (Exod 3:15). This name may mean "I Am" (Exod 3:14). It may also mean "I Will Be What I Will Be," which has been interpreted by some as "My nature will become evident from my actions." The liberation program begins.

Why should a person feel reluctant to become a leader? How do you feel about your role in your family or church?

p. 76 *p. 81*

Day 2: Exodus 13:17–15:21

Crossing boundaries for freedom

Reaching Canaan from Egypt by taking the most direct route, which ran parallel to the Mediterranean Sea, would have taken about ten days. But fearing that the people would be disheartened by the expected opposition from the Philistines on the coast, God decided to lead the people through the wilderness (Exod 13:17-18). The Philistines actually settled in Canaan in the twelfth century BCE, later than the period of this story, so the mention of Philistines here reflects a detail from the author's own time rather than from the time of the story itself. The Sea of Reeds (not the "Red Sea," which comes from a mistranslation in the Greek Bible) is the final boundary before reaching freedom.

A final obstacle must be faced. As in many stories where the hero seems safe and the villain is supposed to be dead—where the villain somehow comes back to threaten the hero only to meet his final demise—Pharaoh decides to pursue Israel to bring them back to servitude.

In this story, Israel's enemies are drowned. Since we value life, even that of our enemies, what does this biblical story tell us about the value of human life?

Day 3: Exodus 20–24 *p. 87*

Sinai covenant

The culmination of the liberation from Egypt is the establishment of a covenant between God and Israel (compare Exod 6:6-7) to make Israel a holy people (Exod 19:6). This is the ultimate purpose of the ethical Decalogue (or Ten Commandments; Exod 20:2-17), of the Covenant Code (Exod 21:1–23:19), and of the covenant ceremony itself (Exod 24:1-15*a*). The biblical God is a covenant God, who previously made a covenant with Noah, all of his descendants, and nature itself (Gen 9:1-17), and with Abraham and his descendants (Gen 15 and 17).

Of all these biblical covenants, the Sinai covenant on a mountain dominates the landscape of the first books of the Bible. Its instructions begin here in Exodus and continue throughout the books of Leviticus, Numbers, and Deuteronomy. It is the Old Testament's fullest description of covenant life and the covenant responsibilities that define the relationship between God and Israel. Covenant language is also an essential Christian concept in the New Testament (compare Exod 24:8; Heb 9:20; 1 Cor 11:25).

A covenant requires the fulfillment of its stipulations by the parties in order to remain valid. No community of faith that understands itself to worship the biblical God should ever forget that there are always stipulations. Not following the instructions is tantamount to breaking the covenant with God. The authors of the great history of Israel in Deuteronomy–2 Kings explain the tragic events of the fall of the northern kingdom, the destruction of the temple, and the exile in Babylon as the consequences of Israel's not complying with such stipulations.

How do you view your responsibilities within your relationship with God? What do you think are the consequences when you disregard these responsibilities?

Day 4: Leviticus 19–22 p. 132
Holiness Code

Leviticus 18–26 is called the Holiness Code. In this code, the priests urge Israel to imitate God: "You must be holy, because I, the Lord your God, am holy" (Lev 19:2). This holiness applies to every aspect of Israel's life and is a consequence of faithfully observing all God's teachings (Lev 19:37). Holiness applies to the whole people in an accountable faith community.

The instructions in this chapter are very practical. They address three issues: (1) care and respect for parents, the elderly, immigrants, and the poor; (2) fairness in relationships and in business; and (3) justice in Israel's methods for settling disputes. But biblical Instruction, as an ancient collection of teachings and expectations, was written for a different place and time, and it should be read with caution. Several of these instructions, for example, apply the death penalty for behavior that no Western society would consider a crime.

How do we decide which of these instructions are still valid today and which aren't? How can the call to be holy be implemented in our society?

p. 156

Day 5: Numbers 11–14

In the wilderness

Although the wilderness journey is perceived as an ideal period by other biblical writers (compare Jer 2:2), these stories regard it as a journey marked by rebellion, not only by the people but also by Moses' closest family, Miriam and Aaron (Num 12). The liberated community begins to wonder if it might have been better to stay in Egypt, and they long for the food they enjoyed there (Num 11:4-5).

We see Moses interceding before God as a prophet (compare Jer 7:16; 11:14; 14:11), but the liberated community won't pass the test of the wilderness, and their rebellions will cost them dearly. None of those who left Egypt, except for Joshua and Caleb, will set foot in the promised land. The provisions of the covenant should have been taken seriously.

The promised land isn't always available immediately after the liberation. A long and unpleasant journey usually follows. However, the land is waiting, and only faithfulness leads God's people there.

What are the wilderness tests that face communities of faith today?

p. 132

Day 6: Leviticus 19:1-2

Covenant Meditation: You must be holy because God is holy.

As we read through the books of Exodus, Leviticus, and Numbers, a temptation might surface to skim over details that appear too tedious and antiquated for your attention. For most of us, lists of laws and ordinances leave much to be desired as reading material. But we should remember that these books contain some of the expectations that persist throughout the Old and New Testaments.

For this purpose, we will use the spiritual reading practice of *lectio divina*, sacred reading. *Lectio divina* has been taught and practiced by Christians for centuries. *Lectio* engages scripture through prayer and meditation, rather than study and analysis. Both approaches—study and prayer—are important, but where study informs us about the words, *lectio* forms us as a people who practice God's word. *Lectio divina* can teach us how to encounter God through the living word.

To begin our practice, locate Leviticus 19:1-2. Before reading these verses, relax and settle your breathing into a gentle rhythm. Prayerfully give to God any distractions that might interrupt your focus.

Now slowly read the assigned scripture aloud. When finished, sit quietly for a minute to let the passage rest in you. Before reading the passage for a second time, prepare to listen for a word or phrase in the text that catches your attention (resist analyzing why one word or phrase stands out for you). Read the verses a second time, and after a word or phrase stays with you, silently repeat it to yourself over and over for one or two minutes.

Next, read the scripture a third time, but with this question in mind: "How is my life touched by this word?" What feelings, images, sounds, or thoughts come to mind through the word or phrase given to you? How does your word or phrase intersect with your life right now? Use the next three minutes to consider what comes to mind.

After three minutes, read the passage one last time, asking, "Is there an invitation here for me?" Does your word or phrase invite you toward a change or response in the upcoming days? Does it nudge you toward some action or new direction? Take two or three minutes to consider and receive any invitation that God may have for you. Is there a response that you are being prompted to make?

Finally, ask God to help you hear, receive, and respond to this invitation, then close with "Amen."

Group Meeting Experience

p. 87

Exodus 20:1-17 | *Ten Commandments*

Biblical covenants typically describe the responsibilities of both members of the covenant, God and the people of Israel, toward each other. The Ten Commandments represent the most famous list of such covenant responsibilities in the Old Testament. A closer look at them reveals the obligations Israel considered essential to covenant life.

1. How does the beginning of this covenant text (Exod 20:1-6) describe God's role in the covenant? How does this picture of God compare to the picture you have of God's relation to you in your covenant relationship with God?

2. The opening commandments (Exod 20:3-11) describe the people's obligations toward God. What are they?

3. How do the instructions to keep the Sabbath (Exod 20:8-11) connect with the creation story in Genesis 1:1–2:4*a* and with the account of the Sinai covenant in Exodus 31:12-18? How do these instructions reflect the themes of holiness and the imitation of God from your readings for Day 4: Leviticus 19–22?

4. The concluding commandments (Exod 20:12-17) describe the people's obligations toward each other. What are they? What do you think of this summary of the people's basic social responsibilities?

5. If you were to make a list of your ten most important responsibilities in your covenant relationship with God as you understand it, what would they be? How does your list compare to and differ from this biblical list?

SIGNS OF FAITHFUL LOVE

Even though we often fail in our responsibilities,
God makes a way for Covenant people
to reconcile and restore relationships.

Gospels: Matthew and Mark

GOD'S KINGDOM

Jesus reveals instructions for a new covenant community.

Bible Readings

Day 1: Mark 1–4

Day 2: Mark 12–14

Day 3: Matthew 4–7

Day 4: Matthew 11–13

Day 5: Matthew 18–22

Day 6: Covenant Meditation on Mark 10:13-16

Day 7: Group Meeting Experience with Matthew 9:18-33

Covenant Prayer

For all who cross borders seeking a better life for the ones they love

In tight circumstances, I cried out to the LORD. The LORD answered me with wide-open spaces. (Psalm 118:5)

For all who help keep dreams alive for the orphaned, the lonely, and the abandoned

"Come, follow me," [Jesus] said, "and I'll show you how to fish for people." (Mark 1:17)

OUR LONGING FOR RELATIONSHIP

When our new way of life is at odds with the prevailing kingdoms of this world, we look for a Teacher who has the authority over these kingdoms to reshape our lives by example.

A gospel is similar to an ancient biography.

GOSPELS

The Greek word for "gospel" (*euangelion*) is translated "good news" more than twenty times in Matthew, Mark, and Luke. This Greek word sometimes comes directly into English as *evangel*.

Matthew and Mark are examples of the same type of literature. Mark is probably the earliest of the New Testament Gospels, and so that writer is credited with inventing a new type of literature. A gospel is similar to an ancient biography, which was a very popular art form in the Roman world. Like a biography, a gospel isn't an eyewitness account, though it can be based in part on testimony from individuals who remember sayings or who interpret events they experienced.

Biographies follow the chronology of a life and use episodes to instruct and entertain the reader. The Gospels focus on the sayings and experiences of Jesus. As a framework, a Gospel includes the significant episodes of Jesus' life, death, and resurrection. A Gospel writer selects particular episodes from Jesus' life and then puts these episodes in a particular sequence. The episodes selected and the sequence of the episodes can tell us many things about the early Christian community that originally read the account.

Sometimes a teacher is tempted to harmonize the four Gospel accounts, but a better way to understand how the episodes convey important discipleship insights is to study the sayings and narratives in parallel. See, for example, *CEB Gospel Parallels,* which puts the sayings and stories in all the Gospels next to each other.

In the Bible we have four Gospels that provide distinct but comparable windows into the life of Jesus for early Christian communities. Many other gospels were written in the first two centuries after Jesus, but by the fourth century, church leaders agreed that these four Gospels were the most reliable biographical efforts to convince readers to become part of a new covenant community and thus to mature as followers of Jesus.

MARK AND MATTHEW

The author of Mark wrote the Gospel around 65–70 CE during a revolt by Jewish leaders against Rome. When he makes references to the destruction of Jerusalem in Mark 13, we think that the writer is referring to the devastation of the temple in 70 CE. Hence, the earliest of the Gospels is a work rooted in social and political conflict. The author doesn't mince words about the dynamics at play.

He immediately establishes the authority of God's kingdom at the beginning of his account (Mark 1:15), since the Roman Empire was in conflict with God's kingdom. When the author highlights this ambiguity about who is really in charge, he is expressing the discomfort felt by his church. These followers of Jesus faced the dilemma of trying to live in a world where the ways of the Roman ruling elite were in direct conflict with the way of life taught by rabbinic Judaism and early Christianity. We see this choice in Jesus' response to Jewish leaders: "Give to Caesar what belongs to Caesar and to God what belongs to God" (Mark 12:17).

Mark's church decided how best to relate to the Roman government, but they were also working out their relationship to groups that practiced rabbinic Judaism. What does it mean, for instance, to call Jesus the Messiah (or the Christ), who is David's son? This was a difficult concept for a church that consisted primarily of Gentiles. And how does God's kingdom fulfill the promises of the Old Testament?

Mark's community felt harassed. So Mark's Gospel devotes much attention to suffering and the cross, to help this covenant community learn the right way to be faithful and hopeful. These early Christians read the poems about a suffering servant in Isaiah 41–53 as songs about the faithfulness of Jesus, who suffered on behalf of his people.

Matthew's Gospel probably appeared around 85 CE. It was written for a Jewish audience, probably with some Gentile members in the community. It appears that the author of Matthew had access to Mark's Gospel and used it to shape Matthew's account. (The author of Luke's Gospel also apparently used Mark as a source.) When reading the Gospel accounts next to each other (see *CEB Gospel Parallels*), the similarities (and differences) become obvious.

Matthew uses "kingdom of heaven" language. His phrase "kingdom of heaven" means the same thing as "God's kingdom" in Mark. Matthew uses the concept so often that it dominates his Gospel account. These early Jewish Christians eagerly trusted that God is ruling here and now. They realized that God's reign has radical implications because it establishes a new covenant relationship through Jesus the Messiah, who is also resisted by the Roman rulers as the "king of the Jews" (Matt 2:2; 27:11-37).

Matthew's Gospel sets out a different order of sayings and episodes than we find in Mark's account. Matthew establishes Jesus as the fulfillment of God's promises in the Hebrew scriptures. From the genealogy to the birth narrative to his teachings of the

A Gentile is a person from an ethnic group that isn't Jewish.

Compare Mark 4 and Matthew 13.

> *Jesus is the new Moses or the new Teacher.*

new Torah (the covenant Instruction), Jesus is the new Moses, the new Teacher (Rabbi) from the line of David. Jesus is crowned as the ruler of the "kingdom of heaven" on earth.

Both Matthew and Mark hint at the struggles in early Christian communities who are trying to establish a sense of identity as followers of a new way of life. Matthew points to a world of predominantly Jewish believers, while Mark has an audience of primarily Gentile believers, but both communities must go about their lives in a Roman culture that serves many gods and forces all people to submit to the policies of the empire.

In the contest between two empires, Mark's Jesus comes to suffer and die on the cross as an example of faithfulness. Matthew's Jesus comes as the Teacher of the new covenant (for example, Matt 8:19; 9:11; 10:24; 12:38; 19:16). The Teacher demonstrates authority to deal with the Roman Empire because he heals the sick (for example, Matt 4:23-24; 8:2-17, 28-34; 9:18-33; Mark 20:29-34). The Teacher's power is also clearly established over the whole creation when he takes authority over destructive wind and water during a severe storm (Matt 8:23-27).

In this new kingdom that Jesus establishes, both Gospel accounts agree that the greatest ruler is not the one on the earthly throne (Mark 10:15; Matt 18:4).

When you hear the word kingdom, *what comes to mind? How does your church interact with political causes or rulers?*

Day 1: Mark 1–4

p.47

God's kingdom is near.

Mark's Gospel introduces Jesus as one who inaugurates a new kingdom on earth. This kingdom has come. It is present and near. Those who witness the appearance of Jesus, and hence the presence of God's kingdom, must respond by changing their lives and trusting what has come into existence (Mark 1:15). God's nearby kingdom requires a reaction to it. After presenting this new authority, the Gospel writer then describes how God's reign is different from the reign of the emperor. Jesus speaks of God's kingdom in parables, which are extended metaphors. Agricultural references to farming, sowing, and scattering fill Jesus' teachings about the kingdom (Mark 4:11-34). Metaphors always involve some level of ambiguity, and thereby Jesus maintains that knowledge about God's new kingdom isn't (good news) for everyone. It's a secret (Mark 4:11). This news is reserved for those who follow Jesus in this new way of life.

What does it mean to you when Jesus says, "The secret of God's kingdom has been given to you" (Mark 4:11)? Do you feel like one of the insiders? Is the new kingdom for everyone?

Optional: *An additional video on the parables of Jesus is available for download from* **CovenantBibleStudy.com**.

Day 2: Mark 12–14 p. 65
God's kingdom is not here yet.

In the closing chapters of Mark's Gospel, we encounter an alternative view of God's kingdom. The initial chapter of the Gospel announces a reign that is here right now, but the final episodes point to a distant kingdom—one that is yet to come in the future. When Jesus responds to the legal expert's question about the greatest commandment, he indicates that God's kingdom is a future ideal brought closer when we love God and others (Mark 12:34). While the answer the man gives isn't in actual alignment with then current practices for drawing near to God (sacrifices at the temple), it speaks of both the distance and the nearness of this kingdom's time and place. The kingdom is close, but not so close. Mark's account of Jesus' life makes us realize that some aspects of God's kingdom are not yet evident.

In Mark 14:25, Jesus hints at a new kingdom for a new day. While sharing the Passover meal with the disciples, Jesus specifically states that the wine will be drunk "in a new way in God's kingdom."

What does Jesus mean when he says, "You aren't far from God's kingdom" in Mark 12:34? What present-day actions cause you to think that Christians are or are not far from the kingdom? Does your church act in accord with God's kingdom?

Day 3: Matthew 4–7
p.4

New instruction for a new kingdom

Matthew highlights the difference between the kingdom of this world and the kingdom of heaven. In the temptation episode, Jesus explicitly rejects the devil's offer to bow down to him (Matt 4:8-10). In his sermon on a mountain, Jesus describes how the kingdom of heaven differs from the rule that is practiced in this world. Jesus preaches that the God of heaven has dominion over the earth. This reign has preference for the hopeless, the humble, those thirsty for doing the right thing, and for the people who make peace (Matt 5:3-9). The kingdom of heaven drives with power in reverse. In the kingdom of heaven, those who sit in positions of authority are the weakest, and those who aren't on the throne are able to exercise the greatest strength. Matthew contends that faith, not force, is the test of true leadership.

Not only does Matthew point to the political nature of the kingdom of heaven, but the Gospel account puts the role of Jesus as ruler in a new context. In submitting to the kingdom of heaven, Matthew's community doesn't need to discard traditional Jewish customs and teachings. Instead, fulfilling the Torah means establishing new covenant norms for God's people in a new setting (Matt 5:17). This spiritual and cultural renewal flows from the core teaching of God's covenant with us: to love faithfully and treat others as we want to be treated. Love your neighbor as yourself (Lev 19:18; Matt 7:12).

What does the word happy *mean in Matthew 5:3-11? (Compare the term* happy *in Psalms 1 and 84.) How is this meaning similar to or different from your feeling of "being happy" or "happiness"? Which of the teachings from Jesus' sermon on a mountain is troubling for you? Why?*

p. 15

Day 4: Matthew 11–13
New way of life

Jesus begins this section with more unexpected reversals. John the Baptist is important to these early Christians (he preached about a changed heart and life), but still the greatest person in the kingdom of heaven is the least (Matt 11:11). While living under Roman rule, Jesus and his listeners knew about violence and force, and yet Jesus used that language to talk about the kingdom of heaven (Matt 11:12). This movement toward uplifting the weak and empowering those who have nothing won't come without a cost.

When using parables, Jesus offers additional explanation about the kingdom of heaven. He draws on images from the everyday experiences of his audience. The images of "planting," "seeds," "yeast," "wheat," and "landowner" describe this kingdom and help Matthew's community to see it as a reality within their grasp (Matt 13:24-43). The kingdom of heaven as "treasure" and "net" also speaks to the economic and professional status of some of the listeners in this context. Matthew's Jesus knows how to present the kingdom, the new covenant community, so that people listening will see the benefits of this new way of life. Yet Jesus is clear that not all will understand this offer. There are some who hear but "don't really hear or understand" (Matt 13:13).

Which description of the kingdom of heaven in
Matthew 11–13 is most provocative, perplexing, or
unsettling to you? Why?

Day 5: Matthew 18–22 p. 25
Jesus is the new Teacher.

Jesus uses show-and-tell to make his point regarding the kingdom of heaven as a realm that reverses expectations. The image of a little child sitting among disciples serves to reinforce the idea of God's rule over against Roman rule (Matt 18:2). In this society, children held no political power. They were the most vulnerable, and they were considered a possession like other property. Jesus presents a new expectation for the covenant community that is rooted in childlike action and faith (Matt 19:14-15).

Humility is at the heart of this new reign, which means a practical willingness to share one's possessions. This was just as hard then as it is now (Matt 19:23). Jesus illustrates this teaching by reversing class privileges in Matthew 22. The kingdom of heaven invites the homeless people on the street to the king's banquet.

Matthew 18–22 provides more explanation of the teachings Jesus introduced in his sermon on the mountain (Matt 5). If Jesus is a new Moses, a new Teacher with a fresh set of instructions, then his lessons bear repeating until we learn the expectations of this way of life.

If you are poor, what does it feel like to be near wealthy people in our world? If you are rich, do you invite vulnerable or traumatized people to your home and your gatherings?

Day 6: Mark 10:13-16

Covenant Meditation: God's kingdom belongs to people like these.

For many of us, we are so conditioned to study and analyze scripture for what we want to know about a text that we can miss what God wants us to hear in a passage. Interpreting a reading and listening to a reading are important for our spiritual health and growth. We benefit by learning what an author wrote about life with God in the past. But it's also important to be formed by how God intends for our lives and God's life to connect here and now. Spiritual reading practices help us with this second, life-giving approach to encountering God in scripture.

So for today's meditation we listen for what God is asking us to hear in a text. It may be helpful, although still difficult, to shift from reading with our minds to reading with our hearts. For the first few times, it may feel contrived and awkward because we are not used to setting aside our analytical skills for our spiritual listening skills. So if this practice doesn't at first feel fruitful, remember that any practice takes time.

Turn to Mark 10:13-16, and read the passage silently two or three times. Read slowly, with the intention to hear all the words and to "see" all the scene. Give time to each phrase and sentence. Consider the range of emotions experienced by those in the story—the people bringing the children, the children, Jesus, the disciples, the bystanders.

Now, pray one of these prayers, or one of your own: "God, what do you want me to see?" or "God, help me to hear you through this story," or "Lord, speak; your servant is listening." Then spend a few minutes in silent reflection and prayer, staying open to whatever holds your attention from the scripture—an image, a person, a word, an emotion. Trust that this is God's word for you this day, and close with "Amen."

Group Meeting Experience

Matthew 9:18-33 | *Jesus as deliverer*

One of the government officials installed by the Roman Empire comes to Jesus because his daughter has just died. The loss of a dearly loved child is the most horrible thing any parent can experience. On the way to see the dead child, a woman with chronic bleeding stops Jesus in mid-step when he feels her touch on his clothing. This woman was considered "unclean" by all religious and social authorities for twelve years, and she trusts that Jesus can help her. Then, after delivering the child from death, Jesus heals two blind men.

1. What kind of authority does the ruler grant to Jesus? How does the ruler expect Jesus to apply his authority? What reaction would the woman expect from touching Jesus, a male, in her society?

2. By raising a child from the dead and healing a woman with chronic bleeding, what is Matthew's Gospel saying about people with the lowest status in their community? What does this episode say to the rulers of his day about Jesus' authority? What does this kind of authority mean to rulers in our society?

3. How does Jesus react when he is mocked by people who are mourning the death of the child? What did Jesus mean when he said that the child was not dead?

4. The woman touched Jesus, and Jesus touched the child and then the blind men. What meaning do you perceive in these acts of touching a person who desperately needs help?

5. The words *faith* and *believe* are used in these healing stories. How would you define these words with examples from your spiritual experience? If you believe or have faith, will Jesus heal you?

SIGNS OF FAITHFUL LOVE

Covenant people learn the surprising instructions of a new Teacher, Jesus, who delivers us from suffering, oppression, and death in God's kingdom.

Letters: Romans and Galatians

GRACE

Trusting that the faithfulness of Jesus is enough

Bible Readings

Day 1: Romans 1–3

Day 2: Galatians 1:1–3:5; 5:2-12

Day 3: Galatians 3:6–4:7; Romans 4

Day 4: Romans 5–8; Galatians 5:13-25

Day 5: Romans 9–11

Day 6: Covenant Meditation on Galatians 3:23-29

Day 7: Group Meeting Experience with Romans 14:1–15:2

Covenant Prayer

For parents who live with hardened, unforgiving hearts toward their children

Create a clean heart for me, God; put a new, faithful spirit deep inside me! (Psalm 51:10)

For parents who have learned to love their children unconditionally

Teach me your way, LORD, so that I can walk in your truth. Make my heart focused only on honoring your name. (Psalm 86:11)

OUR LONGING FOR RELATIONSHIP

Each of us is affected by the weakness of sinful desires. Our selfish desires and addictive appetites separate us from God, and thus each of us is guilty of disloyalty in our covenant relationship with God.

51

Christian greetings use words like grace, peace, mercy, *and* love.

LETTERS

Most of the New Testament consists of letters that follow the conventions for sending messages in the first century. Ancient Greco-Roman correspondence served a wide range of purposes, from personal letters dealing with situations among friends and family, to formal missives related to commerce, government, and law. Addressees ranged from specified individuals to general audiences, depending on the letter's intent, content, and tone. Normally a letter would be structured in three parts. First, in the opening, the sender and the recipient would be identified, followed by a greeting and a wish for good health. Second, the body of the letter would introduce its intent, develop the message, and solicit a response. Third, the conclusion would reiterate a wish for health or prosperity before the farewell.

While these features are found in all the letters of the New Testament, the biblical authors also exercise the freedom to depart from convention for the sake of theology and practical pastoral concerns. For example, in addition to proper names, some senders further identify themselves as apostles and slaves of Jesus Christ, and refer to the readers as those called to be God's people or as faithful brothers and sisters in Christ. The simple Greek greeting is Christianized by the use of words like *grace*, *peace*, *mercy*, and *love*. A blessing or prayer replaces a wish for good health. At the close of the letter, instead of a short farewell, it is common to find a doxology (praise of God), a benediction, or even a command for holy kissing.

According to ancient rhetorical conventions, writings fell into three categories: forensic (to accuse and defend), deliberative (to persuade and dissuade), and epideictic (to praise and blame). One or more of these elements can be found in all New Testament letters, as the writers explain the implications of the good news about Jesus Christ, affirm the readers in their faith, warn them of potential danger, and urge them to live like Christians should. Every letter is situational, written to a particular audience to address concerns in actual Christian communities of the first century. These letters substitute for the physical presence and authority of their senders, and so they become important vehicles of encouragement and training in the early church.

Of the thirteen letters attributed to Paul in the New Testament, Galatians and Romans contain the most sustained interpretation of Paul's gospel. Similar vocabulary and themes appear in both letters, such as God's righteousness, God's and Jesus' faithfulness, the works of the Law, or Instruction (Torah), Abraham's example, circumcision of the heart, and freedom made possible through the Holy Spirit. Yet Galatians isn't simply an abridged version of Romans. Each letter distinctly addresses specific issues of concern to its original recipients.

Salvation is a free gift, received solely and entirely through the faithfulness of Jesus.

GALATIANS

Galatians shows Paul's greatest frustrations:

1. "I'm amazed that you are so quickly deserting the one who called you by the grace of Christ. . . . Certain people are confusing you and they want to change the gospel of Christ" (Gal 1:6-7).

2. "You irrational Galatians! Who put a spell on you? . . . I just want to know this from you: Did you receive the Spirit by doing the works of the Law or by believing what you heard? Are you so irrational?" (Gal 3:1-3).

3. "I wish that the ones who are upsetting you would castrate themselves!" (Gal 5:12).

With a sense of urgency, Paul asserts his apostolic authority to correct a grave misrepresentation of the gospel among the churches in Galatia. Paul is the founder of this Christian community, but in his absence some Christian missionaries have taught the Galatian Gentile converts that it isn't enough to become righteous (reconciled with God) through the faithfulness of Jesus on the cross, but that they must adhere to the teachings of the Jewish Law and circumcise all the male believers.

Paul is livid that anyone should attempt to add any requirement for salvation to the sufficiency of Christ's work on the cross. For Paul, imposing the Jewish Law on Gentile believers immediately nullifies the grace that is offered through the gospel, which is a free gift received solely and entirely through the faithfulness of Jesus, and nothing else. Salvation can't be attained by doing the works of the Law (or following the instructions of the Torah). Gentiles are saved as Gentiles, without the need for physical circumcision. Jews are saved as Jews, for whom circumcision rightly marks their election through their ancestor Abraham. There is but one gospel, one saving Jesus Christ, who addresses Jewish and Gentile believers from their different cultural and spiritual starting points.

ROMANS

Paul wrote to the Christians in Rome for a number of reasons:

1. He planned to go to Spain to preach the gospel, and he wanted the churches in Rome to support the mission (Rom 15:22-24, 28).

2. He wanted to collect money for the mother church in Jerusalem, since it was out of Jerusalem that salvation had come to the Gentiles (Rom 15:25-27).

3. If the churches were to support Paul's endeavors financially and spiritually, they would need to know what Paul's gospel entailed. Romans is Paul's apology for (that is, defense of) his gospel.

4. There was tension between Jewish and Gentile Christians in Rome, and Paul addressed it as a pastor and a scholar.

The result is a long and thorough interpretation of the gospel that preserves the integrity of God's justice on the one hand, and God's covenant faithfulness on the other.

Paul begins with the universal need for salvation. There are none righteous before God, because every person is bound by the power of sin (Rom 3:22-23). Gentiles worship idols and indulge in immorality. Jews disobey God's Law even though they know what is expected of them. Without salvation, death awaits all (Rom 5:12).

A just God must deal with sin. A God faithful to the promise to Israel must save, so that other nations will also receive blessings through Israel. Both necessities are fulfilled in Jesus, Israel's anointed one (*Messiah* in Hebrew; *Christ* in Greek). Through Jesus' righteous obedience, "God displayed Jesus as the place of sacrifice where mercy is found by means of his blood" (Rom 3:25), and his resurrection has overcome forever the deadly power of sin. All who have faith that God raised Jesus from the dead, whether Jew or Gentile, can trust God as much as Abraham did (Rom 4:22-25). Following the pattern of Abraham's faith, they are made right with God and transferred from slavery under sin to freedom in the Spirit.

Therefore, God kept God's promise by sending Jesus as Israel's deliverer, the Messiah. The painful question arises as to whether Israel will be cast aside because of their rejection of Jesus. Paul is convinced that God won't go back on the divine promise because God is faithful. As long as there is a part of Israel, no matter how small, that trusts God, Israel will be redeemed and its elect status will remain intact. Paul makes this point emphatically in Romans 3:3-4: "What does it matter, then, if some weren't faithful? Their lack of faith won't cancel God's faithfulness, will it? Absolutely not! God must be true, even if every human being is a liar."

Romans and Galatians insist that salvation is a gift of grace initiated by a covenant-making and covenant-keeping God. Because grace can't be earned, no one can boast. It's only by sharing the same grace with others who trust in God's faithfulness that the unity of the church in all its diversity can be maintained.

Day 1: Romans 1–3
God's solution for the human condition

Paul begins his articulation of the gospel by putting all human beings on a level playing field when it comes to guilt before God. Paul describes sin not as a list of wrongful transgressions, but as a power that enslaves fallen humanity. Paul personifies Sin. Gentiles sin by idolatry and immorality. Jews are indicted for their pride, hypocrisy, and disobedience even with the Instruction given by God through Moses. If nothing is done about this guilt, the result is ultimate destruction for all sinners.

Out of divine grace, God has provided a universal solution for all people, Jew and Gentile, though Paul will always give priority to the Jews: "to the Jew first and also to the Greek" (Rom 1:16). Those who profess faith in Jesus Christ will be justified (made right with God), sanctified (made holy by separation from sin), and saved (from eternal destruction). This salvation is the manifestation of God's righteousness, a gift that is given apart from what is expected by the Law.

The word *righteousness* (or *right*, or *righteous*) comes from the Old Testament, and it often defines a relationship between us and God or us and others. "God's righteousness" means more than proper moral behavior. It expresses God's saving actions. "Being righteous" means that we are restored to a right relationship with God. The Old Testament God who has participated in covenant now enters into the broken world of human existence by sending Jesus to offer salvation to sinful people, so that all may be made right with God through Jesus.

In your reading of Romans and Galatians this week, when you encounter terms such as *righteousness* and *righteous* (in the CEB; or if you see the word *justification* in another translation), try reading those verses by keeping God's relationship with humankind in mind. You are saved through God's faithfulness in raising Jesus, and through Jesus' faithfulness on the cross.

How did you define righteousness *before? Does this definition change your ideas about what righteousness is?*

Day 2: Galatians 1:1–3:5; 5:2-12
The sufficiency of Christ's sacrifice for salvation

Yesterday's selection from Romans 1–3 provides a baseline for comparing the gospel that Paul preaches with a distorted version that is circulating among the churches in Galatia. Note that the point of contention is between some Jewish Christians and some Gentile Christians, not between Jews and Gentiles in general.

Some Jewish Christian teachers have insisted that the Gentile converts in Galatia should follow the Jewish Law so that their salvation is deemed complete. For the men, circumcision is the beginning sign of these works, but the expectation is to keep the whole Jewish Law. The misleading teachers are Christians, so they understand that salvation comes by trusting the faithfulness of Jesus Christ on the cross. Their error, however, lies in adding adherence to the Law on top of salvation through Jesus, as though Jesus' death and resurrection were somehow deficient and in need of supplement.

Paul's ire is understandable. To deny the sufficiency of Christ's work on the cross for salvation immediately reduces God's good news to a non-gospel. If following the teachings of the Law is required for all believers, then salvation is no longer a gift freely given and freely received. The Jerusalem Council had already settled this dispute and decided not to impose such demands on Gentile Christians (Gal 2:1-10). Yet the deception of Cephas and Barnabas shows how easy it is for even well-meaning disciples of Jesus to compromise God's free gift to stave off criticism and harassment (Gal 2:11-14).

What does the desire to do something to contribute to our salvation (for example, in good works or by requiring agreement with additional beliefs) say about us and the culture in which we live?

Day 3: Galatians 3:6–4:7; Romans 4
Righteousness: Abraham's trust in God's promise

Imagine the missionary opponents of Paul imposing circumcision on their Gentile counterparts by invoking the example of Abraham. They might say something like this: "Since Christians now enjoy the benefits of God's promise to Abraham, the men must be circumcised like us, the descendants of Abraham. After all, circumcision is the mark of the covenant."

Remember, Paul himself was a Jewish Christian (or, more precisely, a Christian Jew), so his debate with his fellow Christian Jews is heated. To argue that Gentile Christians don't need to be circumcised, Paul links Gentile Christians to Abraham by way of Abraham's exemplary faith. He bases his counterargument on the historical sequence found in Genesis. In Genesis 12, God calls Abraham and declares that through his descendants the nations will be blessed. In Genesis 15, God promises Abraham offspring. In Genesis 17, God seals God's covenant with Abraham by establishing the rite of circumcision. Hundreds of years later, God gives the Torah (Instruction, or Law) to Israel.

In Galatians 3, Paul emphasizes the order of these events. God's promise came first, and Abraham responded faithfully. Circumcision and the Law followed. Circumcision is not a prerequisite but a confirmation of God's promise. In Romans 4, Paul repeats this point and further highlights Abraham's trust in God in spite of his and Sarah's ages and barrenness. Abraham was deemed righteous before he was circumcised, not after. Since Jesus is the final fulfillment of God's promise to Abraham, Gentile Christians receive the status as Abraham's children because they have their spiritual forefather's faith, not because of a physical mark on their bodies.

Imagine how difficult it was for Abraham to trust in God's promise, given his circumstance as a wandering immigrant. When do you find it difficult to trust God's promise?

57

Day 4: Romans 5–8; Galatians 5:13-25

Reconciliation with God; freedom in the Spirit

What changes when a person is saved? In today's selection, Paul describes our condition before and after trusting in Christ. For example, a person who trusts God is no longer alienated from God but is reconciled to God. Every person goes from being like Adam (who disobeyed God's instruction and experienced death) to following Christ (whose faithfulness results in righteousness and eternal life). Without Christ, a person is ruled by sin, but with Christ, a person is liberated from sin to become God's servant. Only God's power that raised Jesus from the dead is strong enough to deliver sinners from the death-dealing power of sin and place them under God's benevolent rule. Life redeemed by God's grace is now empowered by the Spirit. The transfer of allegiance (from sin to God) leads to a transformed life.

What about the Law? Paul now recognizes the limited function of the Law. The Law exposes sin and shows Israel how to live. But it is a temporary custodian of our relationship with God until Christ's arrival (Gal 3:24; Rom 10:4). Even though the Law helps Israel, including Paul, to do the right thing and work toward the good of others, Paul says it doesn't have the power to save us from the effects of sin, because even the Law can be manipulated by sin to cause human beings to violate the teachings in the Torah.

What selfish desires or weaknesses have separated you from God? What does Christ's faithfulness and power over sin mean for you?

Day 5: Romans 9–11

God's faithfulness to Israel

Some claim that the Christian church replaced Israel as God's chosen people because the Jewish leaders rejected Jesus as Messiah. Paul, a Christian Jew, doesn't excuse Israel's rejection of Jesus, nor does he insist on seeking righteousness through the Law. Paul laments the misplaced zeal and ignorance of the Jewish leaders, a zeal that he once possessed. In heart-wrenching prose,

Paul expresses his deep love for Israel as he counts on the fact that "God's gifts and calling can't be taken back" (Rom 11:29).

Paul's hope for Israel is based in God's faithful love. God is merciful. Israel's special purpose is based in God's mercy and not in Israel's achievements. In the Old Testament, even when Israel was most deserving of God's wrath for breaking the covenant, God preserved the few who remained faithful. While God makes the Jewish leaders stubborn, this allows time for the good news about Jesus' faithfulness on the cross to be preached to the Gentiles. When and how will Israel be saved? Only God knows, but Paul expects that "all Israel will be saved, as it is written" in the scriptures (Rom 11:26).

Paul doesn't take sides between Jews and Gentiles. Neither one is better than the other. Both are found guilty before God, and both need salvation.

In what ways does spiritual superiority about salvation appear in our churches today?

Day 6: Galatians 3:23-29

Covenant Meditation: All are one in Christ Jesus.

This week's readings explored our relationship with God as a gift that none of us deserve. We don't deserve grace because every human being falls short of God's expectations. Grace is evident through the faithful love that God shows each of us, and God expects that we also will share this gift with others.

The message about God's grace can be shared through teaching, preaching, serving, caring, witnessing, and praying. Here we learn to pray a fragment of scripture until we realize that we are all God's children through faith in Christ Jesus. We all belong to Christ.

To begin, find a quiet place where you can spend time in meditative, uninterrupted reading. Get comfortable and focus on your breathing so that you can be fully present at this time. Turn to Galatians 3:23-29. Read these verses silently and slowly two or three times. After you have completed these readings, look back over the verses you have read, and from the words found there, form a brief, one-line prayer for your life. Some examples: "God, unlock my heart," or "I am God's child."

It's only by sharing the same grace with others who trust in God's faithfulness that the unity of the church in all its diversity can be maintained.

59

You could pray, "Lord, help us be one in Christ," or simply "Clothe me with Christ." Your prayer can come from any of the words or phrases in this text, because it is *your* prayer for *your* life and circumstances. Take the time you need to form this small prayer. You may need to write a few in the margin before one rises to the top for you.

Once you have a prayer in mind, sit quietly and repeat your prayer to yourself again and again for a few minutes. Trust that the prayer that comes to you is a prayer from God for you. Allow God's word to make a home in you this day through your prayer. Imagine writing this prayer on your heart. When you are ready to end praying through this scripture, simply close with "Amen."

Group Meeting Experience

Romans 14:1–15:2 | *Practicing grace*

In the five daily readings, we looked closely at God's grace toward humankind as demonstrated in the gift of salvation through Jesus Christ. But grace doesn't stop there. Only by extending the grace we have received from God to others can we truly claim to understand what God has done for us.

Extending grace in human relationships isn't avoidance of conflict or leniency without standards. When there is disagreement within the body of Christ, the integrity of grace is tested. This situation faced by the Roman congregation is a case in point. While we may no longer argue over eating food sacrificed to idols, the principle behind Paul's advice is still highly relevant if we want to grow together into a grace-filled community.

1. Many Gentile Christians in the Roman faith community, even though they were followers of Jesus Christ, had relatives and coworkers who were not. In social functions and family gatherings, these Christians came into contact with idol food, because pagan celebrations often took place in temples. At times, meat sold in the market had also been sacrificed to idols. The question arose as to whether Christians may eat food sacrificed to idols. Paul's answer seems to be, "It depends." In your reading of Romans 14:1–15:2, what underlying principle can you glean from Paul's advice? How does grace work hand in hand with sound judgment?

2. Even though the issues may not concern eating food sacrificed to idols or the observance of special days, what practices and opinions may become points of contention in churches today? What are appropriate ways to engage these disputes?

3. Paul writes, "Each person must have their own convictions" (Rom 14:5). Can this phrase be taken out of context and misused?

4. Unity is a goal and a challenge in the Christian witness to the world. What beginning steps can you take, within your own heart and your sphere of influence, to practice Christian charity and accountability without denying the diversity within the body of Christ? At its best, what does grace look like in your Christian community?

SIGNS OF FAITHFUL LOVE

Covenant people trust that the faithfulness of Jesus on the cross is all that we need to restore our broken and disloyal relationship with God.

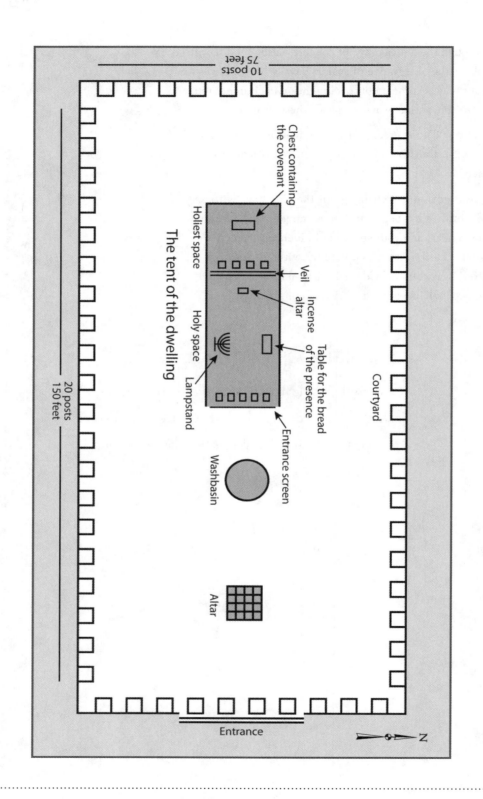

God's dwelling, a meeting tent, as described in Exodus 25 and 26

Hebrews

WITNESS
Showing gratitude and loyalty to God

Bible Readings

Day 1: Hebrews 1–2; Psalm 8

Day 2: Hebrews 3–4; Numbers 14

Day 3: Hebrews 4:14–7:28; Psalm 110

Day 4: Hebrews 8:1–10:18; Leviticus 16

Day 5: Hebrews 10:19–13:25

Day 6: Covenant Meditation on Hebrews 6:10-11

Day 7: Group Meeting Experience with Hebrews 5:11–6:12

Covenant Prayer

For those who aren't sure of God's presence or favor

He did this so that we, who have taken refuge in him, can be encouraged to grasp the hope that is lying in front of us. (Hebrews 6:18)

For those who share the gift of hospitality

Don't neglect to open up your homes to guests, because by doing this some have been hosts to angels without knowing it. (Hebrews 13:2)

OUR LONGING FOR RELATIONSHIP

When gratitude goes missing from our lives, sin separates us further from everyone we love.

HEBREWS

The principal theme of Hebrews is captured in its final exhortation: "Since we are receiving a kingdom that can't be shaken, let's continue to express our gratitude" (Heb 12:28).

Hebrews focuses on three main, interrelated topics: (1) the benefits that have come or will come to the person who puts his or her trust in Jesus; (2) the status and quality of the giver of these benefits; and (3) appropriate and inappropriate responses to such a giver's selfless generosity. The author creates a catalog of ways in which God has graced the converts in Christ:

• Providing freedom from slavery to the fear of death (Heb 2:14-15)

• The timely help of God's Son as mediator of God's favor (Heb 2:17-18; 4:14-16)

• The gifts of enlightenment and the Holy Spirit (Heb 6:4-5)

• Hope that gives them a steady anchor in life's storms (Heb 6:19-20)

• The removal of every defilement that has kept them apart from God (Heb 8:7–10:18)

• The promise of entering into the place of God's rest and full presence (Heb 4:1; 9:24), arriving where Christ has gone (Heb 2:9-10; 6:19-20), where they will enjoy their "better and lasting possessions" in their true homeland (Heb 10:34; 11:16; 12:28; 13:14)

> **Optional:** *An additional video on grace and response is available for download from* **CovenantBibleStudy.com**.

Mixed into this topic of how we benefit from grace, the author dwells on the exalted status of Jesus throughout God's cosmos. The writer stresses Jesus' matchless honor and status and Jesus' use of that status to provide reliable mediation between his followers and God (Heb 1:5-14; 3:1-6; 4:14-16; 7; 10:19-23). Both of these topics—the benefits of grace and the status of Jesus—provide the foundation for the third topic: the necessity of responding to such a giver and such gifts and promises in a way that shows appropriate gratitude, and of avoiding any response that would dishonor, and thus provoke, such an exalted figure who acted so generously.

Hebrews is anonymous. While it was attributed to Paul fairly early in its life in the church, it probably wasn't written by him but rather by one of the many other members of his team. This was someone who was much more highly skilled in public speaking and not afraid to show it (contrast Paul's philosophy of preaching in 1 Cor 2:1-5). Since it was written by a member of the Pauline mission, it was probably written to a church founded or nurtured by this mission—and therefore to a mixed congregation that had brought together both Jews and Gentiles into one church and not, strictly speaking, just "Hebrews."

This congregation, personally known to the author (Heb 13:19), had displayed exemplary faithfulness to Jesus and to each other in the face of their neighbors' hostility. These neighbors viewed the converts' new commitment to this strange Jewish splinter group as representing an insult to the many gods they once acknowledged (if they were Gentile) or a serious departure from loyal observance of the Torah (if they were Jewish). The neighbors tried a wide array of shaming techniques to bring the deviants back in line (Heb 10:32-34). Despite the shame, pain, and loss inflicted on them, the converts remained bold in their witness to the value of God's gifts through Jesus and bold in their support for each other.

With the passing of time, however, it became harder to live with the loss of status and place in society. Some converts began to withdraw from the group (Heb 10:24-25), and the author is concerned that this will further erode commitment. Such withdrawal, the author argues, is "anti-witness." It says loudly and clearly to the world that God's gifts and favor aren't worth the cost of keeping them. Hence, from beginning to end, the author magnifies the value of what the hearers have in Christ and what benefits are yet to come, so that they will want to act in a way that shows gratitude for God's costly favors and loyalty to the one, Jesus, who promises even more.

Although traditionally called a "letter," Hebrews is really a sermon that has been written down since the author couldn't preach it in person. It doesn't open with the typical letter formula seen in Romans, Galatians, 1 Peter, or 2 John (though it does transition into greetings, prayer requests, and announcements at its close). We should listen to it, therefore, as a stirring speech meant to convince and motivate. Like all effective public speaking in the classical world, this sermon aims not only to present logical argument (which it does quite well), but also to stir the hearers' emotions, to arouse confidence in the preacher's credibility, and to keep the audience's attention from beginning to end.

> One of the early church writers, Origen, asked: "Who wrote this letter? Only God knows!"

> The preacher wants the hearers to feel fear when it comes to choosing a course of action that would insult or bring dishonor to the God who had given so much to them.

The preacher wants them to feel confidence when they choose courses of action that show their loyalty to and alignment with Jesus, the surest mediator of God's favor. He wants them to feel a high-minded jealousy of the fame of the heroes of faith, so that they will walk in their footsteps. The emotional impact is as important as the logical content, since the preacher is looking for commitment to particular behaviors and not merely for assent to his statements.

As any strong sermon would, Hebrews calls us to deeper reflection on our lives.

How fully does your life reflect gratitude and loyalty to God? Think about a personal, spiritual, relational, or work-related issue facing you. How would a sense of gratitude (or thankfulness) affect this issue?

Day 1: Hebrews 1–2; Psalm 8
Praise for God's Son

The author's celebration of the Son's honor in Hebrews 1 serves an argumentative purpose that emerges only in Hebrews 2:1-4. The degree to which the Son is superior to the angels (established in Heb 1:5-14) is the degree to which the preacher's audience needs to pay closer attention to the word announced by the Son (Heb 2:1-4). This is the degree to which those same hearers face greater danger than that faced by people who violated the first covenant. At the same time, the Son's honor anticipates the glory that will belong to Christ's faithful followers, whom he leads to glory in fulfillment of the vision of Psalm 8 (Heb 2:5-10), and who belong to the same exalted family (Heb 2:11-13). It also underlines the exalted status of the one who has committed himself to help the converts arrive at that good end (Heb 2:14-18). The opening chapter incidentally gives a sampling of how the author finds that the "many" pieces of God's revelation in the ancient scriptures come together in the decisive revelation made in God's Son.

Who is Jesus according to the preacher, and how does he use his power and status?

Day 2: Hebrews 3–4; Numbers 14
Faithfulness and loyalty

These two chapters parallel Hebrews 1–2 in many ways. The comparison of Jesus and Moses (Heb 3:1-6), like the comparison of Jesus and the angels (Heb 1:5-14), underscores the importance of responding to Jesus' word of promise with greater faithfulness and obedience. Otherwise, one may suffer even greater loss than those who responded poorly to God under Moses (see the story of the exodus generation's failure in Num 14).

Bear in mind that the pressing issue for the preacher's audience concerns whether or not to persevere in Christian commitment (see Heb 2:1-3; 3:12-13; 4:1, 11; 6:4-8; 10:24-25, 32-36), given all it has cost them in terms of worldly standing and resources. The author places them at the threshold of entering the greater "rest" that God has prepared for God's people, namely, God's eternal realm. "Rest" is a new image for the "glory" mentioned in Hebrews 2:10 that is the believer's destiny. Jesus has already entered into this place of "rest" as their forerunner—just as his followers will if they keep running faithfully (Heb 2:9-10; 4:1; 6:19-20)!

What was the exodus generation's failure? How does the preacher use their story to interpret his own audience's situation?

Day 3: Hebrews 4:14–7:28; Psalm 110
Jesus is our covenant mediator.

One of the greatest gifts the converts have received is assured access to God through an unfailing mediator (Heb 4:14-16). The preacher offers proof of the validity of Jesus' high priesthood on the basis of a Christ-centered reading of Psalm 110 (Heb 5:5-6, 10), which leads eventually to reflection on the obscure figure of Melchizedek as Jesus' prototype (Heb 7:1-10). This foundation, together with other reflections on Jesus' sinlessness and personal acquaintance with trial and suffering, undergirds the author's promotion of the greater value of Jesus as our mediator with God. For the writer of Hebrews, Jesus is even superior to the only other available mediators in the scriptural tradition—the priests from the tribe of Levi (Heb 7:11-28).

The preacher interrupts his argument with a digression that is just as important as the main line of the sermon (Heb 5:11–6:20). He snaps the hearers to renewed attention (Heb 5:11-14), and the fact that some of their congregation have begun to slip away is proof of his hard words. In this digression, he stresses that perseverance in gratitude and in bearing fruit that pleases God is the only safe response to God's generous cultivation of the community of faith.

What reasons does the author give for confidence in Jesus when it comes to winning God's favor for us?

Day 4: Hebrews 8:1–10:18; Leviticus 16

Jesus grants us entrance to the most holy place.

The central idea in this passage hinges on understanding how limited our access to God's space was under the first covenant because of the danger that faced those who entered God's space with the contamination of sin or other pollutions (Heb 9:6-8). It hinges also on the belief that God wanted more for God's relationship with the people (Heb 9:9-10), as John captures so beautifully in Revelation (Rev 21:3-4, 22-23; 22:3-4). The ritual for the Day of Reconciliation (Lev 16) is essential background. In this ritual, the defilement of sin is removed from the people and also from the most holy place, to restore the status quo between God and Israel.

The preacher uses a ritual for the Day of Reconciliation as a model for what Jesus achieved for his followers in his death and his ascension into the heavenly realm of God. The author invokes the idea that the meeting tent was just a model of the divine realm: Jesus now plays out the ritual of reconciliation decisively on this cosmic canvas. The result is that not only the high priest, but all the people attached to this priest can enter the most holy place—no longer the cramped space in the meeting tent, but "heaven itself," God's eternal realm and full presence.

Are you confident about access to God's presence?

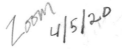

Day 5: Hebrews 10:19–13:25
Faith hall of fame

This section contains the famous "faith chapter" (Heb 11), which extends forward to the example of Jesus as faith's pioneer and perfecter (Heb 12:1-3) and backward to the community's own earlier example (Heb 10:32-39). Trusting God and remaining faithful requires (1) looking ahead to the unseen, future acts of God; (2) looking to the unseen but eternal homeland to which God calls us; and (3) often acting contrary to our interests in terms of this world's enjoyments. This section invites us to dig deeply back into the Old Testament and even into some of the writings between the Testaments in the Apocrypha (such as 2 Macc 6:18–7:42 for Heb 11:35*b*). Think about how each of the examples selected and crafted by the preacher reinforces these lessons.

The author continues to warn the hearers that God's investment in them, costly as it was, requires similar investment and commitment on their part (Heb 10:26-31; 12:25-29). Anything less would mean making light of God's gift and what they cost the Giver. This investment is to be shown largely in the converts' continued investment in each other (Heb 13:1-6), and in their continued willingness to bear shame for Jesus, even as Jesus bore shame for them (Heb 12:1-2; 13:12-14).

How does your congregation reflect the preacher's vision for committed community, and where does the sermon to the Hebrews challenge you to grow?

Day 6: Hebrews 6:10-11
Covenant Meditation: Grateful love serves.

Earlier in this week's episode, we learned that Hebrews was experienced as a sermon. When we read the content of Hebrews silently to ourselves, we are likely to skim, risking the loss of the poetic and oral rhythm that is often present in a sermon. The meanings of sermonic words are conveyed from speaker to listener through inflection, intonation, and emotion.

Today we will slow down and return to the spiritual practice of speaking the scripture aloud, allowing two short verses from Hebrews to become a spoken prayer. As you prepare for this practice today, find a quiet place where you can comfortably vocalize the text.

To begin, locate Hebrews 6:10-11 in your Bible. Then, very slowly, read the text out loud. Take your time; don't rush through this reading. Speak the words as though to someone who longs to hear what you have to say. Pause for a minute of silence after verbalizing the scripture, then repeat this practice. Resist going quickly, even if the pace seems awkward to you. Allow the words to form in you and from you, paying attention to emotions or memories evoked by the text. When you have completed speaking the scripture a second time, rest within a silent prayer, of gratitude.

Group Meeting Experience

Hebrews 5:11–6:12 | *Honor*

The following questions will help you dig into this passage:

1. In light of the defection of some converts from the congregation, what kind of intervention does the preacher expect from the more grounded members (Heb 5:11-14)? Where else does he call for such intervention in the lives of shakier believers?

2. Think about the audience's situation (Heb 10:24-25, 32-36). What is the connection between their perseverance and the honor or dishonor of God and Christ in this world (Heb 6:6)?

3. How does the agricultural analogy of Hebrews 6:7-8 reinforce the point of Hebrews 6:4-6?

4. What indication does Hebrews 6:9-12 give that the audience has been bearing good fruit in response to God's cultivation? In what direction does this motivate them?

5. Where do you find yourself and your congregation challenged by this passage?

SIGNS OF FAITHFUL LOVE

God sent us the perfect mediator, Jesus, whose victory urges us ahead and restores us on the right path among the cloud of witnesses who live faithfully.

1 and 2 Corinthians

LOGIC OF THE CROSS

Consider what Christ accomplished.

Bible Readings

Day 1: 1 Corinthians 1–4 ✓

Day 2: 1 Corinthians 7–10

Day 3: 1 Corinthians 11–14

Day 4: 1 Corinthians 15; 2 Corinthians 1:1-11; 4–6

Day 5: 1 Corinthians 16; 2 Corinthians 7–9

Day 6: Covenant Meditation on 2 Corinthians 4:7-12

Day 7: Group Meeting Experience with 1 Corinthians 13:4-8

Covenant Prayer

For the brokenhearted and grieving

Come to me, all you who are struggling hard and carrying heavy loads, and I will give you rest. (Matthew 11:28)

For the newly baptized, confirmed, and for those who have recently professed their faith in Christ

There is one God the Father. All things come from him, and we belong to him. And there is one Lord Jesus Christ. All things exist through him, and we live through him. (1 Corinthians 8:6)

OUR LONGING FOR RELATIONSHIP

At some point in life, we each will experience the lack or loss of love. We can't live without love.

1 AND 2 CORINTHIANS

Fools for Christ. That's what Paul calls the Corinthians to become (1 Cor 4:10). But they are too caught up in their posturing, their competing, their bickering, and their so-called "wisdom" to hear Paul keenly. Paul founded this church in Corinth in the early 50s CE. Corinth was no backwoods. In fact, it was the capital of the province of Achaia, and it supported a diverse population. It had much of what one would expect in an urban center: sports, conspicuous wealth (alongside much poverty), social hierarchy, diversity of religions and peoples, and all forms of entertainment, including those distractions of the seedy sort.

The Corinthian believers lived within a culture that put a high value on honor or prestige, where public boasting and puffing up oneself were key to a person's self-worth and public value. In such a culture, the loss of honor meant shame and worthlessness.

The Corinthian believers also lived in a world where there were patrons and clients. The patron was expected to take some responsibility for the client, but only if the client recognized the superiority and honor of the patron. The patronage system implies a moral obligation to help others, but the person being helped would be considered inferior.

The apostle Paul had his work cut out for him when he tried to urge the early Christians in Corinth to stop behaving like patrons toward clients. Instead, Paul insisted that these Christians become followers of a crucified Christ who offers a different kind of life. This way of life means equality for the members of the body through covenant relationships.

Paul stayed in Corinth a year and a half teaching and preaching the principles of the way of Jesus (see Acts 18:11). The Corinthian converts carried into their church many of the unhealthy social behaviors that were learned from the culture. Consequently, a few years after planting the church, Paul begins receiving letters and reports of problems (1 Cor 1:11; 16:17-18). First and Second Corinthians represent Paul's response to these issues of division and confusion that afflicted the community. He addresses questions and problems that include sexual immorality (1 Cor 5–6), lawsuits (1 Cor 6), relationships between spouses and betrothed couples (1 Cor 7), food sacrificed to idols (1 Cor 8–10), problems in worship (1 Cor 11–14), spiritual gifts (1 Cor 12), resurrection (1 Cor 15), and the collection for the believers in Jerusalem (1 Cor 16:1-4).

However, each of these situations is a symptom of the larger issue Paul must confront: This church needs a lesson in how to solve problems. Paul teaches them to stop using human reason to sort out their conflicts. Instead, he urges the Corinthian church to reason with the "mind of Christ" (1 Cor 2:16). He seeks to destroy intellectual and spiritual "fortresses," to "destroy arguments, and every defense that is raised up to oppose the knowledge of God. They [disciples] capture every thought to make it obedient to Christ" (2 Cor 10:4-5).

When in doubt about anything, defer to the cross.

The pivotal solution to doubt, immoral behavior, improper worship, and conflict in 1 and 2 Corinthians is found at 1 Corinthians 1:18. Paul directs the Corinthians to the "logic of the cross." Most translations read the Greek (*logos*) as "message of the cross." However, Paul's teaching here contains more than a communication between a sender and a recipient. It's a mentality: When in doubt about anything, defer to the cross.

If anyone had room to boast, to lord his power over others, to be arrogant, surely it was Jesus. However, Jesus chose the path of humility (Phil 2:5-8) in order to build up others. "Knowledge makes people arrogant, but love builds people up" (1 Cor 8:1). Paul himself will model this Christlike humility for the immature Corinthians and then call them to "follow my example, just like I follow Christ's" (1 Cor 11:1). While he could have come among them in a lofty way, "preaching God's secrets to you like I was an expert in speech or wisdom," instead he decided "not to think about anything while I was with you except Jesus Christ, and to preach him as crucified" (1 Cor 2:1-2). In 1 Corinthians 9, Paul notes that he has all kinds of rights as an apostle (to be married; to be paid a salary): "However, we haven't made use of this right, but we put up with everything so we don't put any obstacle in the way of the gospel of Christ" (1 Cor 9:12*b*).

No doubt, like many of us converts, when the Corinthians first heard the gospel from Paul, they were bowled over to find that the gospel was all about them, that it spoke into their own lives in very compelling ways—enough to convince them to adopt this new, if strange, faith. But eventually you must grow up and learn that the gospel isn't really all about you after all. It's about being one part in a huge community across time and space. It turns out that getting over yourself can actually be a liberating experience, a gain rather than a loss. Finding yourself in a covenant community is the end goal. That goal is not based in "self-actualization." For Paul, and for Jesus before him, you find yourself only by losing yourself in the gathered community of Christ-followers.

Getting over yourself can actually be a liberating experience, a gain rather than a loss. Finding yourself in a covenant community is the end goal.

Paul opens the letter as expected, with a greeting that names the senders (Paul and Sosthenes) and the receivers (the church of God in Corinth). Notice that Paul here says "church," not "churches" as he does elsewhere, because the Corinthians need extreme emphasis on unity. He then offers a thanksgiving section in which he gives thanks to God for them, renews the bond across the distance, and announces the main themes of the letter. He then treats the issues mentioned above and concludes with greetings.

An earlier letter is mentioned in 1 Corinthians 5:9, but that letter is now lost to us. So our 1 Corinthians is really at least the second letter Paul sent. Clearly, 1 Corinthians didn't resolve all of the problems. Other issues appeared or became urgent, namely, the arrival of the "super-apostles" who tried to turn the Corinthians against Paul.

The second (or third) letter to the Corinthians has four broad sections. Second Corinthians 1:1-11 is the greeting. In 2 Corinthians 1:12–7:16, Paul defends his actions and his credibility as an apostle (one sent by God), and he affirms his love for the Corinthians. In 2 Corinthians 8:1–9:15, Paul gives instructions for the collection to the poor in the Jerusalem church. In 2 Corinthians 10:1–13:10, Paul offers a defense of his apostleship and closes the letter with a greeting.

In 1 and 2 Corinthians, Paul's correspondence is tied together by his desire to cultivate a covenant relationship where each person in the community depends on the other. This new mind-set (the logic of the cross) governs how the Corinthians imagine themselves as Christ's body when solving the problems we encounter in relationships.

Day 1: 1 Corinthians 1–4

Immature boasting

After offering his thanks (1 Cor 1:4-9), Paul immediately launches into a critique of the fractured nature of the Corinthian community. According to "Chloe's people," one faction has clung to Paul, another to Apollos, another to Cephas. Then there's the group that outdoes them all by claiming that they follow Christ! Paul insists that this type of competitive boasting is a sign of the Corinthians' spiritual immaturity and their tendency toward jealousy and strife. Rather than bask in the adoration of his devotees, Paul defers to the cross and makes a move toward community and humility. Models of leadership, the insignificance of their difference, and the lure of power associated with a favored leader distract the Corinthians. Paul finds their petty concerns disturbing because they limit his ability to dispense spiritual knowledge and diminish the Corinthians' opportunities to live into God's promise for their lives.

Contrary to worldly wisdom that encourages exaggerated self-promotion and selfish claims to power, spiritual wisdom is characterized by learning to depend on each other with the kind of love that can't be repaid.

Is there this kind of division in your own church? Is there this kind of division between your church and other churches in your community? Based on this passage, how do you think Paul would address the things that divide the church in your community?

Day 2: 1 Corinthians 7–10

My freedom is good, but it's not always good for others.

The Corinthian Christians believed and declared, "I have the freedom to do anything" (1 Cor 6:12). Paul agrees to this freedom, but this freedom must function according to the logic of the cross. So while "I have the freedom to do anything," it turns out that "not everything is helpful" (1 Cor 6:12). Here Paul doesn't add the personal qualifier "to me." So the issue isn't whether the action merely benefits the individual as much as whether it builds up and seeks to understand how one's individual actions might serve the community's common good (see also 1 Cor 10:23-24).

In 1 Corinthians 6, Paul advises the Corinthians to stop having sex (with prostitutes), and the next chapter (1 Cor 7) counsels other Corinthians to start having sex (with their partners). Not surprisingly, Paul indicates the normal first-century idea that a husband has authority over his wife's body; but, shockingly, he also claims that the wife has authority over her husband's body. And then another surprise: As a good Jew in a Roman society that emphasized and rewarded procreation, Paul advises against marriage if at all possible. The one concession he makes is for lust. To those who were engaged, he counseled them not to get married, because Paul believed Christ was coming back very soon (1 Cor 7:31). This also seems to have affected his advice that slaves should not bother trying to become free (1 Cor 7:21-24).

The Corinthians' questions about food sacrificed to idols is tackled in 1 Corinthians 8–10. Some Corinthians were apparently questioning whether they were "free" to attend meals at pagan temples. They argued that God is the one God, and therefore there are no such things as idols, so that food is morally neutral. However, other Corinthian believers weren't as convinced. Attending these meals at pagan temples alongside other Corinthian believers compromised the so-called "weak" believers' moral consciences. Paul uses this question to restate his position on freedom in Christ. According to Paul, your freedom as an individual follower of Jesus can't be separated from the social and moral effects of your behavior on others. All believers possess knowledge, argues Paul. But knowledge minus love results in individual conceit rather than the building up of community.

The issue in 1 Corinthians 10 is slightly different from that in 1 Corinthians 8, but the same policy prevails: When making an ethical decision, your choice depends on how it might affect the particular person or people witnessing your behavior. In one setting, it might be perfectly fine to eat the meat; in another setting, the same action might wound the conscience of a "weaker" Christian who is superstitious or ignorant. In a stunning and memorable statement, Paul says, "The weak brother or sister for whom Christ died is destroyed by your knowledge" (1 Cor 8:11). Such a person may appear to us primarily as an ignorant nuisance; to God, that same person is one for whom Christ died. As Christians, instead of insisting on our own rights, we are to be willing like Paul to "become all things to all people, so I could save some by all possible means" (1 Cor 9:22).

Sometimes we talk about our freedom in terms of "rights." Give some examples of where your right to do something infringes on the well-being of another person.

Day 3: 1 Corinthians 11–14

No person is better than another.

Two issues are addressed in 1 Corinthians 11: proper head coverings during worship and eating the fellowship meal. On the issue of head coverings, Paul lifts up three major points. First, he affirms that both men and woman may pray and prophesy so long as both reflect God's glory. Second, his argument seems to preserve, even within the sphere of Christian identity, female and male gender distinctions. At first glance he seems to follow a common cultural understanding of viewing men as having authority over women. However, in the same breath he argues for a mutual interdependence between men and women that is more horizontal than vertical (1 Cor 11:3-16).

In 1 Corinthians 11:17-34, Paul invites the Corinthians to rethink how they treat each other during the holy communion meal. Paul warns that their coming together to eat the Lord's Supper has turned into a display of divisive greed and inequity. Those who partake in the Lord's Supper with no regard for the well-being of the poor or less wealthy individuals in their community are responsible for instances of sickness and death among members of the community, and they also merit the Lord's judgment.

Spiritual gifts are addressed in 1 Corinthians 12, emphasizing their source from God and their purpose of building up community. Everyone is gifted, no gift is better or more important than another, and each gift is just that—a gift—so no one has grounds for boasting. Some gifts lend themselves to more showiness than others. Consider "speaking in tongues" (*glossolalia*), for example. That's a highly dramatic gift that draws attention. For the gift to serve the church and its witness rather than the individual, the congregation needs a translator or an interpreter. The church should always have the "visitor" in mind when it plans and conducts its worship.

How do you feel about praising someone for his or her gift?
Do you think Christians should honor celebrities?

Day 4: 1 Corinthians 15; 2 Corinthians 1:1-11; 4–6

Our faith is pointless without Christ's resurrection.

In 1 Corinthians 15, Paul responds to those who deny that there is a resurrection of the dead. He begins by reminding deniers of the tradition that he has already learned from those before him regarding Christ's resurrection and appearances. He also refers to the scriptural witness. Though the argument that Paul makes for the next fifty verses can be difficult to follow, Paul is convinced that Christ has been raised; we will be raised; death will be thoroughly defeated; we will have a sort of body that we can't yet fully discern; and God will be "all in all" (1 Cor 15:28). Nothing will exist outside of God. Ponder that.

The themes of death and resurrected life are also examined in 2 Corinthians. Notice the emphasis on affliction and consolation. Paul is afflicted, God consoles, and Paul extends that consolation to other sufferers. Who among us hasn't been rescued or at least encouraged by 2 Corinthians 4:7-9 (our "treasure in clay pots")? And as Paul has encouraged and inspired his listeners, so he expects the Corinthians to let the old things fade away and to become creatures of this new covenant (2 Cor 5:16-18).

What do you think it means to be reconciled with God so that you become a new creation?

Day 5: 1 Corinthians 16; 2 Corinthians 7–9

Cheerful generosity

In 1 Corinthians 16:1-4, Paul reminds the Corinthians about the collection of money for God's people in Jerusalem, and he provides brief instruction on taking up an offering in the Christian community. In 2 Corinthians 8–9, Paul offers more detail about the cultural and theological importance of making a contribution to support God's people in Jerusalem. First, salvation came to the Gentiles through the Jews, so the Gentiles owe something to the Jews (see Rom 15:26-28). Second, as demonstrated in Galatians 2, the collection symbolizes the unity of the church's mission, even though various branches of the church may have different people that they can see, know, or reach (Paul evangelizes Gentiles; James and John evangelize Jews). Third, those who have more than others are to give for the sake of those who have less (2 Cor 8:12-15). God loves a cheerful giver (2 Cor 9:7).

How does 2 Corinthians 8–9 affect your behavior? Reflect on the ways you give to your church and the ways that your church gives to the world.

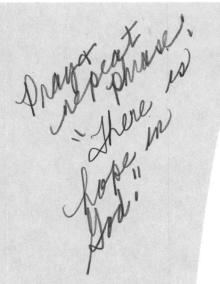

Day 6: 2 Corinthians 4:7-12
Covenant Meditation: God will rescue us.

We return to the ancient spiritual practice of *lectio divina*, by spending time with a few verses of scripture. The intent of scripture meditation is not to teach us about a text, but to teach us from the text—to let the text transform us, rather than inform us. Both ways of accessing God's word are important for our spiritual lives—to be informed and transformed by scripture.

Our text is 2 Corinthians 4:7-12. After locating this passage, take a few moments to become quiet. Take a few deep, slow breaths, paying attention to the rhythm of inhaling and exhaling. Remember that God is as close to you as breath. Now read the whole text one time to get the feel of the passage, and then pause for a minute of silence before your second reading.

As you read these verses again, listen for a word or phrase in the passage that catches your attention. Resist any temptation to analyze or discount the phrase or word that strikes you. Contemplative reading practices are grounded in the belief that through scripture, God has a word for us, for our particular and unique circumstances, and that we can, through practice, learn to hear God's word for us. While keeping this practice in mind, spend two minutes silently repeating the word or phrase that draws you in.

Now prepare a third reading, but focus on the question, "How is my life touched by this word?" After reading the text again, take several minutes to consider how the word or phrase intersects with your life right now. What is a connection between your life and the part of this scripture that has come to your attention? Be open to any possibilities that arise.

Finally, as you read 2 Corinthians 4:7-12 one last time, do so asking, "Is God inviting me to respond in some way to this reading? Is God inviting me to some action through this word?" Ask God to help you respond. If an invitation doesn't seem clear, ask God to connect your life to the scripture in some way. Conclude this reading by placing your life in God's hands and resting there.

Group Meeting Experience

1 Corinthians 13:4-8 | *Love never fails.*

The "love chapter" is often read when a marriage covenant is affirmed during a wedding. The importance of faithful, patient, and kind love is just as crucial to a lasting commitment in the home as it is in the covenant community at church.

This faithful love requires discipline, as much work as it takes to develop deep knowledge of any subject. Our feelings about "love," a word used to describe our attachment to someone, won't last or sustain our relationships if those emotions are shallow, impulsive, convenient, or self-centered.

1. Describe a time when someone told the truth but did it in a way that seemed harsh or arrogant. Choose a couple of role models who can demonstrate for the participants how to say something hard and yet preserve love in the relationship or community.

2. What do you think is more important: to believe the right things or to do the right things?

3. Think of a time when you were jealous. What does that tell you about the relationship with the person who made you jealous? While you might recognize the feeling in a situation, how do you define *jealousy*?

4. In more than one translation, compare how Deuteronomy 5:9 is stated. What does God experience when we follow or become attached to substitutes for a relationship with God? In our

covenant with God, what evidence do we have of God's faithful love, and what evidence do we offer of our loyal love?

5. In several places in the Old Testament, a list of God's attributes is recited, which demonstrates the biblical behaviors that characterize God's covenant love. The first occurrence is at Exodus 34:6 when God passed by Moses on the mountain to offer the covenant and the Ten Commandments. Moses responds, "The LORD! The LORD! a God who is compassionate and merciful, very patient, full of great loyalty and faithfulness." Look up and discuss the contexts for several other passages that cite this covenant response: Numbers 14:18; Nehemiah 9:17; Psalms 86:15; 103:8; 145:8; Joel 2:13; Jonah 4:2; Nahum 1:3.

SIGNS OF FAITHFUL LOVE

Our hearts and lives are changed by the logic of the cross, which proves Jesus' faithful love for us.

Deuteronomy, Joshua, Judges, 1 Samuel

COVENANT RENEWAL
Refreshing our relationships

Bible Readings

Day 1: Deuteronomy 5–9

Day 2: Deuteronomy 29–32

Day 3: Joshua 1–2; 23–24

Day 4: Judges 1–2; 19–21

Day 5: 1 Samuel 13–15; 28:3-25

Day 6: Covenant Meditation on Deuteronomy 6:4-9

Day 7: Group Meeting Experience with Deuteronomy 6:1-19

Covenant Prayer

For those who feel adrift and overwhelmed

Your word is a lamp before my feet and a light for my journey. (Psalm 119:105)

For those who long to grow in love for God and neighbor

LORD, the world is full of your faithful love! Teach me your statutes! (Psalm 119:64)

OUR LONGING FOR RELATIONSHIP

We yearn for healthy relationships that generate satisfying, loyal love. Our selfish desires make it difficult to sustain relationships.

DEUTERONOMY—1 SAMUEL

Deuteronomy ends the Pentateuch and begins the History.

The introduction to the Torah and Genesis (Episode 1) notes that one of the four major authors who contributed to the Pentateuch was responsible for Deuteronomy. The name Deuteronomy comes from the Greek translation of Deuteronomy 17:18—a verse that requires the king to make a copy of the Instruction. The Greek translators seemed to think the Hebrew word for "copy" meant "second," and so they translated this phrase as "second instruction" or "second law."

The book of Deuteronomy is very much a second version of the Hebrew Torah (or Instruction, as it is translated in the CEB), and it includes extensive repetition of the events and Instruction in Exodus and Numbers. But this repetition is not word for word. Much new content appears in Deuteronomy. As a "copy," it is far from an exact replica. Indeed, the combination of what is old and what is new in Deuteronomy makes the book a fitting and climactic conclusion to the first five books of the Bible (the Pentateuch) because it summarizes and reiterates so much of what comes before. This summary points toward Israel's pending life in Canaan—which is taken up in Joshua and the other books that follow.

Despite its concluding and climactic function within the Pentateuch, Deuteronomy is also a hinge or pivot. On the one hand, it ends the Pentateuch, especially by recording the death of Moses (Deut 34), who has dominated the Torah since his birth (Exod 2). On the other hand, Deuteronomy opens up all that follows: the books of Joshua through 2 Kings (excepting Ruth, which in the Hebrew text of the Old Testament doesn't follow Judges). These six books—Joshua, Judges, 1 and 2 Samuel, and 1 and 2 Kings—with Deuteronomy as their introduction, are often called the "Deuteronomistic History" because they seem to inhabit the world created by Deuteronomy. They often reflect its language and themes, for example, through the repetition of key words.

An example of Deuteronomy's influence on the history books that follow is found in the way kings are evaluated in the later history of the Israelite monarchy. In the Deuteronomistic History, the kings of the northern kingdom of Israel and the southern kingdom of Judah are often deemed righteous or unrighteous, based on whether or not they centralize worship in the temple by closing down the local "shrines," which were elevated places of alternative worship. The criticism of Manasseh in 2 Kings 21 is a clear example. The imperative to center worship in one location is stipulated in Deuteronomy 12. So quite early in Deuteronomy, a test is already provided by which many later monarchs are judged and typically found wanting, leading to the nation's judgment and ultimately its exile.

These books are called history because Joshua, Judges, and 1 Samuel are concerned with the settlement of Canaan and Israel's early expansion there, first under the official leaders (or judges) and then under King Saul. But these books may also be defined by the other word used to describe this material in the present study—namely, the word *covenant*.

Covenant is a rich notion in the Bible and elsewhere in the ancient Near East. The concept is found early in Genesis in the covenants with Noah (Gen 8:20–9:17) and the ancestors (for example, Gen 15), but especially in Exodus and the covenant at Mount Sinai (which Deuteronomy calls "Horeb"). Covenant is a formal way to describe the relationship between God and God's people, in which both parties bind themselves together. It's easy to see how these covenants, but especially the one at Sinai (Horeb), undergird all that follows in the Old Testament. The covenant idea explains, for example, why the people are called to account by prophets when they go astray, as well as why the psalmists felt so free to call for God's help in prayer, especially when they felt God had neglected them. Covenant also explains:

- why Israel succeeds in the book of Joshua when they are faithful, but fails when they are not (Josh 7);

- why Joshua renews the covenant with Israel before he dies (Josh 24);

- why Israel suffers in the book of Judges when it goes astray, and how God responds to their changed hearts and lives by sending leaders as deliverers (Judg 2:11-23); and

- why obedience to God's word, especially as it is presented by the prophets, is so important in 1 and 2 Samuel, whether the king is Saul or David (1 Sam 13–16; 2 Sam 11–12).

Deuteronomy's "second" version of the covenant at Sinai/Horeb affects all else in Joshua through 2 Kings (the Deuteronomistic History). The people are judged according to the exclusive demands of

Deuteronomy 6:5 is part of the memorable passage in 6:4-9, known as the Shema ("Listen!") in Judaism.

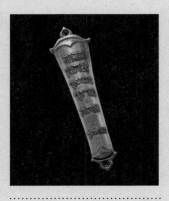

the first commandment to worship one God alone (Deut 5:6-19; 6:4-9), and the monarchs are judged by the requirement to worship in one central place. The history presented in these books, like all history, has a point of view. This history is a passionate and even biased history, which simply means that it is *covenant history*. The presentation sounds like a sermon because it makes crucial points about what the covenant is and what it means, and what it means to be faithful to the covenant or to break the covenant. While there is more to these books than the covenant theme, everything in these books can be seen through the lens of covenant.

The notion of covenant in Deuteronomy and the Historical Books that follow includes some of the most powerful and important aspects of covenant in scripture:

1. the fundamental importance of relationship (Deut 5:2-4);

2. the sense of unmerited graciousness in the covenant relationship (Deut 7:7-8);

3. the deep commitment between the members of the covenant (Deut 6:1-9);

4. the ethical principles at the heart of the covenant community (Deut 5:6-22); and

5. the importance of loyalty or the consequences of betrayal (Deut 8:11-19).

Yet, in its ancient setting, the covenant in Deuteronomy also includes two of the most problematic ideas in all of scripture:

1. a rigid theology of retribution in which the righteous are rewarded and the wicked punished, leaving little room for God's graciousness or human failure (Deut 7:9-11); and

2. a vicious exclusion of the foreigner, so extreme at times as to mandate genocide (Deut 7:5, 16, 23-26).

The challenge for the believer now is to consider carefully how the valuable elements of covenant can be embraced at the same time that its negative applications are confronted and critiqued.

Day 1: Deuteronomy 5–9 ✓

The Ten Commandments and the greatest
commandment

The Ten Commandments are the centerpiece of the covenant at Mount Horeb, also called Mount Sinai in Exodus (19:11, 23). In Deuteronomy 5, Moses retells some of the events at God's mountain and then repeats the Ten Commandments, alternative forms of which are found in Exodus 20:1-17. The importance of the Decalogue (or "ten words," another term for the Ten Commandments) is underscored in several ways. One way is that the ten words are repeated in both Exodus and Deuteronomy. Another way is that in Exodus and Deuteronomy the Decalogue appears first, in pole position, before all other Instruction. "Case laws" (Deut 6:1) that follow, for instance, are instructions that apply to specific situations, unlike the more general instructions of the Decalogue. A third way is that the ten words are also said to be the only commandments that Israel hears directly from God. That experience is overwhelming, and so, after Israel's request, all subsequent Instruction is mediated through Moses (Deut 5:22-31).

> **Optional:** *An additional video on teaching through story and interpreting the Ten Commandments is available for download from* **CovenantBibleStudy.com**.

Deuteronomy underscores the importance of the Decalogue in yet more ways. One of these is how Deuteronomy 6:1–11:32 seems to be an extended sermon based on the first and second commandments (Deut 5:6-10). Note how the great commandment of Deuteronomy 6:5 is a positive articulation of the first commandment of having no other gods. But note also how the threats to Israel's ultimate allegiance to God are discussed in Deuteronomy 6–9. They include foreign deities (Deut 7:4-5) but are mostly about other threats, including militarism, money, and morality.

Read the Ten Commandments, which are explained in Deuteronomy 5:7-21. Recall a time or two when you disobeyed these commandments.

Day 2: Deuteronomy 29–32 ✓

Old and new covenants

Deuteronomy's repetition of previous Instruction—the Ten Commandments included—isn't simple and unwavering. Moses in Deuteronomy knows that time and circumstances matter. Life in the land will be different precisely because it is life in the land, not in the wilderness. So the instructions in Deuteronomy's central collection in chapters 12–28 are often different from older teachings, repeating some earlier instructions but also revising them and updating them for life in Canaan (see Deut 12:1). Furthermore, the Instruction in Deuteronomy 12–28 seems to be developed on the basis of the Ten Commandments, another way in which Deuteronomy underscores the importance of the Decalogue. Yet even the Ten Commandments are revised! Their presentation in Deuteronomy 5 is different from that in Exodus 20, as you can see by setting them side by side and comparing them.

> **Optional:** *An additional video on the Moab covenant is available for download from* **CovenantBibleStudy.com**.

The ultimate "revision" that Deuteronomy attempts is found in Deuteronomy 29–32, which is often called the Moab covenant. This covenant is "in addition to" the one at Sinai/Horeb (Deut 29:1). Here, too, we find Deuteronomy repeating and revising—not just material from Exodus or Numbers but from its own previous chapters! Note how the Moab covenant includes future generations (Deut 29:15) in a way that the Sinai/Horeb one did not (Deut 5:3; 11:2). The Moab covenant imagines a future where humans no longer fail to obey (compare Deut 30:6 with Deut 10:16 and 6:5) because God will directly intervene to help Israel be faithful.

Over time, in the relationships that really matter to you, think about the changes or revisions needed to keep the relationship fresh, faithful, and fruitful.

Day 3: Joshua 1–2; 23–24 ✓
Moses reinvented

Today's readings form the bookends for the book of Joshua. The opening chapters pick up where Deuteronomy 34 left off, with the death of Moses. The final chapters recount Joshua's words to Israel before his own death. In both cases, Deuteronomy and its presentation of Moses has impact on the presentation of Joshua. Joshua is to be rooted in the Instruction that Moses commanded (Deuteronomy), and that will lead to success (Josh 1:7-9). Joshua is, as it were, Moses reinvented, not necessarily an upgrade (since no one compares to Moses; see Deut 34:10-12), but a new version. The balance of Joshua 1–2 shows how Joshua's fidelity (loyal love) rubs off on Israel (Josh 1:10-18) and how Israel's fidelity, in turn, affects the inhabitants of the land, even leading to Canaanite "professions of faith" (Josh 2:8-13; 6:25).

Joshua 23 and 24 comprise Joshua's last will and testament, and are quite similar (though much shorter) than Moses' final words in the book of Deuteronomy. Like Moses, Joshua is at pains to ensure that the people remain faithful to God after his death. Israel's obedience is a response to all that God has done (Josh 23:3, 9, 14), but is nevertheless mandated and essential (Josh 23:6, 11), lest things end in disaster (Josh 23:15-16). This is why Joshua puts the covenant question to Israel in Joshua 24 with his famous statement, "Choose today whom you will serve," and also why he follows Moses' example once more by setting an example himself: "But my family and I will serve the Lord" (Josh 24:15).

Whom do you serve? How do you know?

Day 4: Judges 1–2; 19–21
Downward spiral

Judges tells the story of Israel after Joshua, and it isn't always pretty. The first chapter comes as a surprise after reading Joshua. Not everything went smoothly in the settlement of the land. Instead, much work remains to be done (Judg 1:1). Moreover, the official leaders (also called judges) are chieftains who arise to deliver Israel from its oppressors after it has gone astray from God.

89

These deliverers are charismatic military and religious leaders who rarely "judge" in the formal, legal sense (for example, Judg 2:16-19), and they never attain to Joshua's status, let alone Moses'. If anything, the leaders whose lives are described in this book seem to get worse as time passes. After the successful leaders Othniel, Ehud, and Deborah, we read stories about the ambiguous careers of Gideon and Jephthah, as well as the seemingly self-centered exploits of Samson, who "delivers" Israel only at the end of his life and then only, it would seem, as an act of revenge (Judg 16:28).

The ultimate decline is found in the final chapters of Judges, which recount the horrific story of the rape and dismemberment of a Levite's secondary wife, which leads to intertribal warfare and the near annihilation of the tribe of Benjamin for its role in the atrocities. The Benjaminites are saved by actions that are every bit as disturbing as the Israelites' conquest of Canaan, though this time the Israelites turn inward against Israel's own territory and people (Judg 21:1-12, 16-24). Observe the marked absence of God's direct activity in these chapters—the exception being God's approval of punishing action against the Benjaminites for their crime (Judg 20:18, 23, 28, 35; 21:15). It is as if God stands back at the end of Judges, leaving Israel to its own devices (and vices). We see, in the process, the terrifying results of life lived outside of covenant.

Think of a harmful leader at work or at school or in government. Which of this leader's deeds have seemed to violate expectations and relationships? Now think of a leader who inspires. What behaviors have exceeded expectations?

Day 5: 1 Samuel 13–15; 28:3-25

Tragedy of King Saul

The end of Judges portrays Israel in dire straits, with each person doing "what they thought to be right" (Judg 17:6; 21:25). That's a far cry indeed from Deuteronomy's emphasis on careful obedience to God's covenant, rather than to one's own whims. This phrasing in Judges, then, is proof of Israel's covenant disobedience.

But the end of Judges also indicates that this situation was due to the fact that "in those days there was no king in Israel" (Judg 17:6; 18:1; 19:1; 21:25). Israel is not only disobedient but unruly (un-ruled), guided neither by God nor by a representative of God such as a king or a prophet. First Samuel recounts the rise of both kinds of representative leaders.

> **Optional:** *An additional video retelling the story of Hannah and the infant Samuel is available for download from* **CovenantBibleStudy.com**.

The opening chapters tell of the birth and early career of Samuel, who is the last of the chieftain leaders and the first of the prophets. He is also God's kingmaker, anointing Saul the first king of Israel. From its inception, kingship is portrayed as a highly ambivalent institution, one that is ultimately in tension with God's rule (1 Sam 8:7). Not surprisingly, then, the first king, Saul, is a tragic figure from the start. It does come as a surprise, if not an act of mercy or grace, that he comes from the tribe of Benjamin (1 Sam 9:1, compare the end of Judges).

Saul sacrifices when he shouldn't have (1 Sam 13), makes a rash solemn pledge that could have led to the death of his own son (1 Sam 14), and then breaks the rules of holy war and lies about it after the fact to Samuel (1 Sam 15). All this leads to Saul's rejection as king (1 Sam 13:13-14; 15:23), because God is seeking a man "of his own choosing" (or, "after his own heart"; 1 Sam 13:14). That turns out to be David, of course (1 Sam 16), but note that the prediction of Saul's demise is made long before David is anointed and even longer before David's own significant disobediences to God's commands (2 Sam 12). In the end, Saul breaks the very religious rules he himself instated by consulting a spiritual medium in order to get dead Samuel's advice one last time (1 Sam 28:3-28). Saul dies a dishonorable death thereafter (1 Sam 31).

When human beings form a community, why do we seek a chief, or king, or president? How does this affect our covenant relationship with God?

Day 6: Deuteronomy 6:4-9
Covenant Meditation: Renewing the covenant

Again we have an opportunity to experience scripture by allowing the word to form us through and in our hearts. To mature spiritually, our heads and hearts must be engaged by the living word.

This spiritual way of reading scripture has been practiced in Christian communities for centuries. The classic name for this ancient way of reading the Bible is *lectio divina*, which in Latin means "divine reading." Traditionally in divine reading, there are four key movements through which we listen to a brief selection of scripture: reading, meditating, praying, and resting (contemplating) in God's word.

The meditation is Deuteronomy 6:4-9, in which Moses reaffirms that the holy covenant between God and God's people for all generations is forged and sustained in the commandment to love God always and completely. Open your Bible to this scripture, and mark its location. Go to as quiet a place as possible for this reading, and get comfortable where you are seated. Place both feet on the ground and breathe slowly in and out until you have a sense of calmness and have, as best you can, set aside distractions that are on your mind about other matters.

Read the passage slowly, aloud or silently, paying attention to the whole text—every sentence, phrase, and word. Approach the scripture as though it is new to you. When finished, wait in a minute of silence.

Read the passage again, now listening for one word or phrase that catches your attention. Try not to analyze why a specific word or phrase stands out to you, but receive it as something God invites you to hear. If desired, write this word or phrase in your workbook. Take three minutes of silence to reflect on what caught your attention. What does this word or phrase bring to mind for you? Let your mind engage with the word or phrase and consider what it means to you right now. Resist editing your thoughts, and do not rush through this silent time. It may feel like an hour to you at first, but stay with the full three minutes if you can. For some, this silent time is easy, but for others it can seem to take forever. Try to grow in this practice of silence before God with the scripture.

Read the scripture one last time. Now reflect on feelings or memories your word or phrase evokes. Does your word or phrase point to something that you or someone you know longs for or needs? In as much or as little silent time as you need, write down any reflections that come to your mind or heart.

When you are ready, in prayer offer back to God all that you have heard, thought, and felt in this spiritual reading practice. Entrust to God any insights, questions, worries, or longings that this scripture brings to light for you. Before you end this time of praying the scripture, ask yourself if you sense an invitation from God to act or respond in some way. There may be a small invitation (for example, to attend worship) or a broad one (to pray each day), or you may not yet sense an invitation. You may discover later in the day or week that something comes back to you from this experience. A word or phrase may drift up from your heart or memory for you to reflect upon at another time. There is no right or wrong way to do this practice. It is simply one way to spend time with God and God's message in quiet, personal reflection.

Group Meeting Experience

Deuteronomy 6:1-19 | *A portrait of the covenant*

The book of Deuteronomy provides us with yet another way of describing the covenant between God and God's people and defining the nature of community within such a covenant. Because this covenant provides the theological lens for the historian's evaluation of Israel's faithfulness in the books that follow—Joshua, Judges, 1 and 2 Samuel, and 1 and 2 Kings—it plays a major role in the way we understand much of biblical history and thought.

1. Biblical covenants describe community relationships in which members share mutual care for and obligations to each other. What are the human responsibilities and obligations in this covenant? What are the divine responsibilities and obligations?

2. In what ways is Deuteronomy's covenant similar to and different from the biblical covenants you have already studied in Genesis and Exodus?

3. "Love" in Deuteronomy 6:5 is a term taken from kinship and family relationships in the ancient world. What role does it play in the

relationship between God and Israel in the Deuteronomic covenant? What attitudes and actions does it include?

4. How do you think the author of Luke intends us to understand this kind of covenant love when he quotes Deuteronomy 6:5 in his introduction to the parable of the good Samaritan (Luke 10:25-37)? Compare Matthew 22:34-40.

5. This covenant is built on a theology of rewards and punishments (Deut 6:3, 14-19). What do you see as the strengths and weaknesses of such a theology?

6. What aspects of Deuteronomy's covenant and of its ancient world do you find problematic for our understanding of covenant today? What aspects do you find life-giving and insightful for faithful community life?

SIGNS OF FAITHFUL LOVE

We don't deserve *(betray)* God's love because we are unfaithful, but Covenant people are restored and reinvented through God's unexpected favor.

Well done!

You have completed the first participant guide, *Creating the Covenant*. You studied daily from scripture about the importance of establishing a covenant with God and others. In your Covenant group, you planted the signs of faithful love that are present among friends. Relationships are growing.

About now you are probably wondering whether to continue the daily readings from scripture. Even if you are feeling stress from a hectic life, you can probably see the spiritual benefit of sharing expectations, divine promises, and personal yearnings with your Covenant group.

Keep going! You can do it. The Bible is a big, ancient collection of books, and getting the "big picture" for the whole Bible will help you grow (produce fruit) and become more faithful as a friend, parent, co-worker, or leader. The loyal relationships that can be cultivated in a Covenant group will produce fruit for the rest of your life.

Whether your group takes a break or continues right away, *Living the Covenant* is waiting for your input. You now understand how the biblical God relates to us through covenant. In the second participant guide, you will learn effective strategies for covenant living with others.

LIVING
the covenant

Participant Guide

Episodes 9–16

Abingdon Press

Contents

Living the Covenant

Other Covenant Modules

Creating the Covenant

Trusting the Covenant

Bible Readings at a Glance

Sign up with your group at CovenantBibleStudy.com to get daily readings by e-mail from your group leader.

Episode 9

Day 1	Ruth 1–2	Famine, loss, and exile	❑
Day 2	Ruth 3–4	Redemption and restoration	❑
Day 3	Esther 1–4	Plot	❑
Day 4	Esther 5–8	Counterplot	❑
Day 5	Song of Songs 1–2; 4:1-7; 5:10-16	Love unplugged	❑
Day 6	Covenant Meditation on Song of Songs 8:6-7a	God loves you.	❑
Day 7	Group Meeting Experience with Ruth 1:8-18	Solemn promise for life	❑

Episode 10

Day 1	Luke 1:1–4:30	Jesus fulfills hopes and confounds expectations.	❑
Day 2	Luke 10:25-37; 13; 15; 16:19–17:19; 18:1-17; 19:1-10	Jesus proclaims God's kingdom.	❑
Day 3	Luke 22–24	Jesus, the rejected prophet, dies and rises again.	❑
Day 4	Acts 1–4	Jesus' followers receive power from the Holy Spirit.	❑
Day 5	Acts 8:1b–11:18	Unlikely newcomers join the church.	❑
Day 6	Covenant Meditation on Acts 2:42-47	Teaching, prayers, and shared meals	❑
Day 7	Group Meeting Experience with Luke 4:14-30	Jesus preaches in his synagogue.	❑

Episode 11

❏	Day 1	2 Samuel 7; 9; 11–12	David's use and abuse of power
❏	Day 2	1 Kings 11–13	Loss of Israel
❏	Day 3	1 Kings 17–19; 21	King versus prophet
❏	Day 4	2 Kings 17–19	The fall of Samaria and the northern kingdom
❏	Day 5	2 Kings 22–25	The fall of Jerusalem and the southern kingdom
❏	Day 6	Covenant Meditation on 2 Kings 5:1-14	Who is the leader?
❏	Day 7	Group Meeting Experience with 2 Samuel 7:1-17	Covenant with David

Episode 12

❏	Day 1	1 Thessalonians 1–5	Encouragement for faithful living
❏	Day 2	2 Thessalonians 1–3	Harassed
❏	Day 3	1 Timothy 1:1-2; 2–4; 6:1-2, 11-15	Discernment
❏	Day 4	2 Timothy 1–4	An ethical will
❏	Day 5	Titus	Baptism and the Holy Spirit fuel faithful living.
❏	Day 6	Covenant Meditation on 2 Timothy 3:14-17	Scripture is useful.
❏	Day 7	Group Meeting Experience with 1 Thessalonians 1:2-10	Thanksgiving

Episode 13

❏	Day 1	Proverbs 1–4	Learning discernment
❏	Day 2	Proverbs 10–15	Speaking the truth
❏	Day 3	Proverbs 25–29	Using power and influence wisely
❏	Day 4	Ecclesiastes 1–4	When life seems pointless
❏	Day 5	Ecclesiastes 9–12	Everyday moments of joy
❏	Day 6	Covenant Meditation on Ecclesiastes 3:1-8	What is good for my life?
❏	Day 7	Group Meeting Experience with Proverbs 2:1-19	How to become wise

Episode 14

Day 1	Philemon	Reconciliation of "brothers"	❏
Day 2	Philippians 1–4	Reconciliation and the fellowship of believers	❏
Day 3	Colossians 1:1–3:17	Reconciliation as the hidden treasure of God	❏
Day 4	Ephesians 1:1–5:20	Reconciliation as the cosmic reality	❏
Day 5	Colossians 3:18–4:1; Ephesians 5:21–6:9	A reconciled household	❏
Day 6	Covenant Meditation on Philemon 1:4-7	Reconciled in Christ	❏
Day 7	Group Meeting Experience with Ephesians 2	From death to reconciled life	❏

Episode 15

Day 1	James 1–2	Faith and impartiality	❏
Day 2	James 3–5	Penitence and patience	❏
Day 3	1 Peter 1:3–4:11	New life guided by Christ	❏
Day 4	1 Peter 4:12–5:14	Waiting for the last days	❏
Day 5	Jude and 2 Peter	When the great day is delayed	❏
Day 6	Covenant Meditation on James 1:22-26	Doers of the word	❏
Day 7	Group Meeting Experience with 1 Peter 2:4-10	Chosen people	❏

Episode 16

Day 1	Isaiah 1; 5:1–7:17; 9:2-7; 11:1-10	Royal prophet	❏
Day 2	Hosea 1:1-9; 2; 11:1-9	How can I give you up, Ephraim?	❏
Day 3	Amos 1:1–3:8; 5; 7:10-17	A lion has roared.	❏
Day 4	Micah 1:1–3:12; 6:1-8	What the Lord requires from you	❏
Day 5	Zephaniah 1; 3; Malachi 3–4	The great day of the Lord is near.	❏
Day 6	Covenant Meditation on Micah 6:8	Justice, love, and humility	❏
Day 7	Group Meeting Experience with Amos 5:7-24	Seek good.	❏

LIVING
the covenant

Covenant Creative Team

Video Cohosts

Christine Chakoian, Senior Pastor,
First Presbyterian Church, Lake Forest, IL

Shane Stanford, Senior Pastor,
Christ United Methodist Church, Memphis, TN

Writers: Living the Covenant

Episode 9   Judy Fentress-Williams, Professor of Old
Testament, Virginia Theological Semi-
nary, Alexandria, VA

Episode 10   Matthew L. Skinner, Associate Professor
of New Testament, Luther Seminary, St.
Paul, MN

Episode 11   Roy L. Heller, Associate Professor of Old
Testament, Perkins School of Theology,
Dallas, TX

Episode 12   Audrey L. S. West, Adjunct Professor of
New Testament, Lutheran School of
Theology, Chicago, IL

Episode 13   Christine Roy Yoder, Professor of Old
Testament Language, Literature, and
Exegesis, Columbia Theological Semi-
nary, Decatur, GA

Episode 14   Michael J. Brown, Academic Dean, Payne
Theological Seminary, Wilberforce, OH

Episode 15   David L. Bartlett, Professor Emeritus of
Christian Communication, Yale Divinity
School, New Haven, CT

Episode 16   Francisco García-Treto, Jennie Farris
Railey King Professor Emeritus of Religion, Trinity University, San Antonio, TX

Ruth, Esther, Song of Songs

FAITHFUL LOVE
Committed relationships

Bible Readings

Day 1: Ruth 1–2

Day 2: Ruth 3–4

Day 3: Esther 1–4

Day 4: Esther 5–8

Day 5: Song of Songs 1–2; 4:1-7; 5:10-16

Day 6: Covenant Meditation on Song of Songs 8:6-7a

Day 7: Group Meeting Experience with Ruth 1:8-18

Covenant Prayer

For those who are suffering in the midst of a dysfunctional family

Your faithful love is priceless, God! Humanity finds refuge in the shadow of your wings. (Psalm 36:7)

For those who celebrate their identity in God's family

Heaven thanks you for your wondrous acts, LORD—for your faithfulness too—in the assembly of the holy ones. (Psalm 89:5)

OUR LONGING FOR RELATIONSHIP

A covenant creates a new identity, making a family out of unrelated individuals. A covenant expects faithfulness but also the possibility for love.

[handwritten: Also our church family]

9

The marriage covenant creates a new identity, making a family out of unrelated individuals. A marriage covenant expects faithfulness but also allows the possibility for love.

POSSIBILITY OF LOYAL LOVE

The biblical understanding of the covenant relationship between God and God's people, and among God's people themselves, is shaped and informed by the actual covenants, or agreements, common in Israel's social life. The books of Ruth, Esther, and the Song of Songs explore the committed relationships that are the basis of a covenant.

Sometimes we wonder why these books (especially Song of Songs) were included in the scriptures. But they are an important part of the canon because they use marriage as an analogy for God's covenant love. The marriage covenant creates a new identity, making a family out of unrelated individuals, and unlike economic or political contracts, a marriage covenant expects faithfulness but also allows the possibility for love. Some think a covenant is a contract. A contract, however, is usually a last resort, invoked after a relationship has already failed and is unlikely to recover.

By exploring these stories of marriage relationships and the loyalty and love within them, we can learn more about the nature of covenant relationships in the Bible. We can also learn more about the relationship of women and men in biblical society. While biblical society was patriarchal, investing men with primary prestige and power, these are stories of strong women who work in and around male structures with strength, dignity, and integrity. For Ruth and Esther, their futures and the futures of their people lay in their hands.

RUTH

Ruth is a beautifully written story of loss and recovery, famine and harvest, death and new life. The family of Elimelech and Naomi experiences a series of tragedies. Naomi loses the things that define her and faces an uncertain future. The family's very survival is in jeopardy. As a woman and an outsider, Ruth is the unlikely heroine. Her faithfulness to the covenant she made with her husband and with Naomi's family enables the family to survive.

The narrative of this family's destruction and reconstruction can be dated to the time of the exile, the time of Israel's national destruction. The exiled people of Israel were worried about survival and identity. In the narrative of Ruth, they heard a story of a foreign woman who ensures the family's survival and allows for a renewed identity. The story invites its hearers to consider whether God's covenant relationship is for Israel and Israel alone.

ESTHER

The book of Esther takes place in the Persian court. It was written when the people of Israel were no longer in their homeland. The events in the narrative take place during the fourth or third century BCE, the time of the Jewish diaspora, when Jews had been dispersed throughout the countries of the Mediterranean world. Many of the practices unique to Judaism were lost over the years as later generations of Jews took on names and practices that reflected the languages and cultures of their conquerors. In this new situation, assimilation was necessary for survival. Once assimilation became a way of life, the community had to determine what the core elements of Jewish identity were when their nation, king, temple, and priesthood were long gone. What were the terms of the covenant in Persia? Would God be faithful?

> **Optional:** *An additional video on Ruth and Esther is available for download from* **CovenantBibleStudy.com**.

Esther can be described as a court tale, a narrative that portrays Jews living under foreign rule and subject to the laws of a king who doesn't know their God. In the majority of these stories, a crisis arises when the rules of the king stand in opposition to the covenant practices or God-given commands that are unique to Jewish identity as God's chosen people. In Esther, the reader is introduced to a community whose lives are in danger. The community is threatened not only with the loss of life but with the loss of identity, essential to survival. Esther finds herself in a place of privilege and must decide if she will identify with her people and thereby expose herself to the dangers they face as a community under foreign rule.

SONG OF SONGS

The Song of Songs, also known as the Song of Solomon, is a collection of love poems that has long intrigued and confused its readers. Written in the late fourth or third century BCE, the expressions of affection and desire between the two lovers form a dialogue, or a call and response between the woman and the man. The poetry is sensual. It appeals to the senses of taste, touch, smell, sound, and sight, describing a human love that is without restraint. The sensuality of the poetry and the imagery of the garden evoke Eden's garden, with two people in a sanctuary where all their needs are met. However, as the poetry reveals, the lovers aren't always together. When they aren't together, the energy of the poetry is focused on being together. The lovers fill the space that separates them with language, imagining the dearly loved partner, making promises for the next meeting, or simply expressing the all-consuming desire to be reunited.

Both the woman and the man use symbolic language to praise the dearly loved partner and to convey the urgency of longing and desire. Metaphor and simile are used in analogies. The lovers use the language of familiar things to describe the indescribable. This symbolic language invites us to enter the garden of delights and experience agony with the lovers. Like the speakers, we know the experience of closeness and separation in our own relationships.

And like Israel, we also know what it is to be intimate with and alienated from God. Over the years, interpreters have taken the real and intense human love reflected in this poetry as symbolic of the love between God and God's people. The dialogue of the poetry invites us to embrace the dynamic of longing that comes from being apart and the joy that comes from being united because it sheds light on our relationship with the creator.

The Festival Scroll—Purim, Weeks, and Passover: In the Hebrew text of the Bible, Ruth, Esther, and the Song of Songs are grouped together within the festival scroll known in Hebrew as the *Megilloth*. These three narratives are associated with specific festivals that are a part of the Jewish calendar. Esther is associated with the celebration of Purim. The celebration of this holiday includes the reading and retelling of Esther's story. Ruth is associated with the Festival of Weeks (Hebrew *Shavuot*), a harvest celebration, and the Song of Songs is read during Passover. These three books continue to be part of the ongoing life in communities of faith. They demonstrate that the covenant is more than a contract. Rather, these books vividly present in story and song the responsibilities and privileges of a committed relationship.

Ruth, Esther, and Song of Songs are grouped together in the Megilloth, *or festival scroll. Ruth's story is retold during the Festival of Weeks (a harvest celebration commemorating the gift of Torah instruction at Sinai). Esther's story is told during Purim (celebrating deliverance from Haman's plot to kill the Jewish people in the Persian Empire). Song of Songs is recited during Passover, celebrating the rescue and liberation of the Hebrew people from slavery in Egypt.*

Day 1: Ruth 1–2
Famine, loss, and exile

The book of Ruth is a beautifully constructed narrative with shifts in location and plot twists that create a crisis for the family of Elimelech and Naomi. These elements are also signs of comedy. In the story of Ruth these elements are used to explore the theme of identity. The characters in the story are subject to loss of identity through famine, migration, and death. For them (and us), key markers of identity are name, homeland, and people (including family, tribe, and nationality). In Ruth 1, the family moves away from their homeland, the men die, and—since lineage and descent are reckoned through males—the name or identity of this family is facing certain extinction.

The names of the characters provide clues to the reader: *Elimelech* means "my God is king." His wife's name, *Naomi*, means "full and/or pleasant." The names of the sons are *Mahlon* and *Chilion*, meaning "sickly" and "destruction," or "frail," respectively. *Orpah* means "back of the neck," and *Ruth* means "to saturate" or "to water." As you read, consider the extent to which the characters live up to their names or reputations.

> **Optional:** *An additional video retelling the story of Ruth is available for download from* **CovenantBibleStudy.com**.

Ruth's ethnicity as a Moabite is important. Though this story doesn't speak disrespectfully of the Moabites, they were despised by some Israelite writers. When the text describes Ruth as a Moabite, it is identifying her as a person who some would have considered an outsider of the worst kind. Early hearers of this story would have had contempt for the Moabites. Ruth's story forces us to think about how God may work through those we designate as "outsiders," "opponents," or "enemies."

What type of person would you (or the people in your zip code) think of as an outsider?

Day 2: Ruth 3–4
Redemption and restoration

The second half of the narrative about Ruth is focused on levirate marriage as a form of redemption. Levirate marriage is a practice that allows for the closest living male relative to "marry" a childless widow. This is for the purposes of providing a male child and ensuring that there is someone to inherit on behalf of the deceased for his surviving family members. It is a useful image of redemption because redemption means to buy back that which was lost. Boaz is the closest male relative who is willing to play the role of redeemer, but in this role he marries Ruth, a Moabite. Ruth's first marriage to an Israelite, Mahlon, occurs under the circumstances of famine, death, and displacement for the Israelite family. Her second marriage takes place during the season of harvest. Boaz is a dutiful redeemer, but he is impressed by Ruth's faithfulness. The term "faithfulness" is often used to describe God's undying commitment to Israel. In this story, a Moabite woman embodies that faithfulness and undying love that God has for God's people.

It shouldn't be lost on the reader that the redemption and restoration of the family involves a plan that takes place under the cover of darkness in Ruth 3, and at the city gate, a public place, during the day in Ruth 4. Similarly, God's work of redemption and restoration can take on a variety of patterns and include unlikely characters. David's genealogy at the conclusion of the book includes a Moabite woman.

How does Ruth's relationship to Israel's dearly loved king change the way Israel feels about the Moabites?

Day 3: Esther 1–4
Plot

This story is a court tale, a literary form used for the narratives in Daniel 1–6 and for the book of Esther. In this story type, the hero or heroine is in the court of a foreign king who is temperamental and easily manipulated by his advisors, who are enemies of the Jewish people. A crisis arises when the advisors convince the king to issue an edict that goes against a covenant practice central to the Jewish faith. In the book of Daniel, the king forces the main characters to take a stand on issues such as dietary teaching and worship practices and to risk their safety in order to abide by the instructions of God's covenant. The story ends with the triumph of the hero (Daniel), and the message to Jews in the diaspora is that God is faithful to the covenant and to God's people who are loyal to the covenant.

Esther is a court tale with a heroine and with a twist. When Esther, or Hadassah (her Hebrew name), becomes queen, she finds herself in a position of privilege, but her identity as a Jew is unknown. We don't have any indication that she is observant of Jewish Instruction and practices. When Haman plots to kill the Jews and a crisis arises, Esther must decide whether or not she will reveal her Jewish identity and risk her life. If she doesn't, she can't save her people (Esth 4:13-14).

The narrative uses elaborate and excessive detail to describe the Persian Empire. By contrast, there is no mention of God. In Esther 4, Mordecai takes on the traditional signs of mourning, and Esther fasts. The turning point in the narrative comes when Esther decides to disclose her Jewish identity and face the king on behalf of her people. Her fate and the fate of her people lie on her shoulders.

Think of a time when you had a choice about disclosing personal information to a group or to another individual. Perhaps it was at school, at work, with friends, or in a congregation. What are the risks of disclosing or not disclosing identity?

Day 4: Esther 5-8
Counterplot

Once Esther accepts her role as a champion for her people, the narrative moves quickly to resolution. The action of the narrative is connected with banquets. The opening banquet in Esther 1 leads to Queen Vashti's expulsion. In the second half of the narrative, Esther's disclosure of her identity takes place through two banquets that she prepares for the king. The book concludes with the festival banquet of Purim, celebrating God's salvation of the people (Esth 9).

At the beginning of the story in Esther 1, the king and his queen are at separate banquets, and he sends a request to her, which she refuses. In the second round of banquets, the queen Esther invites the king and Haman to one banquet for the purpose of inviting them to a second one, where she makes her request known. Esther's decision to identify with her people leads to Haman's demise and allows for an edict that permits Jews to defend themselves against any who would attack them. This self-defense looks like revenge at the end of the book, and it raises concerns about how the experience of oppression can lead to similarly oppressive behavior when the power is reversed.

In an environment where God isn't readily apparent, how do we as readers discern God's presence in the story of Esther?

Day 5: Song of Songs 1–2; 4:1-7; 5:10-16

Love unplugged

"Set me as a seal over your heart . . . for love is as strong as death" (Song 8:6). The Song of Songs means "the best of all songs." It is about unrestrained, passionate love. The lovers talk to each other, and their dialogue celebrates the joy of being together. When they are apart, theirs is the language of longing, and their words fill the void created by the absence of the dearly loved partner.

It's hard to ignore the lush imagery of this poetry and how it evokes Eden's garden—the place where humanity and God were together. In the ancient Near East, gardens were walled for protection and often elevated. For this reason, in biblical tradition the garden also becomes a metaphor for Jerusalem, the holy city on a hill, where the temple is the point of contact for God and God's people.

The unmitigated passion and longing of this poetry has caused Jewish and Christian interpreters to gravitate toward allegorical and symbolic readings, seeing this human love as symbolic of the divine-human relationship. However, the experience of human passion and longing is a fitting lens through which to explore the power of relationship and the meaning of the covenant. Through the Song of Songs, we see with new eyes the depth of the agony we experience when we are separated from our dearly loved partner. The experiences of exile and life in the diaspora were challenging not only because of all the practical uncertainties. They were also times of deep longing for what was lost and for restoration of union with God in the garden, that place where the lovers are unencumbered and free to satisfy their desires.

Jot down some feelings or images that describe a time when you were passionate about a relationship, or deeply loved through a relationship. Now imagine what it would feel like to physically lose a relationship with that person. List some words that describe this feeling.

Day 6: Song of Songs 8:6-7a *Thurs*
Covenant Meditation: God loves you.

Before you begin today's reading practice, make the space in which you will be reading as quiet and separated from distractions as possible. You will be using Song of Songs 8:6-7a as the text for your reading. Locate these verses and mark the place so that when you begin, it is easy to find. Now get as comfortable as you can, choosing a position in which you can be most relaxed and at ease with your imagination. If this means that you would rather sit or lie on the floor, don't hesitate to do so. Sometimes a change in posture or position can help us to move into a new way of living with God's word. (In several psalms we read about thinking of God's word as the psalmist lies in bed at night.)

Now, recall that our theme for this week is "Faithful Love." Our readings led us into stories and poetry about God's faithful love for human beings and about faithful love between humans arising from a deep, faithful love for God. Covenant love is at the center of our love for each other and for God.

With this in mind, now read aloud Song of Songs 8:6-7a. When you have finished this first reading, imagine that these verses are God's request to you. Imagine God speaking these words to you, describing the love God has for you, asking that you set God's love for you as a seal upon your heart. Read the verses again, aloud or silently, as though you are hearing God telling you about the depth of love God has for you. Take this to heart. Live as deeply as you can with this idea of how much God loves you.

Now take a minute or two of silence and rest, then read these verses again, aloud or silently. But this time, let this be your prayer in response to God. Offer these same words back to God, asking that God place your life and love upon the divine heart so that you might grow in your love for God, one love bound to the other. Ask God to help you grow in such unrelenting, unquenchable love for God and for others. Let your imagination help you form an image of this fierce and passionate love that you and God have for each other, out of which your love for others and for all creation can live and move and have presence. Close with "Amen."

Group Meeting Experience

Ruth 1:8-18 | *Solemn promise for life*

On the way back to Bethlehem, the widowed Naomi offers her widowed daughters-in-law a unique opportunity. She gives them the option to return home to their families of origin. Ruth responds with a solemn promise that expresses her covenant commitment.

1. Look for repetition in this passage. Are there actions or motifs that we have seen in other parts of the Ruth narrative? How often do we see terms like "return" or "go back"? What themes does the repetition evoke?

2. Ruth's solemn promise to Naomi is a turning point in the narrative. What are the elements of Ruth's promise, and how do they reflect the aspects of the marriage covenant Ruth made when she married Mahlon and joined the family of Elimelech and Naomi? What do the elements of the covenant tell us about the "family values" of the time? In other words, based on what Ruth promises, what are the markers of family?

3. The exchange between Naomi and her daughters-in-law takes place in between Moab and Bethlehem. What is the significance of this location?

4. Ruth seals her promise by pledging, "May the LORD do this to me and more so if even death separates me from you" (Ruth 1:17). When she invokes this curse, she makes it impossible for Naomi to send her back. What are the theological implications of this part of the story? How would Israelite audiences have responded to a Moabite making a solemn pledge in the Lord's name?

5. How do the major women characters in this story, Ruth and Naomi, reflect the love, loyalty, and faithfulness that exemplify true covenant relationships in the biblical world?

SIGNS OF FAITHFUL LOVE

Covenant people say to God, "Wherever you go, I will go. Wherever you stay, I will stay."

Luke and Acts

THE SPIRIT-LED COMMUNITY
To change our hearts and lives and tell others about it

Bible Readings

Day 1: Luke 1:1–4:30

Day 2: Luke 10:25-37; 13; 15; 16:19–17:19; 18:1-17; 19:1-10

Day 3: Luke 22–24

Day 4: Acts 1–4

Day 5: Acts 8:1*b*–11:18

Day 6: Covenant Meditation on Acts 2:42-47

Day 7: Group Meeting Experience with Luke 4:14-30

Covenant Prayer

For all who feel like God's saving love is reserved for a select few

I really am learning that God doesn't show partiality to one group of people over another. (Acts 10:34)

For those who use their gifts to help and bring people together in a spirit of compassion, justice, and sharing

Treat people in the same way that you want them to treat you. (Luke 6:31)

OUR LONGING FOR RELATIONSHIP

We are afraid of strangers and people who are different from us.

21

LUKE AND ACTS

You can see how Matthew, Mark, and Luke share some of the same materials by studying the CEB Gospel Parallels.

Luke's Gospel presents Jesus Christ as the savior who announces and brings God's salvation. This salvation is concerned with physical, social, and spiritual well-being.

The Acts of the Apostles adds to the gospel story by describing Jesus' ministry as it continues in the lives of his followers. In Acts, the Holy Spirit creates communities united in faith and service and leads followers outward to bring the good news about Jesus into many cultural settings.

As the openings to both books (Luke 1:1-4; Acts 1:1-2) make clear, Acts was written as a sequel to Luke. The same person composed both of these books, probably between the years 80 and 95 CE. In many ways the two books connect to each other in their themes and emphases. For example, both have the whole Roman Empire in view, and they see the Christian gospel as something relevant for the whole world—at least the world known to people living under Roman rule. While introducing John the Baptist, Luke mentions the emperor and other regional rulers (Luke 3:1-2). In Luke's Gospel, Jesus brings God's salvation to "all peoples" (Luke 2:29-32). Acts begins with Jesus' followers huddled together in Jerusalem, but ends with Paul in the imperial capital, Rome, awaiting an audience with the emperor. In between, the gospel travels into major cities and through remote areas across the empire. (See the map in the back of the *CEB Study Bible* for an overview of where Paul traveled.)

Even as Luke and Acts tell of salvation brought to new and sometimes exotic places, they insist that the source of this salvation is very familiar. Luke's opening chapters use phrases and themes from the Old Testament to reassert God's continuing faithfulness. Jesus speaks of his ministry—and his death and resurrection—as fulfilling scripture. Characters in Acts also frequently cite Old Testament scripture to make sense of what God has done through Jesus and what God is continuing to do in their midst. Luke and Acts present themselves as the continuation of the stories about God that began in the Old Testament.

Although Luke shares much in common with Matthew and Mark, the perception of Jesus in Luke's Gospel is quite distinctive. A good amount of the material in Luke 3:1–9:50, as well as most of the account of Jesus' final fateful visit to Jerusalem in Luke 19:28–23:56, resembles passages found in Matthew and Mark. At the same time, most of the stories in Luke 9:51–19:27, a section initiated by a statement about Jesus' determination to travel to Jerusalem, appear in no other Gospel. There readers find, among other things, several noteworthy parables and challenging teachings about wealth and possessions.

Luke names Jesus as "Lord," "savior," "Messiah" (or "Christ"), "God's Son," and other familiar titles. This Gospel also places a special accent on Jesus' identity as a prophet. Jesus, in Luke 4:25-27, compares himself to great prophets in the Old Testament (see also Acts 3:22). He performs deeds, such as raising a widow's only son from the dead, that recall these prophets (Luke 7:11-17; compare 1 Kgs 17:17-24). He also utters a lament about Jerusalem in Luke 19:41-43 with words reminiscent of Old Testament prophets. Depicting Jesus and his followers as prophets emphasizes his role as one who announces God's actions on behalf of God's people. Sometimes this prophecy announces the upending of the status quo (as when Mary, Jesus' mother, speaks of the overturning of social orders in Luke 1:51-53). Sometimes the prophecy calls for changed hearts and lives (Luke 5:32; 13:3), imploring people to adopt a new perspective on God and their accountability to God.

Jesus announces God's salvation frequently during meals. See Luke 5:27-31; 7:36-50; 10:38-42; 24:36-49.

Jesus announces God's salvation frequently in intimate settings and for the sake of those who most need God's helping love and power in their lives. Many scenes occur around communal meals. This Gospel includes nineteen references to meals. Often these settings provide opportunities for transformations to occur, or for outsiders to be recognized as coming into a group of insiders. Similarly, no other Gospel pays as much attention to people who lacked power in ancient society. Frequently in Luke, Jesus speaks about or interacts with women, the poor, the ill, and the outcasts.

When we move into Acts, Jesus, after his ascent into heaven, bestows the Holy Spirit on his followers, empowering them for ministry and knitting them together into communities of mutual care and worship. Just as Luke gives special attention to the roles of the Holy Spirit and prayer in Jesus' ministry, Acts regularly reminds readers that worship, prayer, and service are aspects of Spirit-led churches. Jesus' impact on the world doesn't end or pause when he ascends into heaven after his resurrection. Rather, his story continues in the Christian communities that live out and proclaim his salvation, guided by the Holy Spirit. Even when these groups and their leaders encounter resistance from powerful people—which happens often in Acts—the Lord's word is nevertheless proclaimed, sometimes in unexpected ways.

In Acts, the Spirit empowers all Christians to be prophets (Acts 2:17-18), interpreters of God's action, of God's salvation on behalf of the whole world. Nevertheless, they do their work

> *The Holy Spirit empowers all Christians to be prophets.*

without knowing all the answers. Regularly the Spirit surprises them, such as when God brings non-Jews (Gentiles) into the church, the community of God's people (Acts 10:1-18; 15:1-35). The book tells of responsive churches—communities of people who must discern God's leading as they are called to bear witness to Jesus with boldness in their lives.

We learn about the purpose of Luke and Acts in the prologues (Luke 1:1-4; Acts 1:1-2). The books are addressed to a man named Theophilus, about whom nothing else is known. He may have been a patron, someone who commissioned the author to write both books for his or his community's benefit. Even though the author, whom church tradition names as "Luke," is aware of other Gospels and was himself not an eyewitness of Jesus' ministry, still he deems it worthwhile to provide another account. He does this for the sake of Theophilus and other believers, to give them "confidence in the soundness of the instruction" (Luke 1:4) they have already received. This indicates that Luke writes about Jesus and the early church, not necessarily to convince skeptics, but so that he might strengthen existing faith.

Luke and Acts don't understand personal religious commitments or spiritual lives as being separate from who people are as members of society and participants in a community. People changed by Jesus become part of his ongoing work in the world.

Day 1: Luke 1:1–4:30 √

Jesus fulfills hopes and confounds expectations.

The first two chapters of Luke describe Jesus coming to people who are eager for and amazed by his arrival. Three characters in particular respond to what God is doing in these events by singing songs (Luke 1:46-55, 67-79; 2:28-32). Each song is composed of phrases and themes taken from the Old Testament. The songs are prophecies because they celebrate God's will and name God's activity. In the conceptions and births of John and Jesus, Luke asserts that God is doing a new thing, giving light and guidance (Luke 1:79) that brings about salvation for "all peoples," both Jews and non-Jews, or Gentiles (Luke 2:31-32). At the same time, these actions of God are hardly new. God has, in the past, regularly shown mercy (Luke 1:50) and has made reliable promises to God's people (Luke 1:54-55, 72-75). Luke tells the next chapter of an ongoing story.

In Luke 3, John's ministry begins. He calls for changed hearts and lives (repentance) and promises judgment. In the following chapter, Jesus must discern what it means for him to be "God's Son." Will Jesus seek privilege and glory, or will he submit himself to a different way? Luke then introduces Jesus' public ministry with a story of an incident in his hometown. The scripture Jesus reads and the comments he makes serve as a kind of mission statement for his ministry in Luke.

What has Jesus come to do? Why do the people of Nazareth turn on him?

Day 2: Luke 10:25-37; 13; 15; ✓ 16:19–17:19; 18:1-17; 19:1-10
Jesus proclaims God's kingdom.

Sample some of the most loved—and most challenging—passages in Luke's Gospel. Together, they provide an overview of the topics Jesus addresses in his teachings. Note in particular how outcasts or powerless people figure in these stories.

In what ways is Jesus merciful and reassuring? In what ways is he, like the prophets, hard on those who misuse power and wealth to oppress others?

It's common to read stories like these and ask ourselves, "How should we be more like Jesus?" or, "How can we act like the people Jesus commends?" While those questions are useful, consider this one instead: "What does Jesus promise in these stories?" That is, think about what Jesus says is true about himself, people, life, and God.

Day 3: Luke 22–24 ✓

Jesus, the rejected prophet, dies and rises again.

Every Gospel tells about Jesus' death and resurrection, but Luke tells these stories in several unique ways.

How would you describe the mood around Jesus' crucifixion in Luke?

Luke mentions the presence of people who support Jesus and mourn his death (Luke 23:27, 48). Only in Luke does one of the criminals appeal to Jesus on the cross (Luke 23:39-43). Jesus promises salvation to him, even as both of them suffer miserable deaths. Jesus dies speaking words of trust in God (Luke 23:46). This message demonstrates his faithfulness, even on the cross.

Luke, along with John, contains the most stories about the resurrected Jesus' appearances to his followers. Notice how Jesus, risen from the dead, is both hidden from his followers and recognizable to them. Their belief doesn't come automatically. Their eyes have to be opened. Their memories have to be jogged. They need to encounter him directly and personally.

How do you recognize Jesus directly and personally two thousand years after his resurrection?

As the Gospel draws to a close, Jesus calls his followers "witnesses" of all that has occurred (Luke 24:48). The book of Acts will reaffirm the importance of that term. The word *witness* brings to mind legal settings.

What does it mean to bear witness to Jesus?

Jesus instructs people to proclaim "a change of heart and life" (or repentance) for "forgiveness" (or "release"; recall Luke 4:18) from sins.

How do you think forgiveness or release stems from Jesus' death and resurrection?

Day 4: Acts 1–4

Jesus' followers receive power from the Holy Spirit.

Acts, a story packed with adventures, begins with waiting. Jesus commissions his followers as his "witnesses," not just where they are but also as far as "the end of the earth" (Acts 1:8). But first they must wait for the Holy Spirit's power.

What does it mean to associate the Holy Spirit with "power"? What kind of power is Jesus talking about?

The Spirit arrives, with much fanfare, in Acts 2. This is the first of many stories in Acts in which the Spirit launches new movements in the church's life and witness. Peter announces that the strange events of Pentecost give evidence of the Spirit, a Spirit promised to all members of the community (Acts 2:17-18). The coming of the Spirit, claims Peter, is a sign that Jesus has ascended to God's right side, meaning he now possesses all God's authority over creation. Mention of Jesus' death prompts the crowd to react, and Peter tells them, "Change your hearts and lives" (Acts 2:37-38). As the chapter ends, the Spirit creates a community unified by its fellowship, worship, and charity. Acts 2 indicates the Spirit's presence outdoors as people proclaim the gospel, and indoors as the church organizes its common life.

What is the source in your church fellowship, worship, and charity? Are you comfortable with speaking about the Spirit inside and outside the church?

In Acts 3–4, we glimpse the church in action, continuing Jesus' ministry of healing and teaching, describing Jesus as fulfilling what God promised in advance, and encountering opposition from religious authorities. A major theme in these chapters is the power of Jesus' "name" and God's "word."

What does it mean to you to bear "the name" of Christ? How is the message or good news about Jesus "God's word" for you?

Sun 9/13/20

Day 5: Acts 8:1*b*–11:18 √

Unlikely newcomers join the church.

> **Optional:** *An additional video retelling the story of Peter and Cornelius is available for download from* **CovenantBibleStudy.com**.

The book of Acts is full of surprises, including events that seem to catch the people in the story unaware and that are interpreted as God's actions. This section of Acts begins with Jesus' followers having to leave Jerusalem in response to harassment. What might look like a setback quickly becomes an occasion for the church to expand. Samaritans, people usually considered enemies or rivals of those from Judea (where Jerusalem was) and Galilee, respond positively to the gospel message. So, too, in an astonishing scene, does an official of the royal court in Ethiopia. Then Jesus reaches out directly to Saul (later known as Paul), the church's archenemy. Just when things couldn't get much stranger, God prompts Peter and an official in the Roman military to find each other, resulting in the salvation of Cornelius and his household. Acts 10:1–11:18 is a pivotal scene, told with much repetition and great care to make its point. As a result, the church in Jerusalem (which at this point appears to be composed entirely of Jews) declares that God (not Peter) acted to give salvation to Gentiles, bringing about in them changed hearts and lives (repentance). As a result, the community of Jesus' followers would never be the same.

As you read these stories, note all of the places where Acts describes God, Jesus, or the Spirit doing something. Note also where characters in the story name God, Jesus, or the Spirit as the agents behind events or ideas.

Why do faithful people understand God as the primary force leading the community of believers in new directions? Give an example of an event where God was plainly the cause of what happened.

Day 6: Acts 2:42-47

Thurs 9/17/20

Covenant Meditation: Teaching, prayers, and shared meals

We will experience a reading from Acts through the spiritual gift of imagination. In the introduction for this week, our author writes, "People changed by Jesus become part of his ongoing work in the world." Since the beginning of the church, Christians have helped each other figure out and grow into what it means to live in community day by day. Our text for this time of spiritual reading invites us to see and join with these early brothers and sisters of faith.

Turn to Acts 2:42-47 and mark this reading so that you can find it easily. Before you begin to read, close your eyes, quiet your breath, and set aside distractions as best you can. Then, when you are ready, read these verses slowly and imagine yourself as part of each community activity. Take each phrase and sentence to heart, placing yourself in the community as an active member. What does it look like for you to "devote" yourself to the apostles' teaching? What do you bring to the meals? Who else is at the table? For what are you all praying? Who is offering the prayers?

What does it look like to experience with others "awe" for what God is doing? What are community members sharing? What do they need from each other? What do you have to share and to whom do you give it?

As you slowly work through this reading, take time to notice what you see (colors, expressions, interactions); what you hear (voices, laughter, table noises); and what you smell and taste and touch. Then close this time of reflection by examining your thoughts and feelings about this community of believers. What caught your attention? What troubled you? What will you take with you from this reading, from this community to whom we are connected by faith?

When you are finished, offer a prayer of gratitude for these brothers and sisters who, like us, had to find their way as Christ-followers. Offer as well a prayer of gratitude for a community of faith that has helped to shape your spiritual life.

Group Meeting Experience

Luke 4:14-30 | *Jesus preaches in his synagogue.*

Following his temptation in the wilderness, Jesus returns to Galilee "in the power of the Spirit" (Luke 4:14). He heads to his hometown of Nazareth, where a Sabbath visit to the synagogue finds him doing what he's always done: reading from the scriptures. As he reads aloud the scroll from Isaiah the prophet, he reaffirms God's clear and present favor for those living with impoverishment, bondage, blindness, and oppression. Then, in his address, Jesus extends this favored status to Gentiles outside the traditional boundaries of the covenant people—and it almost costs him his life.

1. What do we learn about the role of the Lord's Spirit in Luke 4:14-18? Why is it important to understand that the Holy Spirit is active in Jesus' ministry? What does it mean for us, then, that we possess the same Holy Spirit? How does the Holy Spirit assist the church as we work on God's behalf in the wider world and seek to be a community that embodies mutual love and support? How does your understanding of the Holy Spirit, as the book of Acts has informed you this week, affect your reading of Luke 4:14-30?

2. The scripture Jesus reads in the synagogue comes mostly from Isaiah 61:1-2a, with a portion of Isaiah 58:6 added. The release and liberation spoken about in these passages strikes an echo with the "Jubilee year" described in Leviticus 25:8-55. Jesus speaks in Luke 4, then, of fulfilling themes that already have deep significance in his people's hopes and memories. How would you summarize or reword these themes? What do these themes mean to you? What do you think he means when he says, "Today, this scripture has been fulfilled just as you heard it" (Luke 4:21)?

3. The scriptures from Isaiah that Jesus reads describe people being restored. What does it mean to you to be restored or released? What does a community of restored people look like to you? What challenges does such a community face? Is there any cause for worry in these images of powerless people suddenly becoming empowered? How might such radical transformations affect a wider society, or the world at large?

4. The people of Jesus' hometown, those who probably know him very well, try to kill him at the end of this incident. What motivates them to do this? Why does Jesus seem uninterested in diffusing

the tension or lessening the offense they feel? What do these people expect from him, and why won't he give them what they want? Where is the root of the misunderstanding or hostility in this passage?

SIGNS OF FAITHFUL LOVE

Covenant people rejoice and multiply when the Holy Spirit forms us into a dynamic and growing community. We grow by revealing the good news of Jesus Christ to unexpected groups of people.

2 Samuel, 1 and 2 Kings

LEADERSHIP
Potential and peril of leadership

Bible Readings

Day 1: 2 Samuel 7; 9; 11–12 ✔

Day 2: 1 Kings 11–13

Day 3: 1 Kings 17–19; 21

Day 4: 2 Kings 17–19

Day 5: 2 Kings 22–25

Day 6: Covenant Meditation on 2 Kings 5:1-14

Day 7: Group Meeting Experience with 2 Samuel 7:1-17

Covenant Prayer

For those who lead powerful governments and institutions

He has told you, human one, what is good and what the LORD requires from you: to do justice, embrace faithful love, and walk humbly with your God. (Micah 6:8)

For those who are at the mercy of power brokers

My God, rescue me from the power of the wicked; rescue me from the grip of the wrongdoer and the oppressor because you are my hope, Lord. (Psalm 71:4-5a)

OUR LONGING FOR RELATIONSHIP

Staying faithful to the covenant is tested through our ambitions and desires, our illusion of self-sufficiency, the idols of culture, and internal family conflicts.

33

God's covenant promises to David:

I have been with you, from your shepherding days in pastures to leading my people Israel.

I will make your name great.

I will provide a place for my people.

I will give you rest from your enemies.

I will make a dynasty for you.

Your son will sit on the throne.

He will build me a temple.

I will be a father to him, disciplining him when he does wrong.

I will never take my faithful love away from him.

Your kingdom and dynasty will be eternal and established forever.

(See 2 Samuel 7:1-17.)

KINGS

9/20/20

In 586 BCE, Babylonia's King Nebuchadnezzar and his army destroyed the city of Jerusalem. This destruction included not only the wall around the city, the houses, and the palace, but also God's temple, which had been built by Solomon, David's son. Many of the inhabitants of Jerusalem and the surrounding countryside were killed during the siege. The elite were forcibly exiled to Babylon. Most of those exiled died in that foreign land, far removed from their former homes, their former ways of life, and their former religious traditions. It's a tragedy that is difficult for us to appreciate. The effects of Jerusalem's destruction are certainly hard to overestimate.

The disaster of the destruction was made worse because it simply wasn't supposed to happen. The kingdom of Israel was established in a real and vigorous way by David, someone specially chosen and dearly loved by God. Because of God's particular regard for David, he established a covenant with David, promising him not only that God would bless him and make him great but that God would also provide a dynasty after David. God also made one additional promise in that covenant: David's dynasty would be eternal. There would always be one of David's descendants sitting on his throne in Jerusalem. Regardless of the faithfulness or disloyalty of any of the descendants, the covenant would never fail (2 Sam 7). The dynasty of David—and, by implication, David's city—would last forever. However, in 586 BCE Nebuchadnezzar's army destroyed the land and put the promise in doubt.

The books of 2 Samuel and 1 and 2 Kings address the strengths and weaknesses of the Davidic monarchy and its leadership of the people of Israel. How is it that God entered into an eternal covenant with David and his sons? How do David and his descendants successfully rule such a powerful and long-lasting kingdom? Why do they assume such a central place in the lives of God's people?

On the other hand, how could Jerusalem fall to the Babylonians? What are the causes of that destruction? Not merely the immediate causes, such as the rise of Babylonia or the weakness of Judah's final king, Zedekiah. Deeper causes stretch throughout Israel's entire history, all the way back to David and his promised son, Solomon. Are those causes only political and economic, or are they also religious and social? How do Israel's political and religious leaders and the people of Israel themselves contribute to or slow down the deterioration of the nation?

The books of 2 Samuel and 1 and 2 Kings wrestle with the nature of leadership of all types: social, religious, and political. A common refrain throughout the books is the evaluation of each of the kings who did "what was right in the Lord's eyes" (that is, keeping their covenant commitments) or "what was evil in the Lord's eyes" (that is, disregarding the covenant).

These stories about Israel's kings are far from simplistic statements about who was good and who was bad. These books illustrate again and again that there is more to a good leader than simply obeying a set of instructions, and more to a bad leader than simply not doing whatever God's instructions state. Leadership involves and combines many different qualities: justice, mercy, compromise, determination, authority, humility, an awareness of the "big picture," and attention to detail. Starting with the crowning of David and ending with the torture and death of Zedekiah, these stories offer us a way to wrestle with the purpose and strategies of leadership.

The stories about the kings also help us understand the prophetic figures who provide an alternative model of leadership that confronts the ruler on behalf of the powerless. The prophets play a major role in these stories, delivering God's word to the kings of Israel and Judah and holding them accountable to the covenant. Like the righteous kings, the prophets also are accountable to the covenant life.

Although the stories in 2 Samuel and 1 and 2 Kings present what looks like history, it is a history that is told for a particular purpose. While a modern historian might want to know more about various Assyrian or Babylonian leaders, or about particular political, economic, or social realities of the ancient world, these stories are wrestling with different issues: What does it mean to live in covenant with God? What does faithful, strong leadership look like? What does unfaithful, weak leadership look like? What are the reasons David's kingdom assumed a central place in God's covenant with the people of Israel and endured for centuries? What role do prophetic figures play in Israel's history? And how are we to understand the various reasons why David's kingdom, which was so full of promise and security, became so fragile and was eventually destroyed?

Leadership involves and combines many different qualities: justice, mercy, compromise, determination, authority, humility, an awareness of the "big picture," and attention to detail.

History with a purpose: portrayals of faithful and weak leadership

Sunday
9/20/20

Day 1: 2 Samuel 7; 9; 11–12
David's use and abuse of power

Prophet-and-king pairs of the Old Testament:

*Samuel and King Saul
(1 Sam 8–15)*

*Samuel and the
shepherd David
(1 Sam 16)*

*Nathan and King David
(2 Sam 12)*

*Shemaiah the man of God
and King Rehoboam
(1 Kgs 12)*

*Ahijah the man of God
and King Jeroboam
(1 Kgs 13–14)*

*Elijah and King Ahab
and Queen Jezebel
(1 Kgs 18–19)*

*Micaiah and King Ahab
(1 Kgs 22)*

*Elisha and King Jehoram
(2 Kgs 3–7)*

*Elisha and King Jehu
(2 Kgs 9)*

*Isaiah and Hezekiah
(2 Kgs 19)*

*For a table with a complete list
of the kings of Israel and Judah,
see the CEB Study Bible, OT
page 543.*

The story of 2 Samuel outlines the ways in which David gained the kingship over all Israel and then almost lost it. After Saul's death, David becomes king over his own tribe of Judah in the area to the south and west of the city of Jerusalem (2 Sam 2:1-7). From this area, David wages war against one of Saul's remaining sons, Ishbosheth, who is king over the other tribes that live north of Judah. In turn, Abner, the commanding general of the northern army, as well as Ishbosheth, are assassinated. David, however, denies that he had any knowledge of the plots to kill these two leaders. The people hear David's denial and are pleased that David, by his own account, is innocent of the murders (2 Sam 3–4). After this, David becomes king over the northern tribes (together called Israel) as well. David finally conquers Jerusalem and sets it up as his own city, making Jerusalem the center of political and religious power (2 Sam 5–6).

> **Optional:** *An additional video on David and the peril and promise of faithful leadership is available for download from* **CovenantBibleStudy.com**.

In 2 Samuel 7, God enters into a covenant with David and promises him that his kingdom will last forever, because after David's death God will raise up one of David's sons to rule on his throne. In 2 Samuel 9 we see how David deals with Saul's one remaining son, Mephibosheth, who is lame and can't walk. Is David being merciful or cautious (or both) here?

In 2 Samuel 11–12, we see the inner workings of the affair between David and Bathsheba and of the tragic judgment that it provokes from God. This is an intimate account of the failure of leadership, and the author draws the reader into its personal details. Is the affair as secret as it appears at first glance? Does Uriah know? In what way does David disregard his covenant obligations and what are the consequences? How does God's judgment "fit the crime"?

As you read, consider how the various characters might understand the situation, whether people are being honest or lying, and how people are using whatever power they might have.

How would you evaluate David's leadership, both in his crime and in his response to Nathan's accusation? How does Nathan provide prophetic leadership?

[handwritten notes: Sun 9/27/20; DAVID'S PSALMS 51; forgiveness 32]

Day 2: 1 Kings 11–13
Loss of Israel

After a long and seemingly prosperous reign, we see Solomon in a negative light here at the end of his life. This is the author's explanation for Solomon's failure to maintain rule over his father David's united kingdom. In chapter 11, Solomon is blamed for disregarding the covenant and for worshipping other gods, the first and most important obligation of the covenant (1 Kgs 11:1-13; compare Deut 5:6-10; 6:4-5). In chapter 12, he is blamed for exploiting the citizens of the north and abusing them through forced labor (1 Kgs 12:1-20).

According to Deuteronomy 17:14-20—a passage that is closely linked to the stories in Kings—a king of Israel was prohibited from having many horses, which probably refers to having a personal army. He was denied a personal treasury. And he couldn't have many wives, probably because intermarrying with the daughters of foreign rulers symbolized the making of treaties with foreign nations. Deuteronomy seems to warn that kings with great power tend to abuse that power for personal ends—as we saw in the reading for Day 1. While 1 Kings 1–10 tells the story of Solomon's reign in positive terms, it's also clear that he builds up his personal army with more than forty thousand horses (1 Kgs 4:26-28; 10:26-29), that he has so much money that he makes "silver as common as stones" (1 Kgs 10:27), and that he has placed some of his citizens into forced labor (1 Kgs 4:6). Yes, he had wisdom (1 Kgs 3:1-15). But which influenced his rule more, his wisdom or his personal power? By the end of his life, it became clear: His absolute power had corrupted him absolutely.

As you read these stories, think about what strengths and weaknesses in Solomon's leadership are reflected in his own son, Rehoboam, as well as in Jeroboam, the son who becomes the new king over the northern tribes of Israel. Prophetic leaders—Ahijah the man of God and the old prophet—also play an important role in these stories.

Considering Nathan in the previous readings and the prophets in these readings, do we still need prophets to hold rulers accountable for their covenant obligations? What covenant obligations in our community right now are in need of a prophet?

[handwritten signature: Rev Franklin Graham]

Day 3: 1 Kings 17–19; 21

King versus prophet

These stories are set in the northern kingdom of Israel and center around the prophet Elijah and the king Ahab. Ahab, like Solomon in the previous reading, also has a wife who is the daughter of a foreign king and sponsors great building projects of a religious nature. Like Solomon, he worships other gods, breaking the first obligation of the covenant (1 Kgs 18), and abuses his power over his subjects (1 Kgs 21). In both instances, the prophet Elijah stands up to the king and demands that Ahab keep his covenant obligations.

On Mount Carmel, Elijah summons all the prophets of the foreign gods Baal and Asherah to a contest, a contest in which Israel's God prevails. In spite of this victory, however, and in spite of the end of the drought, Elijah is terrified by a threat by Jezebel. He runs to Horeb, the mountain where Moses and the Israelites witnessed God's presence and received the Ten Commandments and the Instruction (Torah) about how to live in covenant (Deut 5–9; compare Exod 20–24). Here God appears also to Elijah (but not in the way God did to Moses and Israel) and gives him instructions (but not like those God gave to Moses and Israel).

When Ahab tries to seize the family farm of one of his subjects, Elijah stands up to him again for abusing his power (1 Kgs 21). Clearly, Elijah is presented as an opponent to Ahab and Jezebel. As you read these stories, notice how the kind of leadership exemplified by Elijah is both similar to and different from that of Ahab's leadership.

Does this similarity or difference between Ahab and Elijah tell us anything about the strengths and weaknesses, as well as the purposes and dangers, of leadership?

Day 4: 2 Kings 17–19

The fall of Samaria and the northern kingdom

In 722 BCE, the army of the Assyrian Empire came against the northern kingdom of Israel. The Assyrians destroyed its capital city of Samaria, killed some of its inhabitants, and forcibly moved others back to Assyria, settling them throughout the country. We are told that this occurred because Israel's King Hoshea withheld the yearly tribute that the Assyrian king demanded and made an alliance with Egypt, Assyria's enemy (2 Kgs 17:4). Yet this reason isn't the one that is highlighted by the reading for today. Instead, the text includes a long sermon outlining the various reasons why Israel collapsed from the inside out (2 Kgs 17:7-41). In contrast, the story is also told about Hezekiah, who is held up as a positive role model, and about how God miraculously rescues the kingdom of Judah from an Assyrian attack (2 Kgs 18–19).

The covenant relationship established in Deuteronomy (see Episode 8) provides the lens for evaluating the behavior of the people and their kings. As you read about the destruction of Samaria and the reasons given for it and about Hezekiah and the rescue of Jerusalem, notice how the character of Hezekiah is contrasted with the inhabitants of Israel throughout the long sermon.

What are the specific differences between Hezekiah and the people? What role do prophetic leaders play?

Day 5: 2 Kings 22–25

The fall of Jerusalem and the southern kingdom

In 586 BCE, the army of the Babylonian Empire, under King Nebuchadnezzar, came against the city of Jerusalem, destroyed it, and exiled all but the poorest people to Babylon. The importance of this event and the end of the Davidic dynasty is impossible to overstate in the way it influenced Israelite and Jewish religion and theology, and in the formation of holy scripture itself. The readings for today outline the events of those final decades of Judah's kingdom with an eye toward understanding how such a tragic event occurred.

The reading begins in the aftermath of the reigns of Manasseh and Amon, who had sponsored the worship of foreign gods and religious practices against the clear instructions of the covenant. In a counter to this, Josiah reigned and brought about a religious reform based on a scroll that was found in the temple. Josiah, like Hezekiah in the last reading, is presented as a positive character who ushers in a reign of peace and faithfulness to God (2 Kgs 22:1–23:25). Most scholars believe that the scroll found during Josiah's reign was a version of Deuteronomy, or a version of the Torah, which is now the introduction to the Deuteronomistic History (the books of Joshua, Judges, 1 and 2 Samuel, and 1 and 2 Kings).

> **Optional:** *An additional video on exile and hope is available for download from* **CovenantBibleStudy.com**.

The tragic effects of the long history of unfaithfulness, stretching all the way back perhaps to the very start of the Davidic monarchy with Solomon, or perhaps even to David, couldn't be lessened with a few years of faithfulness under Josiah. The weight was too great, and the effects were too enduring. After Josiah's death, the kings who followed were weak, religiously and politically, and they led the country to disaster.

Think of an example of a leader in recent memory who led his or her people into a disaster. Write the leader's name, and write something you would say to that leader.

Day 6: 2 Kings 5:1-14 ✓
Covenant Meditation: Who is the leader?

Many of us are conditioned to read and interpret history in a particular and focused way: to gather details. Historical writings in the Bible are often read for the predetermined purpose of getting straight in our minds the names, dates, places, and events that formed the community of our spiritual ancestors. But as we have learned this week, details and facts are only a few of the gifts intended by God through the stories found in 2 Samuel and 1 and

2 Kings. Within these same sacred texts, we are also invited into the contours of human relationships as created and known by God. We witness the good and the not so good, as our forebearers sought to lead faithful lives and worship the God who makes a covenant with us.

You are invited to expect something fresh from these stories. Find 2 Kings 5:1-14. Before you begin to read, recall that God not only encountered the people in this story from our past, all of whom exhibit different qualities of leadership within the faith community; but that God is just as present and engaged during this time of reading and reflecting on this text. The same God is addressing you here and now. Aloud or in silence, offer this prayer: "God, help me to seek and follow those you call to lead."

Now, slowly read 2 Kings 5:1-14. As you read, or reread, make a list of any of the characters' leadership qualities, noting especially those qualities valued by God. Be open to different kinds and forms of leadership, formal and informal, official and behind-the-scenes. Set aside assumptions about leadership that you might be carrying with you to this reading, and look for those qualities that lead to the kind of life desired by God. Review your list. Offer these qualities or characteristics of leadership to God in gratitude and remember those in your community who bring these qualities into your shared life together. Be specific as you let leaders come to mind.

> **Optional:** *An additional video retelling the story of Naaman and Elisha is available for download from* **CovenantBibleStudy.com**.

Group Meeting Experience
2 Samuel 7:1-17 | Covenant with David

God makes a covenant with David, promising him that he will become famous, that Israel will live securely, that David himself won't be troubled by any enemies, and that David will have a dynasty. After David's death, one of his own sons will reign in his place, will build a temple for God, and will become God's own son. God further declares that this covenant won't be affected by the obedience or disobedience of the son, but will last forever and be eternal. David will, forever, have a descendant sitting on his throne in Jerusalem.

1. The passage begins with David's wish to build God a permanent house or palace, so that God's holy chest won't stay in a tent. In light of David's character, as seen in the reading for Day 1, why might David want to do this? Are there positive reasons why David might want to do this? Are there selfish reasons? How does David's initial plan here mirror what else we know about his character?

2. The introduction to the covenant begins with a relatively long section about God's history with Israel (2 Sam 7:5-7), God's history with David (2 Sam 7:8-9*a*), and God's plans for both (2 Sam 7:9*b*-11*a*). Why might the covenant begin this way? What role does this introduction play in the larger speech? Do you see any parallels between these three sections? If so, how do those parallels cause us to think about Israel? David? God?

3. The central point in the promise of the dynasty (2 Sam 7:11*b*-16) is that the royal line of David's descendants will last forever. The word *forever* appears three times (2 Sam 7:13, 16). The phrase "will never take my faithful love away" emphasizes this (2 Sam 7:15). The phrase "I will establish" has a sense of permanence (2 Sam 7:13), as does the phrase "will be secured" (2 Sam 7:16). Why does the covenant make such a point about the permanence and eternal nature of David's dynasty? If, as pointed out in the general introduction, these texts reached their final form after the destruction of Jerusalem, the palace, and the throne of David, how does this promise read in light of that eventual disaster?

4. The early Christian church believed that Jesus was a descendant of David and "God's Son." How might those early Christians have read and understood this passage?

5. What is the relationship between God's promises and our responsibility to do what we are called to do?

SIGNS OF FAITHFUL LOVE

God is faithful to Covenant people, even when we fall short.
God's faithfulness comes in many forms: in an unexpected mission,
in an unconditional promise, in the unwelcome rebuke of prophets,
and even in the unwanted appearance of our adversaries.

1 and 2 Thessalonians, 1 and 2 Timothy, Titus

GOD'S HOUSEHOLD
To live responsible, changed, and well-ordered lives

Bible Readings

Day 1: 1 Thessalonians 1–5

Day 2: 2 Thessalonians 1–3

Day 3: 1 Timothy 1:1-2; 2–4; 6:1-2, 11-15

Day 4: 2 Timothy 1–4

Day 5: Titus

Day 6: Covenant Meditation on 2 Timothy 3:14-17

Day 7: Group Meeting Experience with 1 Thessalonians 1:2-10

Covenant Prayer

For all who feel discouraged, unimportant, or isolated from friends and family

Know that the LORD is God—he made us; we belong to him. We are his people, the sheep of his own pasture. (Psalm 100:3)

For pastors, teachers, counselors, and spiritual coaches who encourage others in the faith

*Brothers and sisters, we must always thank God for you. This is only right because your faithfulness is growing by leaps and bounds, and the love that all of you have for each other is increasing.
(2 Thessalonians 1:3)*

OUR LONGING FOR RELATIONSHIP

Often we hurt each other by word and deed in our homes or in our faith communities.

43

PAUL'S LETTERS

The five books in this unit are letters attributed to the apostle Paul, composed over a period of about fifty years. First Thessalonians was probably written around 50 or 51 CE, making it the earliest book of the New Testament. Three of the letters, 1 and 2 Timothy and Titus, were likely written late in the first century CE or early in the second, while the date of 2 Thessalonians remains uncertain.

Although the letters span a lengthy time period and were written to different communities, they share a concern to encourage the followers of Christ to live lives dedicated to God (1 Thess 4:3). As the author tells us, "I'm writing these things to you so that if I'm delayed, you'll know how you should behave in God's household. It is the church of the living God and the backbone and support of the truth" (1 Tim 3:14-15). As we read these letters, we might imagine ourselves flipping through the pages of a family scrapbook, catching occasional and one-sided glimpses of the stories and images preserved there. We will sometimes need to read between the lines in order to understand what is going on in the communities represented in these letters.

In the first decades after the crucifixion and resurrection, the followers of Jesus gathered for worship and fellowship in houses belonging to wealthier members of each community. Attending these gatherings were believers from a wide cross section of the society: rich and poor, slave and free, women and men, Jews and Gentiles. We can imagine from our own experience, as well as from our knowledge of Paul's letters and other New Testament writings, that it wasn't always easy to live in these "cross-cultural" communities, especially when social conventions differed for different sets of people.

Like other teachers of his day, Paul and his companions wrote letters to offer guidance and encouragement to these gathered communities. In a world without high-speed travel, telephones, Internet, or text messages, letters functioned as a substitute for the actual presence of the writer. Because most people in the first century were unable to read or write, these letters would have been read aloud to the communities to which they were addressed. Letters were a way not only to convey information or to stay in touch, but also to express concern, offer instruction, correct misunderstandings, and provide encouragement.

In the first century, letters were a way not only to stay in touch or to convey information, but also to express concern, offer instruction, correct misunderstandings, and provide encouragement.

For a complete chart of Paul's ministry and writing, see the CEB Study Bible, *NT page 244.*

1 AND 2 THESSALONIANS

Thessalonica was a large city in northern Greece, located at a major crossroads. The population included both Jews and Gentiles, although the young church was predominantly Gentile (they "turned to God from idols"; 1 Thess 1:9). They faced a challenge shared by believers of nearly every time and place: how to live faithfully in a political, religious, and cultural setting that doesn't necessarily share the church's values and commitments.

In what ways does your own church or faith community face a similar challenge? How have you resolved that challenge?

Paul himself had faced "a lot of opposition" and was "publicly insulted," but he reminds the Thessalonians that instead of trying to please people, he and his companions "are trying to please God" (1 Thess 2:2-5). The Thessalonians are in a similar situation, having "suffered the same things from your own people" as the churches in Judea did from theirs (1 Thess 2:14). First Thessalonians demonstrates Paul's warm regard and encouragement for this community. God has given them what they need to live faithfully in the face of their difficulties: They are loved and chosen by God (1 Thess 1:4), and God's word is working in them (1 Thess 2:13), even as they are striving "to live lives worthy of the God who is calling [them] into his own kingdom and glory" (1 Thess 2:12). Paul is delighted to learn of their faithfulness (1 Thess 3:8), and he prompts them to continue encouraging each other and building each other up.

Second Thessalonians suggests that life together in God's household is more difficult when people disagree about how to make sense of a hostile world. The first chapter encourages a community that is facing conflict and suffering from "all the harassments and trouble that you have put up with" (2 Thess 1:4). Using stark terms ("blazing fire" and "the penalty of eternal destruction"), the letter asserts that God's justice will prevail, although it won't be revealed until Jesus returns (2 Thess 1:7-10).

Then, as now, some people thought that Jesus' return ("the day of the Lord") was already happening. From our perspective, two thousand years later, it is impossible to be certain how to interpret some of the details found in the letter, such as "the person who is lawless" in 2 Thessalonians 2:3-12. However, it is clear that harassment of the church doesn't mean that the end is here. The letter offers encouragement and support, reminding readers that "our Lord

> *Life together in God's household is more difficult when people disagree about how to make sense of a hostile world.*

Jesus Christ himself and God our Father, loved us and through grace gave us eternal comfort and a good hope" (2 Thess 2:16).

Interpreters are divided about whether 2 Thessalonians was written by Paul and his associates (2 Thess 1:1) or rather by a later author writing in Paul's name. Letter-writers sometimes wrote in another name in order to lend weight and authority to their words.

1 AND 2 TIMOTHY AND TITUS

Collectively called the Pastoral Letters since at least the early eighteenth century, the letters addressed to Timothy and Titus discuss matters of behavior, church structure, and leadership. They are especially concerned with "sound teaching" (Titus 2:1) and how to live a godly life as a member of God's household. For example, 1 Timothy and Titus include explicit instructions for women and men, including slaves (1 Tim 2:8-15; 6:1-2; Titus 2:1-10), while 2 Timothy suggests behaviors and people to avoid (2 Tim 2:22–3:9). These instructions seem to reflect the customs and practices that were common in their day.

In what ways should (or shouldn't) those cultural practices apply today? How might the church decide which practices to eliminate and which ones to keep?

Notice the qualifications for various church leaders. Some debate how organized the early churches were, and this is reflected in the different translations of terms. Should *episkopē* be translated as "bishop" (indicating a highly formalized office) or just "supervisor" (as in the CEB)?

Most interpreters are convinced that all three letters were written sometime after Paul's death (in part because their vocabulary and theology reflect other writings from the second century CE). Does the issue of authorship affect your understanding of the letter or its usefulness for building up the church? Why or why not?

Day 1: 1 Thessalonians 1–5
Encouragement for faithful living

As you read 1 Thessalonians, watch for the ways that Paul builds up the community and indicates his care for and connection to them—for example, in the opening thanksgiving (1 Thess 1:2-10) and in the prayer (1 Thess 3:6-13). Note also the many times Paul uses words like *encourage* and *love*. What impact do you think Paul's language would have on a gathered community that was facing opposition from other people in their city and region?

Especially beautiful and comforting is Paul's message to those whose loved ones have died: "Brothers and sisters, we want you to know about people who have died so that you won't mourn like others who don't have any hope" (1 Thess 4:13). Notice that Paul *never* tells them not to mourn. He absolutely expects Christians to mourn, and he acknowledges the awful pain of separation. But Christian mourning is shaped by the movement toward hope, because we know and trust that the separation isn't ultimate.

If you have lost someone you love, in what ways do Paul's words provide encouragement for you?

One of the ways that Paul shows his solidarity with the Thessalonians is by offering himself as an example: not to brag about himself, but to let them know that he understands the challenges of living out one's faith in difficult circumstances. He encourages them to live "lives worthy of the God who is calling you" (1 Thess 2:12) and to "continue encouraging each other and building each other up, just like you are doing already" (1 Thess 5:11).

What are some of the ways that you can encourage others to remain faithful? What are some of the ways that others encourage you?

Day 2: 2 Thessalonians 1–3
Harassed

Harassment caused some Thessalonian believers to assume that Jesus would return right away, or that he had already come (2 Thess 2:1-3). This was a source of confusion in the church. If you believed that the world would end tomorrow or next week, what would you do? How would that expectation affect your choices and your relationships? Would you quit your job? Among the Thessalonians, it appears that some people stopped working or even taking care of themselves (because they thought the end of the world had come), which meant that others in the community had to pick up the slack (2 Thess 3:6-15). This was a crisis situation for a community that needed to stick together in the face of serious opposition from outside.

The letter promises that no matter what happens, God will give strength to endure (2 Thess 3:3-5; compare 2 Thess 2:17), so that the church might continue to express God's love (2 Thess 3:5; 1:3). Today we occasionally hear dire predictions for the end of the world, but most people don't expect the imminent return of Jesus.

Have you suffered or been harassed by others in your desire to "live a holy life in Christ Jesus" (2 Tim 3:12)? How did you experience God's grace in those situations?

Day 3: 1 Timothy 1:1-2; 2–4; 6:1-2, 11-15
Discernment

First Timothy is an example of a letter from an experienced mentor to his younger charge. The purpose of this instruction is to guide Timothy into a "holy life" (1 Tim 4:7), in part "so that God's name and our teaching won't get a bad reputation" (1 Tim 6:1). Central to the letter is the claim that "Christ Jesus came into the world to save sinners—and I'm the biggest sinner of all" (1 Tim 1:15).

Although 1 Timothy is addressed to an individual, its inclusion in the Bible suggests that early churches found its teaching to be useful for communities as they discerned how to live faithfully in their particular settings. What are some of the teachings from this letter that would nourish the faith community or church of which you are a part? Some of the letter's cultural assumptions (such as slavery as an accepted practice) are no longer accepted by Christians today. Some churches today forbid the ordination of women by citing 1 Timothy 2:8-15.

What do you think about this advice: "A wife should learn quietly with complete submission" (1 Tim 2:11)?

How might you discern which teachings to Timothy (or the behaviors that follow from those teachings) are "reliable" and deserve "complete acceptance" (1 Tim 4:9)?

Day 4: 2 Timothy 1–4
An ethical will

Imprisoned and nearing the end of his life (2 Tim 2:9; 4:6), the author—identified as the apostle Paul—writes to a member of the next generation. Like an "ethical will," the letter testifies to the values that stand at the heart of Paul's faith. It encourages Timothy to "take the things you heard me say . . . and pass them on to faithful people who are also capable of teaching others" (2 Tim 2:2).

Paul points to his own life experiences, particularly his imprisonment and suffering for the sake of the gospel, and sees in them the evidence of God's grace (2 Tim 1:10). He also sees an opportunity to trust in God's power (2 Tim 1:12).

Are there experiences in your life or in the lives of people you know that help you to see God's activity and power?

Paul acknowledges that some people support one's life in the gospel, while other people are destructive to one's life in the gospel and should be avoided (2 Tim 3:1-9). To be sure, he would prefer to have more of the former and fewer of the latter (see, for example, 2 Tim 4:9-18).

Are you hanging out with the right people? People who encourage your faithfulness?

49

Day 5: Titus

Baptism and the Holy Spirit fuel faithful living. Like 1 and 2 Timothy, the letter to Titus probably represents a period late in the first century or early second, when churches needed to figure out how to organize themselves for the long haul. The letter instructs Titus to appoint elders who will "encourage people with healthy instruction and refute those who speak against it" (Titus 1:9). Instructions for men, women, and slaves tell what it looks like when God's grace "educates us so that we can live sensible, ethical, and godly lives right now by rejecting ungodly lives and the desires of this world" (Titus 2:12). The gospel is proclaimed most clearly when the church is well ordered and when people's behaviors show that they have been changed by God's grace. In this way, the world will know that God, through Christ, "gave himself for us in order to rescue us from every kind of lawless behavior" (Titus 2:14).

Most of the ethical instruction mirrors the teaching of (non-Christian) philosophers and moralists of the day. The difference, however, for the followers of Jesus, is that faithfulness to the new covenant is made possible through baptism and renewal by the Holy Spirit (Titus 3:5).

From all the ethical instructions in Titus, write down one behavior that you want to develop more faithfully in your household.

Day 6: 2 Timothy 3:14-17
Covenant Meditation: Scripture is useful.

Throughout our readings for this week, we learned that the Pastoral Letters written to Timothy, Titus, and the Thessalonians offer guidance on how to "behave" as family members who share responsibilities in God's household. Learning to live together as Christians, and to also live as Christians in a "cross-cultural" world that doesn't share the church's views or values, is no easier today than it was when these letters were first written and read to congregations.

Because these letters were read to congregations, our spiritual reading practice for today will, again, ask that you find a quiet place where you can comfortably read aloud. If possible, go to a location where you can close the door or be alone for a little while as you listen for God's word to you from 2 Timothy 3:14-17. Once you are settled in, turn to this passage. Before your read, take a deep breath and, releasing it, ask God to help you set aside any distractions for this time.

Now read aloud these four verses, reading slowly as though you are reading these words not only to yourself but also to others whom you love. Pause for a minute after the first reading, then read aloud again, listening for a word or phrase that catches your attention. Receive this one word or phrase, without analyzing or editing which word or phrase it may be. Take two or three minutes of silence to think about this word or phrase. What images come to mind with it? What feelings or emotions come to you as you silently repeat this word or phrase in your imagination, trusting that God has given it to you for some particular reason today? Take as much time as you want to explore where this word or phrase leads you. If you wish, take time to make notes or to journal.

Before you end your meditation time, read the verses aloud one final time, and as you do, offer these verses as a prayer for your faith community, for your family and friends, and for God's entire household. Place your prayer and life into God's hands, and receive God's prayer for you as you continue to live faithfully as a member of God's beloved family.

Group Meeting Experience

1 Thessalonians 1:2-10 | *Thanksgiving*

Imagine what it might be like if 1 Thessalonians were the only letter from Paul that you ever read. When the Thessalonians received this letter, they could not compare it to Paul's other letters nor to the Gospels because none of these had yet been written. In order to make sense of this letter, the Thessalonians had to draw on their prior experience of Paul, as well as on the content of the letter itself.

As noted in the general introduction to this episode, most people in the first century were unable to read and write. Letters like this one were read aloud to the gathered community. One of the first things those early hearers noticed was that the letter was written to the whole church as a community, and not to its individual members.

1. Like the other books of the New Testament, 1 Thessalonians was originally written in Greek, which distinguishes between singular and plural pronouns (that is, *you*, singular, looks very different from *you*, plural). Although it isn't obvious in the English translation, every time the word *you* appears in this letter, it refers to *you*, plural. Invite one person in your study group to read 1 Thessalonians 1:2-10 aloud, substituting the words *you all* each time he or she encounters the word *you*. (If you prefer, you may use whatever word or words indicate the plural *you* in your local dialect: *y'all, yous, you guys,* and so on.) What stands out for you as you hear all those *you all*'s in these opening verses? Are there images or phrases that you hear differently now as they emphasize the plural form of *you*? How do these verses speak to your church, faith community, or Bible study group as a whole?

2. Read through the "thanksgiving" passage (1 Thess 1:2-10) again, this time paying close attention to the details. What information do you learn about Paul? What do you learn about the Thessalonians? What do you learn about God, Jesus, and the Holy Spirit? Imagine that Paul is writing or speaking directly to you and your faith community: How do you see yourselves in this passage? How is the passage inviting all of you to grow or to change?

3. The "thanksgiving" passage functions like a preview of the whole letter, drawing attention to topics that will be addressed later. For example, notice the emphasis on activity that occurs in this passage. Look at the things that Paul and the community have done, how people act, and the impact of their behaviors on other people. (We see a similar emphasis on behavior and action in the other letters that we have read in the Covenant Bible Study.) The *work . . . effort . . .* and *perseverance* highlighted in 1 Thessalonians 1:3 comes from *faith . . . love . . .* and *hope*.

4. Compare our group study passage to 1 Thessalonians 3:6-13 and 4:9-11 (and if you have time, to 5:8-24). How do these passages pick up themes from 1 Thessalonians 1:2-10? Why does Paul place so much emphasis on the behavior of the community? What makes

it possible for the community to live in the ways that Paul commends? Is there a word or phrase from these passages that stands out for you? If so, how might you incorporate it into your life?

SIGNS OF FAITHFUL LOVE

Covenant people live responsible, changed lives at home and
in the community. Our lives display the same grace and goodness
toward others that we experience through God's love and faithfulness.

Wisdom: Proverbs and Ecclesiastes

DISCERNMENT
Finding what is good for my life

Bible Readings

Day 1: Proverbs 1–4

Day 2: Proverbs 10–15

Day 3: Proverbs 25–29

Day 4: Ecclesiastes 1–4

Day 5: Ecclesiastes 9–12

Day 6: Covenant Meditation on Ecclesiastes 3:1-8

Day 7: Group Meeting Experience with Proverbs 2:1-19

Covenant Prayer

For those of us blinded by greed, power, and selfish desires

You will understand the fear of the LORD, and discover the knowledge of God. (Proverbs 2:5)

For people trying to make sense of the world so they can live well in it

OUR LONGING FOR RELATIONSHIP

Wealth, knowledge, and power aren't satisfying. Our path to well-being is paved by God's wisdom.

Teach us to number our days so we can have a wise heart. (Psalm 90:12)

WISDOM LITERATURE

Ecclesiastes, the Teacher, is described as working hard to find the wise word for his community.

Proverbs, Ecclesiastes, and Job are the wisdom literature of ancient Israel. These books ponder in various ways the question: "What is good for my life?" They respond by drawing primarily from human experience, passing on the wisdom of elders and ancestors. They point to the natural world, confident that nature can teach us something about how to be wise as God's creatures; for example, "Go to the ant, you lazy person" (Prov 6:6). They also include and engage the wisdom of other cultures, such as Agur (Prov 30) and King Lemuel's mother (Prov 31:1-9), neither of whom are Israelites. In short, Israel's wisdom literature, which was part of a broader wisdom tradition in the ancient Near East, wrestles with how to live well in a world formed by God's wisdom.

The most celebrated wise person of ancient Israel is Solomon, the second and last king of the united monarchy (who probably lived from 966 to 926 BCE). Tradition tells us that Solomon's wisdom was granted by God, exceeded that of all others, and was celebrated by world leaders of his day (1 Kgs 3–11). Like David with the Psalms and Moses with the Torah (the Instruction), Solomon is identified with wisdom. Proverbs as a whole, or at least three of its sections, are attributed to him (Prov 1:1; 10:1; 25:1). So is the book of Ecclesiastes (Eccl 1:1). Although most interpreters think it is unlikely that Solomon wrote much, if any, of either book, his name gives significance and authority to both.

As the famous story of Solomon's judgment between two women quarreling over a baby suggests (1 Kgs 3:16-28), wisdom requires discernment. A wise person must be able to understand a situation and respond appropriately. It isn't enough to know traditions and texts. One must also know how to interpret contexts accurately. Notice how often Proverbs celebrates a word spoken at the right time. For example, "to give an appropriate answer is a joy; how good is a word at the right time!" (Prov 15:23). Other proverbs compare fitting speech to valuable and beautiful ornaments, such as gold apples in a silver setting (Prov 25:11) and gold earrings (Prov 25:12). The timely word is exquisite. Perhaps that is why Ecclesiastes, the Teacher, is described as working hard to find the wise word for his community. He listened and studied. He searched for "pleasing" words—speech that is at once appropriate and compelling. And he wrote "truthful words honestly" (Eccl 12:9-10). By contrast, fools are notorious for throwing words around, using proverbs willy-nilly. As a result, they harm others and themselves (Prov 26:7, 9). Fools don't take the time to understand the world around them.

PROVERBS

The wise know that every proverb is complex. A proverb is a brief statement of an apparent truth that is based on human experience and endures in a community over time. The term "proverb" is used for different forms of speech, from one-line sentences to longer poems. The most common form is the two-line proverb. The first line makes an observation or claim, which the second line develops, contrasts, or motivates. Other forms include "better than" proverbs (Eccl 7:1-3, 5, 8), numerical proverbs (Prov 30:18-19), "happy" proverbs (Prov 3:13; 28:14), commands (Prov 16:3), and prohibitions (Prov 22:22-23). Although proverbs are brief, they are packed with artistic insight. Proverbs often feature vivid images and play with words, sounds, or rhythms. And every proverb has more than one possible meaning. A proverb will convey a different meaning depending on who says it and how, to whom, or in what circumstances it is said. So discernment is required to use proverbs effectively.

The book of Proverbs contains some of Israel's wisdom as the community discerned and reinterpreted it over centuries, often at significant moments of building or rebuilding. The book is a collection of collections, nearly all of which have a separate title (for example, Prov 1:1; 10:1; 22:17). Proverbs 10–30 contains the oldest sections. They generally include oral folk proverbs that wise persons—sages who were associated with the royal court—gathered and edited. The process started perhaps as early as the time of Solomon (mid-tenth century BCE). Reference to "the men of Hezekiah, king of Judah" (Prov 25:1) suggests the work continued in the late eighth to early seventh centuries BCE, perhaps as part of Hezekiah's religious and political reforms. Finally, Proverbs 1–9 and 31:10-31 were added in the postexilic period (late sixth to early third centuries BCE). The assembling of the book thus began during the period of the monarchy, continued over generations, and drew to a close in the aftermath of the Babylonian exile as the community struggled to rebuild itself. Not surprisingly, the community in exile turned to age-old wisdom.

ECCLESIASTES

Ecclesiastes, whose name or title in Hebrew means "teacher" or "preacher," was a sage in Israel during the period after the exile (late sixth to third centuries BCE). The book recounts how he studied the world around him and tried to discern what is good for

> *Proverbs are complex. They are like all the fortune cookies of the community gathered together, their wisdom held in one place. Because proverbs have more than one meaning, discernment is required to know which life situations they fit best.*

humans all of their days "under the sun" (Eccl 1:3). He judges much of what he sees to be pointless (Hebrew *hebel*), which in some contexts can mean "vapor" or "breath," or "that which can't be grasped." Indeed, he repeatedly observes that "everything is pointless, a chasing after wind" (Eccl 1:14; 2:26; 4:4). He points to such difficult realities as hard work and profits that don't satisfy (Eccl 5:10-17), injustices (Eccl 4:1-3; 5:8; 8:14), everyday hazards (Eccl 10:8-9), and the certainty and finality of death for everyone (Eccl 3:19-21). He describes how the world is turned upside down, with "slaves on horseback, while princes walk on foot like slaves" (Eccl 10:7). And he notes that even wisdom, which he still considers an advantage, can't guarantee success (Eccl 7:12). So what does Ecclesiastes conclude is good for the human? To seize and savor moments of joy—to eat and drink with a merry heart, to enjoy one's family and community, to find pleasure in one's labor (for example, Eccl 3:13; 5:18; 9:7-10). One must be quick to recognize and relish those moments as gifts from God.

Day 1: Proverbs 1–4
Learning discernment

The prologue to Proverbs (Prov 1:2-7) makes clear that the book's purpose is to teach wisdom. The prologue nearly bursts with vocabulary central to the work, such as *discipline*, *instruction*, *guidance*, *justice*, and *righteousness*. The terms are, on the one hand, clear and familiar. On the other hand, they name concepts that are complex and often contested. What is justice? What does righteousness look like? Whose discipline? Answering such questions in everyday circumstances requires discernment. Perhaps that is why the prologue insists that the book's audience is everyone—the young and the naive, the wise and those who understand (Prov 1:4-5). People never outgrow the need for instruction.

Set in a household in a city, Proverbs 1–9 contains the instructions of a father to his son(s). The setting is common in ancient Near Eastern wisdom literature. The father wants his children to choose the wise path, so he commends the teachings of parents and elders (Prov 1:8). He describes Wisdom as a woman who stands in the city and offers life-giving instruction (Prov 1:20-33). He urges the youth to search for wisdom as for "hidden treasure" (Prov 2:4) and declares that wisdom is a gift from God (Prov 2:6). The father also warns about the foolish path. He cautions about a street gang (Prov 1:10-19), wicked men (Prov 2:12-15; 4:14-19), and the "mysterious woman" (Prov 2:16-19), all of whom compete for the youth's attention. Pay attention to how the parent portrays the two paths and the consequences for choosing them.

How would you define some of the words that are central to Proverbs? What is discipline, instruction, guidance, justice, or righteousness? Can you imagine how someone else might define these words differently?

> **Optional:** *Additional videos on Woman Wisdom and the wise wife are available for download from* **CovenantBibleStudy.com**.

Day 2: Proverbs 10–15
Speaking the truth

The landscape changes significantly at Proverbs 10:1. Whereas Proverbs 1–9 contains long poetic instructions by a parent, Proverbs 10:1–22:16 consists primarily of two-line proverbs one after another. Each proverb stands on its own and seems, at least at first, disconnected from the proverbs around it. There is no apparent order. The arrangement can be disorienting.

Without the parent's guidance, readers now have responsibility for making sense of each proverb. We are invited to consider them slowly, one at a time, pondering whether we believe the proverb and imagining in what situations we might use it. We learn quickly that proverbs, like fine spices, have different senses; they "taste" different depending on the circumstances. So a wise person is careful about when and how she speaks. Notice how many proverbs in these chapters are about the power of speech. The wise word is honest (Prov 12:17) and life-giving (Prov 10:11, 17; 13:14; 14:25). It promotes peace (Prov 10:10; 15:1) and inspires joy (Prov 15:23). The foolish word, by contrast, harms oneself and others. Fools and the wicked lie, gossip, and stir up violence (Prov 10:6, 11; 11:9). Unlike the modern-day proverb that says, "Sticks and stones can break my bones, but words can never hurt me," the ancient sages recognized that speech can do real and significant damage.

When have you seen words do more damage than "sticks and stones"?

Day 3: Proverbs 25–29
Using power and influence wisely

Proverbs 25–29 focuses on the royal court and government. Indeed, some interpreters believe that portions of these chapters were used to prepare young men for leadership. The world that these proverbs describe appears more complicated than earlier in the book. We learn how to contend with kings, officials, bosses, enemies, gossips, sluggards, and liars. And for the first time, the sages warn about the precariousness of power. A morsel of bread buys injustice (Prov 28:21). Those who do right can be led astray (Prov 28:10). Wicked rulers trample the poor (Prov 28:15), steal from their people (Prov 29:4), and leave wrongdoings unpunished (Prov 29:16).

By this point in Proverbs, we are also aware that wisdom offers several perspectives on most topics. Skim through the book and identify proverbs that differ or even conflict about an issue. For example, some proverbs say that wealth is always good (Prov 10:15, 22; 14:20; 22:4). Others say it can be a liability (Prov 11:28). Some proverbs associate poverty with laziness (Prov 10:4; 24:33-34). Others point to violence and deceit (Prov 13:23; 21:6). The best example of different perspectives side by side is Proverbs 26:4-5: "Don't answer . . . Answer . . ." So what do we do? That requires discernment and paying close attention to one's particular situation. Both proverbs are wise in the right circumstances. See if you can list some modern-day proverbs that offer conflicting points of view, such as "Look before you leap" and "He who hesitates is lost"; or "Out of sight, out of mind" and "Absence makes the heart grow fonder."

When has someone passed on wisdom to you that helped you figure out a new situation (a new job, a new living situation, or a different culture or context)?

Day 4: Ecclesiastes 1–4
When life seems pointless

Ecclesiastes, the Teacher, wrote during a turbulent time in ancient Israel. In the Persian/early Hellenistic period (late sixth to third centuries BCE), the economy became increasingly commercialized and competitive, and taxes and interest rates were high. The result was a very slippery socioeconomic ladder. Some people got ahead quickly. Others lost everything overnight (Eccl 5:13-16). There were no guarantees that hard work would produce security. That reality prompts Ecclesiastes' central question: "What do people gain from all the hard work that they work so hard at under the sun?" (Eccl 1:3).

The Teacher responds that "everything is pointless" (*hebel*, or "vapor"; Eccl 1:2). It can't be grasped. It is pointless. He comes to that conclusion by discernment. He looks at the world around him and reflects on what he sees. Notice how often the phrases "I said to myself," "I applied my mind," "I saw," and "I observed" repeat in these chapters. What Ecclesiastes sees is a weary, repetitive world: generations come and go; the sun rises and sets; the winds blow round and round (Eccl 1:3-11). There is constant activity but "nothing new" (Eccl 1:9). Ecclesiastes doesn't see progress or a grand design. Yet humans keep chasing "after wind" (Eccl 1:14; 2:11, 17, 26). They work tirelessly to try to secure their happiness. Ecclesiastes does, too (Eccl 2:1-11). But what the Teacher discovers is that none of it is certain or permanent. Bad and unexpected things happen, and death comes for everyone.

The humble and wise person sees a world that doesn't make sense, where the rules don't work the way they should, and where there are no guarantees. Everyone dies, so living wisely is about finding the moments of joy one has: family, friends, simple meals, and good work done well. Do you make time for this kind of wisdom in your own life?

Optional: *An additional video on the different kinds of proverbs is available for download from* **CovenantBibleStudy.com**.

Day 5: Ecclesiastes 9–12

Everyday moments of joy

Ecclesiastes' observations of the world could leave him in despair. But instead he looks around for signs of hope. Ecclesiastes takes all of his observations to heart (Eccl 9:1) and shares what he can say with certainty about the world. Although death comes for everyone, it is better to live than to die (Eccl 9:4-6). Because time and chance happen to everyone, it is better to eat, drink, enjoy life with those whom you love, and do your work with all your might (Eccl 9:7-10). And while weapons might be powerful, wisdom is still an advantage. It can save a city (Eccl 9:13-18; 10:10). Ecclesiastes studies the world around him and concludes that the "word of truth" his community needs to hear is a call to relish everyday moments of joy (Eccl 8:15-16; 12:9-10).

Ecclesiastes is one of several voices in Israelite wisdom literature that emphasize the limits of human knowledge. Notice how often he asks "Who knows?" and declares that "No one knows" or "You don't know." Consider how frequently he speaks in relative terms, such as "This is better than that." Ecclesiastes recognizes that human understanding only goes so far. Ultimately, it bumps into the mystery of God, whose works and purposes are unknowable despite a sense of "eternity" that God placed in the human heart (Eccl 3:11; 11:5). To claim to know more than we do is simply hubris and folly.

Think of someone in your life who is unafraid to say "I don't know." Why is that difficult for so many? Can it be liberating?

Day 6: Ecclesiastes 3:1-8

Covenant Meditation: What is good for my life?

Today's reading will be Ecclesiastes 3:1-8. For many people in the church, the words of these eight verses of scripture are well known, for they are frequently read at funerals and memorial services. In fact, in the Christian tradition, wisdom literature is commonly placed in services of remembrance. In these times of communal memory, grief, and honor, a proverb or a line of poetry can do in short, clear measure what might otherwise take a paragraph's worth of fresh words.

Our spiritual reading practice will be anchored in the question: "What is good for my life?" Our author for this week's Bible study suggests the wisdom books, including Ecclesiastes, all ponder this question in various ways. Allowing a single question to frame our reading of a passage can help form us in the spiritual practice of discernment, that is, of learning to search out and listen for God's voice, light, and direction in the midst of everyday life's layers and noise. To ask God, "What is good for my life?" while turning to a time-honored scripture, and then to let the scripture prompt stories, people, images, hope, and prayers—trusting that what comes to mind is also on God's heart—is one way to begin to allow scripture to teach us discernment.

For today's practice, begin by reading silently through the eight verses once, just to observe each carefully selected word and phrase. Then, before your second reading, ask God in prayer: "What is good for my life?" Then read each verse one at a time, resting for a few moments at the end of each verse and staying with any thoughts about people, circumstances, emotions, longings, worries, or desires that come to mind for you out of the verse. It may be helpful to pray the question again between each verse: "God, what is good for my life?" Go slowly and try to really trust that what comes to mind, even if it doesn't seem to make sense in the moment, is something between you and God, something that leads toward goodness for your life.

When you have prayed for discernment through all eight verses, offer a silent prayer to God of thanksgiving and for clarity for your life. Close with "Amen."

Group Meeting Experience

Proverbs 2:1-19 | *How to become wise*

In Proverbs 2, the parent encourages the youth to search for wisdom. The chapter is one long speech of twenty-two verse units, the number of consonants in the Hebrew alphabet. The effect is a sense of completeness: This is the description of how one becomes wise. It is a collaborative effort between parents, the youth, and God. By describing the path to discernment for the young, the sage describes the path to discernment for all God's people.

1. Outline the main units of Proverbs 2:1-22. Pay attention to the use of the word *then* to signal the results of the search for wisdom. Look also for repeated images and phrases. How does the parent build his case? What steps does he identify in the quest for wisdom?

2. The parent insists that the youth must actively seek wisdom. What exactly does the youth need to do? What does that suggest about how a person learns?

3. How does a person finally gain wisdom? What is significant about gaining it?

4. Circle the terms the parent uses for wisdom. What exactly do the wise understand? What happens when God gives someone wisdom and discernment?

5. The parent says that the youth will understand "fear of the LORD" (Prov 2:5). "Fear of the LORD" is the refrain of Proverbs. It frames Proverbs 1–9 (Prov 1:7; 9:10) and the book as a whole (Prov 31:30), and it is found frequently throughout. Indeed, the aim of the book is arguably to form "fearers of the LORD," that is, people who revere God, recognize their capacities and limitations, and work for good with insight, energy, and humility (Prov 3:5-8; 15:33). How is the concept of "fear of the LORD," reverence for God, similar to or different from the ways you think about wisdom?

6. How does the parent depict threats to wisdom? What is helpful and problematic about a parent's warnings? Compare the mysterious woman in this chapter with the wise woman in Proverbs 1.

7. How do we encourage the search for wisdom and true discernment today? Would you identify the same steps to wisdom as the parent does in Proverbs 2? Why or why not?

SIGNS OF FAITHFUL LOVE

Covenant people search for wisdom. In the pursuit of wisdom,
we experience well-being and everyday moments of joy.

Philemon, Philippians, Colossians, Ephesians

RECONCILED
Repairing broken relationships

Bible Readings

Day 1: Philemon

Day 2: Philippians 1–4

Day 3: Colossians 1:1–3:17

Day 4: Ephesians 1:1–5:20

Day 5: Colossians 3:18–4:1; Ephesians 5:21–6:9

Day 6: Covenant Meditation on Philemon 1:4-7

Day 7: Group Meeting Experience with Ephesians 2

Covenant Prayer

Thank you, merciful God.

He brought us to life with Christ while we were dead. (Ephesians 2:4)

We are created in Christ Jesus to do good things.

God planned for these good things to be the way that we live our lives. (Ephesians 2:10)

OUR LONGING FOR RELATIONSHIP

We each have flaws in our relationships that pull us apart in our homes and within the body of Christ.

PRISON LETTERS

Paul's Prison Letters give readers a glimpse into some of his closest relationships and his biggest ideas about God's secret plan to bring reconciliation through Jesus Christ. Just as these letters are written "in prison," they also engage what it means to live "in Christ." The theme of knowledge also permeates these letters and is linked to the experience of living "in Christ."

PHILEMON

The shortest and most personal of Paul's letters, Philemon was written from prison (either in Ephesus, Caesarea, or Rome). It's addressed to an individual first and only then to "the church that meets in your house" (Phlm 1:2). Philemon is a wealthy leader in one of Paul's congregations. He probably owned many slaves, perhaps twenty to thirty, if his household was like most large households of the day. Philemon and the congregation are probably located in Colossae, providing a connection between this letter and another we will discuss (compare Col 1:7; 4:10-14; Phlm 1:23).

Paul's purpose in writing this letter is a matter of debate. The most common suggestion is that Paul wanted Philemon to accept his slave Onesimus back without punishment. Runaway slaves were often subjected to severe punishment once recaptured. One common form of punishment was branding the letter *F* (for "fugitive") on a prominent part of the slave's body. So Paul wants Philemon to subdue his potential anger. The alternative suggestion is that Paul was asking Philemon indirectly to free Onesimus so that he could join Paul's missionary team. Paul's letter is crafty and peppered with humor, puns, irony, and double meanings. Philemon, like us, probably read the letter several times to figure out what Paul wanted.

PHILIPPIANS

Again we find Paul imprisoned, although we aren't sure where (Ephesus, Caesarea, or Rome). The congregation sent Epaphroditus to minister to Paul's needs while he was in prison (Phil 2:25, 30). Unlike modern prisons, inmates were dependent upon others for food, clothing, and other needs. This extraordinary effort of the Philippians, to provide for Paul's repeated financial support

(Phil 4:10-20) while he was incarcerated, points to the special relationship that existed between the apostle and this congregation.

Paul has opponents in Philippi. His description of these adversaries is general, so we can't be certain of their identity. They urged circumcision. They also seem allergic to self-denial (Phil 3:19). They appear to focus more on Christ's resurrection than his crucifixion. They apparently even believed that they were perfect. This would account for Paul's denial of his own perfection (Phil 3:12) and for his emphasis on the cross of Christ (Phil 3:8-11). Finally, given Paul's emphasis on his own Jewish identity (Phil 3:5-6) and their emphasis on circumcision, they were probably also Christian Jews.

In addition to this problem with opponents, Paul is also concerned with divisions in the fellowship. Near the letter's end, Paul calls upon two women, Euodia and Syntyche, "to come to an agreement in the Lord" (Phil 4:2). Clearly they are so significant to the leadership of this church that their disagreement matters greatly. These women "have struggled together with [Paul] in the ministry of the gospel, along with Clement and the rest of [Paul's] coworkers whose names are in the scroll of life" (Phil 4:3). If we think Paul insisted that people agree with him on all matters, it may be because his letters usually address problems he considers central to the gospel. Disputes like these demonstrate that in other matters, the apostle recognized that differences were inevitable and that a spirit of reconciliation should prevail.

COLOSSIANS

We do a "double take" when reading Colossians in light of the other letters of Paul. The apostle is credited as the author, but the literary expression seems different, and most interpreters think that Colossians and Ephesians were written by a faithful disciple of Paul in his name. We encounter in this letter several new phrases that are peculiar because of their absence from other Pauline letters. In addition to the new phrases, there is the provocative statement: "I'm completing what is missing from Christ's sufferings with my own body. I'm doing this for the sake of his body, which is the church" (Col 1:24). This language goes well beyond other statements made by Paul where he relates his own suffering to that of Christ.

On the other hand, Colossians' close ties with Philemon seem to suggest that Paul wrote it himself (for example, both send greetings from Aristarchus, Mark, Epaphras, Luke, and Demas; both

Paul, in chains, pleads with Philemon on behalf of the runaway slave Onesimus to be reconciled with him as a brother in Christ.

For a complete chart of Paul's ministry and writing, see the CEB *Study Bible, NT page 244.*

Unlike modern prisons, inmates were dependent upon others for food, clothing, and other needs.

Christ is God's secret plan.

call Archippus a minister; and both mention Onesimus). The congregation was founded by Epaphras in a place where Paul was unknown (Col 2:1). He did this as Paul's deputy (Col 1:7). The purpose of Colossians seems to be a report on the apostle's situation in prison, which would be described more fully by Tychicus, who was most likely carrying the letter (Col 4:8). In the process a vague warning is given to the members of the fellowship (Col 2:8-23). It isn't clear whether the dangers stem from within or from outside the Colossian church.

One of the most defining features of Colossians is its cosmic scope. Elsewhere, Paul cites traditions presenting Christ as preexistent (Phil 2:6-11) and as God's agent in creation (1 Cor 8:6). He also envisions the cosmic redemption of all creation (Rom 8:18-25). In Colossians, however, we encounter a Christ who transcends human boundaries of time and space. He plays an expanded role in creation, and his work of redemption stretches across time. Christ is at the highest level of the cosmic order: "All the treasures of wisdom and knowledge are hidden in him" (Col 2:3). He is God's "secret plan" (or "mystery"; Col 2:2). We as believers are encouraged to delve into this secret plan in order to experience fully the reconciliation that Christ accomplished so that we can be presented to God "as a people who are holy, faultless, and without blame" (Col 1:22).

EPHESIANS

Most interpreters consider Ephesians to be an expansion of Colossians. The words "in Ephesus" are actually missing from the oldest manuscripts, and a convincing argument can be made that this isn't a letter but an encyclical, which is a sermon meant to be shared by many churches. Ephesians has gifted the church with many beautiful themes and memorable passages, including: the lofty potential of the church; the unity of believers across polity, race, and ethnic identity (Eph 3:15); donning the armor of God against destructive powers; and the stunning benediction in Ephesians 3:20-21. Like Colossians, Ephesians has also raised ethical concerns from some modern Christians due to its acceptance of destructive hierarchical relationships, including approval of human slavery (Eph 6:5). It is ironic that just a few verses later the author calls us to resist powers and principalities, not to mention the earlier insistence that Christ has broken down "the barrier of hatred that divided us" (Eph 2:14).

Glory to God, who is able to do far beyond all that we could ask or imagine by his power at work within us. (Eph 3:20)

Day 1: Philemon
Reconciliation of "brothers"

Philemon is unlike other Pauline letters. It avoids theological language in tone and argument. The letter mentions God only twice. Here Paul isn't thinking through the meaning and implications of the death and resurrection of Jesus Christ—if we read this letter quickly. If, however, we read it slowly and deliberately, then we experience a conversation arising from lived theology.

The key to unlocking the theology of Paul's argument is the phrase "in Christ." The number of times Paul refers to Christ in this letter stands out in itself—11 times in 25 verses. Paul speaks of himself as being "a prisoner for the cause of Christ Jesus" (Phlm 1). His boldness toward Philemon has to do with the slave owner's faith in Christ. Paul's order or command rests on how deeply they both are immersed in this "partnership" that characterizes life in Christ. Now that Onesimus has joined this partnership, Paul's main concern is to bring about reconciliation between alienated "brothers," individuals of equal status in the eyes of the Lord. This type of behavior, from Paul's perspective, was as essential to his ministry as preaching the gospel in the first place (see, for example, 2 Cor 5:18-20).

Are you estranged from someone, such as a relative or a friend or a coworker? Even if it seems too late, imagine what reconciliation would look like. How would forgiveness feel?

Day 2: Philippians 1–4
Reconciliation and the fellowship of believers

Like Philemon, the Philippians are Paul's "partners in the ministry of the gospel" (Phil 1:5). So close is the bond between the church and its founder that some have seen this as a friendship letter, a well-defined literary type within the ancient world. Several of the features that typified such letters occur in Philippians: a strong sense of partnership (Phil 1:7); his longing for them (Phil 1:8; 4:1); shared experiences (Phil 1:30); affectionate language

(Phil 4:1); sharing gifts (Phil 4:10-20); and familial forms of address (Phil 1:12, 14; 3:1, 13, 17; 4:1, 8).

One of the dominant ideas in this letter is that of "knowing" (Phil 3:8). Paul's language suggests a kind of knowledge that is different from the mastery of doctrine and more than self-awareness. It is a way of knowing that transforms us even as it reveals who we are. It is the kind of knowledge that makes us transparent before Christ. In fact, it forms the core of our new understanding of ourselves. In one sense, the relationship created is one of spiritual union—being "found in him" (Phil 3:9). In another sense, the relationship created promotes a lens through which we navigate the world— "the participation in his sufferings" and "being conformed to his death" (Phil 3:10). This kind of knowing emphasizes binding together individuals in the fellowship, and binding the fellowship to Christ.

Imagine a close friend. Do you talk often? Are you honest and transparent with each other? Do you suffer when your friend suffers? Do you know Jesus as a friend like this?

Day 3: Colossians 1:1–3:17
Reconciliation as the hidden treasure of God

We can locate this book's purpose in Colossians 2:2-3. This passage identifies a core feature of the letter: At the heart of the faith is the hidden treasure of God's secret plan, whose content is Christ himself. This language suggests that there are many ways of probing, many ways of knowing. Framed in this manner, the secret plan that ends in Christ begins with God.

As in Philippians, reconciliation and knowing are intertwined in Colossians. The letter gives depth to God's character. Although the author says that God is "invisible," God is never entirely out of the picture. The challenge isn't to keep God in mind, as though knowing God were a matter of concentrating solely on God. Knowing God's will is a God-given capacity that comes in response to answered prayer. It is a special gift of discernment (Col 1:9). While this kind of knowledge may be experienced in a flash of insight, it is a knowledge that grows over time (Col 1:10). It may even take a lifetime. While Philippians focuses on Christ giving up the "form of God," Colossians focuses on the cross as the sacrificial death through which God achieved universal reconciliation (Col 1:19-20, 22).

Try to put God's secret plan in your own words. What did Jesus accomplish on the cross?

Day 4: Ephesians 1:1–5:20
Reconciliation as the cosmic reality

When the author uses the word *church*, he normally has a local congregation in mind (for example, Corinth, Philippi, Colossae). Ephesians, by contrast, focuses exclusively on the universal church. In Colossians, the universal church is also emphasized, but the local congregation is sometimes the point of reference (see Col 4:15-16). This difference of perspective helps explain why Paul in his other letters envisions ministries as gifts that are exercised primarily in local churches (compare 1 Cor 12:4-11; Rom 12:3-8). Similarly, duly appointed leadership roles are based in a congregation (for example, Phil 1:1). By reflecting a more comprehensive perspective, Ephesians sees the universal church as built upon a foundation of "apostles and prophets"—an earlier generation—with Christ as the cornerstone (Eph 2:20).

Ephesians also displays considerable creativity with metaphors for the church. Like Colossians, it understands "the body of Christ" to be the universal church (Eph 4:12-13). Christ, as cosmic ruler, is the head of the church, "God's household" where Christians work out the implications of their faith. The most innovative metaphor, however, is the church as the "one new person" formed from the fusion of Jews and Gentiles who are reconciled by the death of Jesus Christ (Eph 2:15-16).

Think of something that divides the church, God's household. Do we still divide over race? Are there other dividing lines that we establish but that the cross makes untenable?

Day 5: Colossians 3:18–4:1; Ephesians 5:21–6:9

A reconciled household

Christ's exaltation in Colossians and Ephesians creates its own form of obedient submission. We as the church (the body of Christ) are subordinate to our head, which is Christ himself. An appropriate posture then emerges. We are to "submit to each other out of respect for Christ" (Eph 5:21), and the church itself lives in submission to Christ (Eph 5:24). Recognizing Christ as head means yielding to Christ's supreme authority. The body metaphor suggests that growth is the maturation that the church experiences over time.

The image of the body of Christ points to a covenant community that stresses unity, mutual commitment, and reconciliation. Note how Christ and the church are imagined in terms of a wife's and a husband's responsibilities. Relationships here are structured hierarchically—wives, children, and slaves are expected to be subordinate and obedient—but these expectations are cast in terms of mutual respect and love (Eph 5:21). Many Christians would argue that hierarchy and equality are in practice mutually exclusive. In the author's own time, the household was structured as a miniature version of the government. Envision a pyramid with the emperor at the top, then the aristocracy, then down to the widest part of the pyramid on the bottom: slaves and other vulnerable populations. One-third of all people in the Roman Empire were slaves.

Should Christian households be organized as miniature versions of the nation or state, or should another structure pertain? What family structure do you think best reflects Christian principles? How does Christ's journey to the cross inform your view of God's household?

Day 6: Philemon 1:4-7
Covenant Meditation: Reconciled in Christ

Our reading on Day 1 this week encourages us not to overlook the "lived theology" of Paul's letter to Philemon. But now we will slow down and reread this text. We will, through prayer, revisit this faithful word between brothers who don't agree but are united by Christ through love.

Begin by turning to Philemon 1:4-7. This is "Paul's prayer for Philemon." Slowly read this text. Now recall someone in your life—perhaps a family member, work colleague, teacher, friend, or acquaintance—for whom you can offer this same prayer. It may be someone with whom you have a difference of opinion or some obstacle in your relationship, or it could be someone who isn't in disagreement with you. It simply should be someone for whom you give God thanks, who shares your faith in Christ, and who serves God and the faith community in a way that you have noticed but perhaps not affirmed before.

Place this person's name at the beginning of this prayer, and offer this prayer for him or her. As you pray, hold this person in your imagination and in God's life-giving light. Throughout the day, lift your brother or sister in prayer whenever possible. At the end of the day, give God thanks for this scripture and this person.

Group Meeting Experience
Ephesians 2 | From death to reconciled life

Our study of these Prison Letters comes near the middle of Covenant Bible Study. In particular, these letters focus on the core challenge of covenant life: being reconciled with God and with God's household. To bring this theme to mind, we started with a concrete instance of reconciliation (Philemon) and moved to the cosmic need for reconciliation (Ephesians).

Ephesians begins with an extended opening (Eph 1:1-23). It ends with a grandiose statement about the cosmic Christ: "God put everything under Christ's feet and made him head of everything in the church, which is his body. His body, the church, is the fullness of Christ, who fills everything in every way" (Eph 1:22-23). This statement sets the stage for all that follows in the letter.

1. Our reading opens with a depiction of our former reality and conduct (Eph 2:1-3). Why were we "at one time" like dead people? What does the author mean when he says, "You followed the rule of a destructive spiritual power" (Eph 2:2)? Is there any suggestion as to who or what this destructive spiritual power is?

2. Ephesians 2:4-7 presents God's act of intervention and the reconciliation it brought. What motivated God's act of intervention? What does it mean that God didn't act because of our lovable behavior but out of a wealth of divine mercy and an abundance of love? "You are saved by God's grace because of your faith," says the apostle (Eph 2:8). How do these verses remind us of the "before" and "after" of salvation? Does this act of grace make our own actions irrelevant, or does it set up an expectation?

3. Ephesians 2:8 serves as a foundation for the popular personal proclamation "I am saved." How is this different from what Paul says in Philippians 2:12-13? How are we to understand or interpret the differences?

4. Ephesians 2:11-22 uses the images of "aliens," "citizens," and "strangers" alongside the religious and ethnic division of Jews and Gentiles. How are these ideas related to "the covenants of God's promise" (Eph 2:12) and those who lack such access? What does it mean that Christ broke down the barrier (Eph 2:14)?

5. Ephesians 2:19-22 proclaims that Gentiles are "no longer strangers and aliens" but are members of "God's household." How does the foundation described in Ephesians 2:20 differ from what we find in Matthew 16:18? What role does Christ as the cornerstone play in this image of the church? How can the church exemplify the barrier-free life discussed here?

SIGNS OF FAITHFUL LOVE

Covenant people know the secret plan of living in Christ,
who reconciles us to God and others, by living life each
day with mutual respect and an abundance of love.

James, Jude, 1 and 2 Peter

ACT LIKE A CHRISTIAN
Practicing what we believe

Bible Readings

Day 1: James 1–2

Day 2: James 3–5

Day 3: 1 Peter 1:3–4:11

Day 4: 1 Peter 4:12–5:14

Day 5: Jude and 2 Peter

Day 6: Covenant Meditation on James 1:22-26

Day 7: Group Meeting Experience with 1 Peter 2:4-10

Covenant Prayer

For all who have been bullied, teased, or ridiculed

I take refuge in you, Lord, my God. Save me from all who chase me! Rescue me! (Psalm 7:1)

For those who stand up to bullies and become a friend to those who are despised

My brothers and sisters, what good is it if people say they have faith but do nothing to show it? (James 2:14)

OUR LONGING FOR RELATIONSHIP

As Christians, we sometimes speak harshly to each other and to others who are watching to see if we practice what we preach.

75

JAMES, JUDE, 1 AND 2 PETER

Each of these four books was written to provide guidance to Christians living toward the end of the first century CE. Each is full of advice for faithful covenant living in light of an unbelieving and sometimes even hostile community outside the church. Each was probably written pseudonymously—that is, a faithful early Christian writer sought to gain authority and credibility for his work by writing in the name of a Christian from an earlier era.

Peter was of course one of the most prominent of Jesus' disciples. He is mentioned in every Gospel and also in the writings of Paul (1 Cor 9; Gal 2). Peter is a nickname meaning "rock" that Jesus gave to his disciple Simon, who, along with his brother Andrew, left the family fishing business to become a disciple. It's no wonder that Christians writing toward the end of the first century would choose to honor Peter by naming their books after him.

Jesus had brothers named James and Jude. It seems likely that the authors of the letters by those names claimed that they stood in such a close relationship to Jesus' own teaching that they could name his brothers as authorities for what they wrote.

It's also striking that both James and 1 Peter read more like speeches or sermons than like conversational letters. They have the beginning salutations that we expect from a letter (compare the letters of Paul, such as 1 Corinthians or Galatians). James, however, lacks the usual farewell greeting of a first-century letter.

Second Peter and Jude were probably written later than James and 1 Peter. Both deal with the particular problem of how to live faithfully when the end of time seems to be delayed almost indefinitely. First Peter is written with the expectation that the end is near. Second Peter is written in realization that this final act isn't coming as soon as Christians had thought. Second Peter and Jude contain much of the same material; one author almost certainly copied from the other.

JAMES

The letter from James is full of good advice for Christian living. It's much like the book of Proverbs in its trust that human wisdom, can understand God's wisdom, and that if we live by that wisdom, we will be faithful to God's covenant with us. "Are any of you wise and understanding? Show that your actions are good with a humble lifestyle that comes from wisdom" (Jas 3:13).

James makes two points with special power. First, James disagrees with those who misinterpret Paul's stress on faith and who think that Paul claims it doesn't matter what you do. James reminds us how important it is to practice what we believe, to act out our convictions: "As the lifeless body is dead, so faith without actions is dead" (Jas 2:26).

> **Optional:** *An additional video on James and Paul is available for download from* **CovenantBibleStudy.com**.

Second, James is concerned that the churches he knows are showing favoritism toward people who are rich and are neglecting the needs of those who are poor. He wants to make sure that powerless people are treated with just as much hospitality as the powerful. Indeed, he shows a profound suspicion of the rich and powerful (see Jas 5:1-6).

Like the book of Proverbs, the letter of James is full of lively pictures that the author uses to make his point. "Think about this: a small flame can set a whole forest on fire. The tongue is a small flame of fire, a world of evil at work in us" (Jas 3:5-6).

> **Optional:** *An additional video on how the book of James speaks about the tongue is available for download from* **CovenantBibleStudy.com**.

If we had only James to read in the New Testament, we wouldn't know nearly enough of the abundant mercy of God in Jesus Christ. If we got rid of James, we wouldn't think hard enough about how to serve that mercy in our relationships with others.

1 PETER

First Peter is a letter written to seven churches in Asia Minor. The order in which the churches are listed in 1 Peter 1:1 may suggest the route that the letter took as it was carried from church to church.

The letter can be divided into two sections: 1 Peter 1:1–4:11 and 1 Peter 4:12–5:11. The first section deals with the theme of the new life that God gives to believers. The stress on new birth is so strong

If we live by God's wisdom, we will be faithful to God's covenant.

The early readers of 1 Peter faced pressure to return to the comfortable ways of their culture's popular religions. Peter wants them to know that if they do this, they misunderstand their own identity as covenant people.

that some have thought that this section of the letter was originally a baptismal sermon. The second part of the letter deals more directly with the threat of harassment and gives advice to Christians in distress. Both sections recognize that the churches are facing some kind of trial.

We have no idea whether the harassment of which 1 Peter writes included physical punishment or even martyrdom. It almost certainly included being shunned and derided by the majority of the people in their towns.

First Peter is written for people who are called immigrants and strangers (see 1 Pet 1:17-18 and 2:11-12). Here the letter may be referring to their actual legal status as persons who arrived from another country, or it may be that these Christians are exiles from their heavenly home. Either way, it's also clear that these Christians feel like immigrants because they have been cut off from the pagan communities and practices where they have been at home.

Strikingly, without explanation or apology, 1 Peter simply takes terms that the Old Testament applies to Israel and applies them to the first-century church.

The whole letter is shaped by the firm conviction that at the end of time God will judge all people fairly and bring history to its consummation. This letter is written to tell Christians how to live in the meantime.

2 PETER AND JUDE

Jude and 2 Peter are probably the last two books to be written in the Bible. Both are concerned with theological inaccuracies and moral failings among self-designated believers. Second Peter, the more thorough letter, apparently knows and uses Jude. The author establishes his authority by claiming (as Peter) to have been present at Jesus' transfiguration. He addresses the problem of Jesus' delayed return by insisting first that God's mathematics aren't like our own and by suggesting that the delay in Jesus' return allows time for people to change their hearts and lives.

These formerly pagan Christians aren't just "like" Israel. In the new era of Jesus Christ, they are Israel.

Day 1: James 1–2
Faith and impartiality

In these chapters, the author warns his readers against two mistakes that are easy for Christians to make. The first mistake results from paying attention too closely to the standards of the world. The second mistake results from misreading one of the great sources of the church—Paul's letters.

James notices that it is too easy for church members to apply the standards of the world to the community of faith. If people have prestige in the larger world, it is easy to give them special prestige in the church. If people are wealthy, it is easy to prefer them over the poor (see Jas 1:9-12 and 2:1-7).

James insists on the centrality of faith for Christian life and community. Faith is a great gift from God. It is tested and refined in difficult times. It is contrasted above all to doubt. Faithful people are single-minded; doubtful people wander and waffle (Jas 1:2-7).

However, James fears that his hearers misunderstand the nature of faith. Either James and his congregation know some of the writings of the apostle Paul, or they have a sense of the kind of gospel that is being preached in Paul's name. James claims that the Christian life always has two movements. First is the movement of belief, and second is the movement of charity and compassion on the part of the faithful. The charity is evidence of the faith (Jas 2:14-26).

Think of examples in your life where your faithfulness or trust in God is evident in your actions.

Day 2: James 3–5
Penitence and patience

Like the book of Proverbs in the Old Testament, James presents a series of wise sayings to help Christians conduct their lives. Like Proverbs, James believes that such human wisdom is a reflection of the divine wisdom that is a gift from God (Jas 3:13-18).

When this letter calls us to wisdom, it calls us to pay close attention to the way the world really goes. A careful look will reveal that in the world—and in the church—the tongue has considerable power to bless, to curse, and to slander. The wise Christian will use the tongue wisely (Jas 3:1-12). In the world—and in the church—jealousy and envy are frequently the cause of strife and even warfare (Jas 3:13-14; 4:1-3).

Because all of us stand in need of heavenly wisdom and fall short of that wisdom, we all are called to change our hearts and lives before a just and merciful God (Jas 4:4-10). James continues to affirm his concern for impartiality by suggesting that the wealthy, who have more goods, will have more need to change their lives (Jas 5:1-6).

The fruit of a changed life is patience. Trusting in the mercy of God, faithful Christians wait for the fulfillment of divine wisdom in God's providential time (Jas 5:7-11).

Reflect on whether you use your tongue wisely. If you are frequently impatient, what needs to change about your relationship with God and with others?

Day 3: 1 Peter 1:3–4:11
New life guided by Christ

These verses are rich in their assertion that lives guided by Christ require and provide a new beginning for our old lives: "Don't be conformed to your former desires, those that shaped you when you were ignorant. But, as obedient children, you must be holy in every aspect of your lives" (1 Pet 1:14-15; see 1 Pet 4:1-6).

When Peter tells the believers that they are "immigrants and strangers in the world" (1 Pet 2:11), he emphasizes that they are now separated from their former way of life and are called to live by new standards of faithfulness and obedience while they await Christ's coming.

It is striking, however, that the new life Peter envisions doesn't really include new social structures. Rather, he suggests that Christians live in the present social structures in ways that are relatively charitable and kind. This becomes a problem when he simply assumes a hierarchical view of the family and tells slaves to bear cruelty patiently.

Yet over against this support for the social status quo, there is a reminder that, read through the ages, suggests a more radical reordering of life in Christ: "Finally, all of you be of one mind, sympathetic, lovers of your fellow believers, compassionate, and modest in your opinion of yourselves. Don't pay back evil for evil or insult for insult. Instead, give blessing in return" (1 Pet 3:8-9).

If someone at school, at work, or in the community suspected you were a Christian, what kind of clues would they gather from watching your life?

Day 4: 1 Peter 4:12–5:14
Waiting for the last days

The New Testament assumes that the future of history is in God's hands and that God will bring history to its conclusion. Moreover, the New Testament claims that the conclusion of human history will be generous, merciful, and just.

First Peter is written for Christians in Asia Minor who are suffering some kind of distress. We have no idea whether there was a general harassment of Christians, or whether a smaller number of Christians were suffering at the hands of the authorities, or whether they were suffering the distance and exclusion from their former pagan friends. It's clear, though, that Christians are to live humbly and faithfully in light of the coming fulfillment of history. Part of that humble living will require a church as orderly as the households Peter admires. Elders—probably both in age and in office—will rule kindly; younger members—probably both in age and in faith—will obey (1 Pet 5:1-5). It's also clear that fulfillment will be God's fulfillment, and full of grace. "After you have suffered for a little while, the God of all grace, the one who called you into his eternal glory in Christ Jesus, will himself restore, empower, strengthen, and establish you" (1 Pet 5:10; see 1 Pet 4:12-19).

Think about whether painful experiences or personal suffering has strengthened your faithfulness.

Day 5: Jude and 2 Peter
When the great day is delayed

The letter from Jude is especially concerned with false teaching and false behavior. In such literature, the opponents are almost always characterized harshly as being wrong intellectually and being inexcusable morally. While it is almost impossible to sort out just what Jude opposes, it's clear what the letter affirms: "Keep each other in the love of God, wait for the mercy of our Lord Jesus Christ, who will give you eternal life" (Jude 1:21).

Second Peter picks up much of the same concern for those who are led astray, but holds fast the hope in God's consummation of history while dealing with a problem: Why is this consummation taking so long? The answer is twofold. First, God's time isn't our time, so we shouldn't put confidence in our own highly speculative timetables. Second, the delay is God's gracious way of allowing time for changed hearts and the conversion of unbelievers.

As with 1 Peter and Jude, the time of waiting is also to be a time of obedience and faithfulness—and hope. The final verse of 2 Peter isn't just a formula; it's an admonition and a promise: "Grow in the grace and knowledge of our Lord and savior Jesus Christ. To him belongs glory now and forever" (2 Pet 3:18).

How do you typically deal with delay when systems or serious flaws are changing slowly? Are you patient? Do you look for greener pastures? Are you an activist who tries to make something happen?

Day 6: James 1:22-26
Covenant Meditation: Doers of the word

Through this week's readings, we studied biblical texts in which the authors offered early Christians guidance for faithful living, especially in difficult or hostile environments. It's just as true today that following the way of Jesus isn't easy. Our choices, behaviors, and responses to daily circumstances must be made in a context where our faith in Christ continues to be countercultural. To follow Christ requires intention, discernment, and practice. With this week's theme, "Act Like a Christian," our spiritual practice invites us to reflect on Christian behavior through prayer.

First, find a space that is as quiet as possible—a place with no interruptions (from phone, computer, coworkers, others). All you need is your source of scripture and the time you can give to this practice (ten to fifteen minutes is adequate). Sit in a comfortable position. Locate James 1:22-26 and mark its place for easy return.

Before you begin to read, relax your breath and body, setting aside as many distractions as possible—task lists, appointments, unfinished conversations. Try to imagine giving these distractions to God for a while. They will wait for you until you complete this time of prayer.

Now read James 1:22-26 aloud, softly, and slowly. When you are finished, take a deep breath in and out. Then read the passage again, reflecting on each word and phrase as you read. At the end of this second reading, return to a word, phrase, or verse that catches your attention for any reason. Repeat this word or phrase to yourself over and over again. Stay with this one part of the text for a few minutes, even if it's only a single word. Resist judging or analyzing the word or phrase that has claimed your attention. Resist trying to make sense out of the choice, but instead, to receive it as a word God is giving you today from this reading.

After two or three minutes of silent reflection on your word or phrase, read the whole passage again, silently or aloud. Do so with this question as your guide: "How am I being called to respond to this word or phrase today?" Is there some invitation in the scripture for you, prompted through the word or phrase that has captured your attention? Something personal, something for someone you know, something you need to do in response, something for God? Do you feel called to change something or to stand firm in something in your life as a Christ-follower?

If you don't experience an invitation at this time, don't worry, but allow this scripture passage to go with you throughout the day. Remain open to how God might prompt an invitation and response at a later time. Spend at least five minutes reflecting on prayerful invitation from and response to the reading. When you feel you are ready to move on, offer a prayer to God for the possibilities of how this scripture may help shape your faithfulness.

Group Meeting Experience

1 Peter 2:4-10 | *Chosen people*

First Peter is written to people who wanted to go back to the loyalties that claimed their hearts and minds before encountering Christ. With this in mind, the writer wants them to reclaim their identity as covenant people. Using passages from the Old Testament with astounding literalism, Peter says to those who are tempted to go back to their old ways: You are the chosen people and heirs of God's faithful, promising love.

1. Here are some of the Old Testament passages that 1 Peter quotes in these verses: Psalms 34:8; 118:22; Isaiah 8:14-15; 28:16; 57:15; Hosea 2:23; and Exodus 19:6. Find these passages and read them aloud.

2. How do you understand the fact that 1 Peter can mix up these verses from all over and combine them into a kind of prophetic stew?

3. If Christians are now the chosen people, what do we understand about Jewish people? You might want to look briefly at Romans 9–11, where Paul wrestles with this question and insists that God is still, as always, the God of Jews as well as of Gentiles.

4. What about the role of God's destiny (or predestination) as implied in 1 Peter 2:8? Does this mean that our fates are determined by God from the beginning? If so, how do we understand our responsibility? If our decision to believe isn't determined by God, what does the passage suggest about those who don't trust God or behave responsibly with a changed life?

5. Look at 1 Peter 1:10-12. Does this passage help us see how our writer interprets the Old Testament?

SIGNS OF FAITHFUL LOVE

Whether God chooses us or we choose God, Covenant people lead changed lives that put faith into action.

Prophets: Isaiah 1–39 and the Book of the Twelve

DOING THE RIGHT THING
What should we do?

Bible Readings

Day 1: Isaiah 1; 5:1–7:17; 9:2-7; 11:1-10

Day 2: Hosea 1:1-9; 2; 11:1-9

Day 3: Amos 1:1–3:8; 5; 7:10-17

Day 4: Micah 1:1–3:12; 6:1-8

Day 5: Zephaniah 1; 3; Malachi 3–4

Day 6: Covenant Meditation on Micah 6:8

Day 7: Group Meeting Experience with Amos 5:7-24

Covenant Prayer

For those of us who are comfortable, whose songs drown out God's call in the cry of the needy

Let justice roll down like waters, and righteousness like an ever-flowing stream. (Amos 5:24)

For those of us who long for lasting harmony between the powerful and the weak

He has told you, human one, what is good and what the LORD requires. (Micah 6:8)

OUR LONGING FOR RELATIONSHIP

When we as God's children ignore our covenant with others and with the Lord, it breaks God's heart.

THE PROPHETS

John the Baptist addresses his audience like a prophet: "You children of snakes! Who warned you to escape from the angry judgment that is coming soon? Produce fruit that shows you have changed your hearts and lives. And don't even think about saying to yourselves, Abraham is our father" (Luke 3:7-8). Challenged, the crowd asks the question, "What then should we do?" (Luke 3:10), and John answers that doing the right thing is required. The right thing includes mutual care and sharing, responsible use of power in society, honesty, and respect for the less powerful.

John the Baptist, like the prophets who came before him, knew that the life-giving covenant that God establishes with God's people isn't a matter of pedigree or entitlement. It's a living relationship that expresses itself in love of neighbor, as well as in love of God. The prophets believed that to be truly religious was to live faithfully and justly. They especially held the wealthy and the powerful accountable, addressing most of their speeches to individuals with status and power and to those who lived in their rich and powerful cities. By their passion for justice, the prophets have become the great voice in the Bible—and in Western culture more broadly—for the ethical life.

John's judgment of his hearers' failures, like the judgments of the prophets before him, was harsh. The eighth-century BCE prophets we will study in this episode saw God's punishment for Israel's failures in the military invasions and widespread destruction of the Assyrian Empire's armies. We may have different opinions about the prophets' view that God is a God of judgment or that God uses one nation to punish another. But we can appreciate the prophets' passion for justice that drove these ideas of judgment. And we can also appreciate the persistent prophetic hope for renewal. Like the eighth-century prophets facing the destruction of Israel's and Judah's political life, and the loss of their religious centers to foreign invaders, John never closes the door of hope. "What then should we do?" is a hopeful and timely question today, as well.

ISAIAH OF JERUSALEM

Numerous men and women became prophets in ancient Israel, but we have available only some words from a few of them, preserved in collections and anthologies compiled and written after their proclamations were spoken. The Isaiah scroll is a compilation of the work of three prophets. Isaiah ben Amoz, active in Jerusalem during the second half of the eighth century BCE, concerns us in this episode (see Episode 21 for Isa 40–66). Isaiah 1–39, with the probable exception of chapters 24–27, contains his words. Unlike the other eighth-century prophets, Isaiah ben Amoz seems to have easy access to Judah's kings. His words are directed primarily to Jerusalem (known also as Zion) and to the Davidic monarchy, to which he appeals for justice. He sees the monarchy as the focus of divine displeasure, and he believes that the Davidic monarchy is central to the hope of restoration. God, after all, still offers a future for the covenant with David's house (2 Sam 7).

THE BOOK OF THE TWELVE

The "Book of the Twelve" is a single book (or scroll) in the Hebrew text of the Bible. It is the fourth book of the Latter Prophets (sometimes called Minor Prophets) following Isaiah, Jeremiah, and Ezekiel. The Christian canon counts the Latter Prophets as separate books. We will read selections from only five prophets, keeping them in canonical and historical order: Hosea, Amos, Micah, Zephaniah, and Malachi.

These prophets were different in time and place, in historical context, location in society, and of course, in personal interests and gifts. Hosea, Amos, and Micah share Isaiah's eighth-century context, while Zephaniah and Malachi are from later periods. It's possible, however, to see in all of them what Abraham Joshua Heschel long ago defined as the essence of prophecy in the Hebrew Bible: The prophets express the "pathos of God." The covenant that God established with Israel is a personal relationship in which both parties are affected by each other. The covenant isn't an impersonal contract. The prophets give expression to God's anger, aroused by social injustice even more than by willful disobedience about God's instructions. They also promise a coming judgment where accounts will be severely settled. At the same time, the "door of hope" (Hos 2:15) will ever be reopened, and restoration will always be possible, because God loves Israel as a parent loves a straying child, as a partner loves an errant spouse.

Prophets in ancient Israel functioned as spokespeople for God and advocates for God's way in the world. Royal prophets had a place in the court and access to the king (Nathan in David's court, Isaiah to king Hezekiah). Others, like Amos and Hosea, came from humble or obscure settings. Together they bring messages of judgment on injustice and idolatry, and a promise that God's faithful love will reclaim a faithless people (such as in Hosea).

For a complete chart of the historical settings of the Prophetic Books, see the CEB Study Bible, OT pages 1156–1157.

> **Optional:** *An additional video on defining a prophet is available for download from* **CovenantBibleStudy.com**.

Day 1: Isaiah 1; 5:1–7:17; 9:2-7; 11:1-10
Royal prophet

Isaiah begins with an accusation in the form of a dispute (Isa 1:2). Calling the heavens and the earth to witness was a traditional way of addressing the elders who settled family conflicts. The voice we hear—"I reared children; I raised them, and they turned against me!"—is that of a grieving parent. His stubborn children have refused to learn from punishment and continue to rebel, to the point that the community risks the fate of Sodom and Gomorrah (Gen 19:23-28). The grieving Lord rejects the sacrifices of the temple as "wickedness with celebration" (Isa 1:13) and insists that "Zion will be redeemed by justice, and those who change their lives by righteousness" (Isa 1:27). What angers God is clear: injustice and oppression of the weak and corruption at all levels of the clan and community.

There's a last offer by God. God is as unwilling to carry out the deserved destruction as God is anxious to keep open the possibility of change and deliverance. Isaiah 1:16-31 represents that offer, a call to "settle this" (Isa 1:18). Rather than trying to mend a broken relationship with God with religious rites, Jerusalem and its rulers have work to do throughout the community (Isa 1:16-17). Isaiah 1:21-23 makes it clear that God requires changes in the areas of public safety, financial integrity, consumer protection (watered-down beer?), honest government, and fair administration of justice, especially to the least powerful: the widows and the orphans. This, rather than more sacrifices, is what God requires, and in the rest of Isaiah 1 the threat of destruction turns into a promise of redemption.

The "song of the vineyard" in Isaiah 5:1-7 returns to the theme of God's disappointed expectations concerning Judah, still within the general framework of a family dispute. Here the prophet is using a bitter parody of a "love song," perhaps a song addressed to the bridegroom at a wedding. Such a song might have celebrated the expected crop of the vineyard (metaphorically, the children to come), but here the prophet turns it into condemnation of the people who have disappointed God (Isa 5:3, 7).

When foreign enemies threatened Judah and Jerusalem, Isaiah viewed their invasion as God's punishment, but he believed that God wouldn't allow his dearly loved city Jerusalem to fall into their hands. For Isaiah, that hope is rooted in God's covenant with David, in the survival of Jerusalem, and in the rule of a future righteous king of the house of David.

Isaiah 7 is spoken during an invasion of Judah by Israel's King Pekah and Syria's King Rezin (see 2 Kgs 16:1-9), who formed a coalition aimed at forcing Judah to join them in a revolt against Assyria. Isaiah tells Judah's King Ahaz that God would protect Jerusalem and preserve David's dynasty, and he confirms this with the sign of Immanuel (Isa 7:14-16). The "young woman" is probably a pregnant wife of Ahaz. By the time she gives birth, she will be able to give her newborn the joyous name "Immanuel" (God is with us) because the crisis posed by the attack of Israel and Syria will be over.

This narrative and other speeches in Isaiah—for example, the lovely prediction of an ideal future Davidic ruler leading to the establishment of a peaceable kingdom found in Isaiah 11:1-9—helped to shape later Jewish and Christian ideas of a messiah, a future descendant of David who would renew God's ancient promises. As we read these passages, remember that the qualities of the ideal king (Isa 11:2-5) represent precisely the values that covenant people are to establish in their social, economic, and political lives. The peaceful and lasting harmony between the powerful and the weak, which Isaiah 11:6-9 so beautifully evokes, is indeed God's will for covenant people everywhere.

Can you think of a time when you felt that God was angry with you or your family or your community? Did that sense of anger give way to forgiveness and hope?

Day 2: Hosea 1:1-9; 2; 11:1-9
How can I give you up, Ephraim?

Hosea's prophetic activity took place in the northern kingdom of Israel (Ephraim) in the years before its capital, Samaria, fell to the Assyrians (721 BCE), beginning in the reign of Jeroboam (Hos 1:1). He was a contemporary of Isaiah, who prophesied to the southern kingdom of Judah and to its capital, Jerusalem.

Hosea chooses images from the sphere of family life and human love (husband and wife; parent and child) to express God's relationship with God's dearly loved people, even if they are less than faithful. Canaanite shrines were devoted to the Canaanite god Baal (whose name means "lord," "owner," "husband"). These worship centers tried to secure fertility for families and crops, and they were popular in Israel and Judah in the eighth century BCE. Hosea condemns the worship of Baal, mingled and confused with the worship of Yahweh (Hos 2:8, 16-17), calling it adultery, promiscuity, or prostitution. To dramatize God's relationship to a faithless Israel, Hosea marries a prostitute (Hos 1:2). Hosea's marriage to Gomer produced three children, whose names symbolize Israel's rejection of its covenant relationship to God: Jezreel (named after the site of Jehu's massacre of members of the previous ruling house in 2 Kgs 9:14–10:11), "No Compassion," and "Not My People." The name of the last child reverses the formula used in Exodus 6:7 and Leviticus 26:12 to signal the establishment of the covenant.

In Hosea 2:2 we find the covenant metaphor extending to marriage and divorce: "She is not my wife, and I am not her husband." Hosea's address to his children in Hosea 2 is also clearly God addressing Israel, and the grief of God over Israel's idolatry shows through the grief of the prophet over Gomer's adultery. Hosea 2:8 poignantly asserts that going after Baal was fruitless, since all along it was Yahweh who "gave her the corn, the new wine, and the fresh oil, and . . . much silver, and gold that they used for Baal." From Hosea 2:14 on, the marriage is renewed (note the reference to the exodus as a honeymoon in Hos 2:15), and Yahweh promises a new covenant that will involve all nature and ensure universal peace. The lovely poetic reversal of the divorce ends with the renewal of the relationship: "You are my people . . . You are my God" (Hos 2:19-23).

In Hosea 11:1-9, the prophet turns to the image of a parent with an errant grown child, who finds that the tender feelings their relationship once evoked are still there: "When Israel was a child, I loved him, and out of Egypt I called my son." Hosea 11:3-4 is heart-rending, and Hosea dares to tell us that it's God's heart that is torn apart. Ephraim (Israel) will suffer, inevitably—but his grieving parent can't bear to give him up (Hos 11:8). In a situation that would destroy a human parent, however, God can decide against anger and the inevitability of Ephraim's destruction (Hos 11:9).

At times, most people will feel estranged or distant from God. If this happens, recall such a time and try to express how God's heart was affected. If it helps, imagine how a parent feels when a child isn't relating or communicating.

Day 3: Amos 1:1–3:8; 5; 7:10-17

A lion has roared.

Amos lived in Tekoa, a village on the edge of the desert near Bethlehem in the southern kingdom of Judah. He wasn't a "professional" prophet but "a shepherd, and a trimmer of sycamore trees" (Amos 7:14). It's unusual that Amos, a southerner, prophesied in Bethel, the royal sanctuary of the northern kingdom. The editorial note in Amos 1:1 places the prophet's words at "two years before the earthquake," a reference to a major earthquake dated by archaeology to 760 BCE. He, too, was an eighth-century contemporary of Isaiah and Hosea.

> **Optional:** *An additional video on Isaiah and Amos is available for download from* **CovenantBibleStudy.com**.

Amos' words about the Lord roaring like a lion in Amos 1:2 and in Amos 3:8 frame six speeches of doom to foreign nations (Amos 1:3–2:3), one to Judah (Amos 2:4-5), and a climactic one addressed to Israel (Amos 2:6-16). The crimes of the six foreign nations—Damascus/Syria, the Philistines (Gaza, Ashdod, Ekron, and Ashkelon), Tyre/the Phoenicians, Edom, Ammon, and Moab—are all war crimes: committing atrocities, selling the defeated into slavery, or betraying treaty obligations. In each case, God will inflict punishment through war, sending fire to destroy fortifications, breaking down gates, defeating armies, and deporting rulers.

Judah's crime is different: "because they have rejected the Instruction (Torah) of the LORD, and haven't kept his laws" (Amos 2:4). They have rejected their covenant responsibilities. The crime of Israel (Amos 2:6-12) is an amplification of Judah's crime. Amos criticizes corruption of justice to the detriment of the innocent poor, oppression of the powerless by the powerful, sexual abuse, worship celebrations financed by illegal gains extorted from the poor, refusal to respect the solemn pledge of nazirites, and failure to listen to the prophets. The most powerful expression of Amos' conviction that the covenant relationship between God and Israel can carry terrible consequences comes in Amos 3:1-2, which is directed against "the whole family that I brought out of the land of Egypt": "You only have I loved so deeply of all the families of the earth. Therefore, I will punish you for all your wrongdoing." That "therefore" bears the weight of the grief and disappointment God feels at the people's betrayal of God's love, and the pain of having to punish their wrongdoing.

What types of behavior in our present-day society would you want God to punish?

Day 4: Micah 1:1–3:12; 6:1-8
What the Lord requires from you

Micah came from Moresheth, a village in the southern kingdom of Judah, which, if it is the village mentioned by the prophet in Micah 1:14, may have been located near the Philistine city of Gath. Micah was an eighth-century contemporary of Isaiah, Hosea, and Amos. Nearly a century later, defenders of Jeremiah, accused of treason for speaking against the king, successfully cited in his defense "Micah of Moresheth, who prophesied during the rule of [King] Hezekiah" (Jer 26:18).

Micah 1:2–3:12 tells of the terrifying destruction that the Lord is already bringing upon the land by the Assyrian invasion of 701 BCE, when many of the towns of Judah were taken. Micah places the blame for the Assyrian invasion on the two capitals, Samaria and Jerusalem (Mic 1:5). He focuses on the guilt of land-grabbing speculators and of political and religious leaders who forbid the prophet from condemning them while they evict women and children from their homes (Mic 2:1-11). Micah sarcastically says that they would rather listen to a false prophet who would preach to them for wine and beer. The sarcasm turns gruesome in the image that opens Micah 3, where the rulers of the northern kingdom of Israel who are in charge of administering justice "devour the flesh of my people" (Mic 3:3). In the southern kingdom, fraudulent prophets, corrupt judges, and venal priests have joined with the rulers "who build Zion with bloodshed and Jerusalem with injustice" (Mic 3:10). The consequence is inevitable: "Zion will be plowed like a field" (Mic 3:12).

Micah 6:1-8 brings back the image of the Lord's dispute with God's people, which includes a recital of God's "righteous acts" in the history of Israel, beginning with the exodus (Mic 6:4). What does the Lord require? Micah answers his own question, first by ridiculing the value of offerings and sacrifices with mounting exaggeration (Mic 6:6-7), and then by stating what fidelity to the covenant really requires in the brilliant words of verse 8: "to do justice, embrace faithful love, and walk humbly with your God."

Can you think of a contemporary example of a person who pursued justice, embraced faithful love, and walked humbly with God? Try to think of someone you know.

Day 5: Zephaniah 1; 3; Malachi 3–4
The great day of the Lord is near.

Zephaniah's editor—whoever compiled Zephaniah in its final form—places him a century later than the prophets above. This makes Zephaniah a contemporary of Jeremiah, who also prophesied during the reign of Josiah (640–609 BCE), Judah's king when the great Babylonian Empire was on the rise. His editor gives him an unusually long genealogy, going back to his great-great-grandfather Hezekiah (Zeph 1:1). There is no evidence that this was the eighth-century King Hezekiah under whom Isaiah prophesied, nor that Hezekiah had a son named Amariah, but some have claimed that Zephaniah was of David's line.

For Zephaniah, "the day of the LORD" (Zeph 1:7) is a day yet to come, but near, in which the Lord will appear to wage victorious battle against God's enemies, and to rule, judge, and heal the earth. As we have seen, not only the foreign nations will come under judgment, but the people of God also risk falling into the same category. Destruction and judgment on Judah and Jerusalem are overwhelming in Zephaniah's speeches, but he sees them as the awful consequences of a covenant failure full of unethical conduct: violence and deceit, corrupt business practices, irresponsible wealth, cruel government, and unfair courts (Zeph 1:9-13; 3:1-3). At the same time, references to the "day of the LORD," even those that promise a thorough destruction of humankind as Zephaniah 1 does, are followed by promises of a few survivors (Zeph 3:9-20) and revival of a faithful people.

Malachi means "my messenger." It is a work written after the exile and addressed to the Jerusalem priesthood sometime during the latter half of the fifth century BCE. This was the period of reconstruction after the fall of Jerusalem (586 BCE) and the Babylonian exile (586–539 BCE).

Like the prophets before him, Malachi calls his contemporaries to covenant faithfulness, reminding them about the life of justice that the covenant relationship requires. In Malachi 3:1, the "messenger of the covenant"—identified as Elijah in Malachi 4:5—is announced, coming

93

before the final judgment to purify the temple and the Levites, to rid society of all who offend against justice, and to call for a return to the LORD, who says: "Return to me and I will return to you" (Mal 3:7).

Do you think we live in a just society, like the world required by the Old Testament prophets?

Day 6: Micah 6:8
Covenant Meditation: Justice, love, and humility

Embedded deeply in the conscience and memory of God's people is a very brief text that states what fidelity to the covenant really requires. These words glisten in Micah 6:8: "He has told you, human one, what is good and what the LORD requires from you: to do justice, embrace faithful love, and walk humbly with your God."

Few scriptures better capture the essence of the human side of our life-giving covenant with God—a covenant into which God invites us. It is a relationship that God establishes with us, not the other way around.

So for our spiritual reading practice this week, we will use this text to form a prayer that we can take with us wherever we go. You may want to rephrase the text into a prayer you can remember by heart, creating a personal prayer such as: "Lord, help me to do justice, embrace love, and walk humbly" or simply, "Teach me to be just, loving, and humble, God." Or you may find that memorizing the text just as it is will strengthen this experience of praying the scripture. Either way, these powerful words from Micah are forever ours to help guide us in the covenant life with God.

Once you have created or memorized your prayer, take some time (at least a few minutes) to repeat the prayer in silence or aloud. As this day and week move forward, recall your prayer with intention, perhaps associating it with an activity that occurs often throughout the day, such as waiting at a yellow light, washing your hands, or sitting down to read your e-mail. In this way, you can begin to develop a more frequent practice of praying the scripture by connecting it to a habit you've already formed.

Group Meeting Experience

Amos 5:7-24 | Seek good.

Of all the prophets, Amos, the earliest writing prophet, was probably the harshest critic of his people's injustices. As is typical of prophetic speeches, this one alternates between criticism of the people's failures and prediction of the consequences of these failures. Amos' aim isn't to consign his people to destruction, but to encourage them to live faithfully (Amos 5:14-15, 24).

1. Outline Amos' speech by identifying which sections critique the people's behavior and which sections describe the consequences of the people's behavior. From the sections of Amos' speech that you've identified as criticizing the people's behavior, list the specific crimes that Amos emphasizes. What would you describe as the modern equivalents of the specific crimes Amos emphasizes?

2. Amos believed the consequences of unfaithful behavior to be the punishment of God delivered by the invading Assyrian armies. How do the images of punishment in this speech reflect such an invasion?

3. If Amos saw God's punishment for injustice in terms of a defeat in war, how do you see the consequences of faithless behavior today? How do we experience the consequences of disregarding covenant responsibility and of not doing the right thing?

4. Amos says, "Seek good and not evil, that you may live" (Amos 5:14). Given his specific criticisms of his people's failures in this speech, what do you think seeking good—doing the right thing—meant for him? What does it mean for you?

5. Dr. Martin Luther King, Jr., often quoted Amos 5:24 in his sermons calling for equality in American society. Whom would you identify as prophetic figures today?

SIGNS OF FAITHFUL LOVE

Covenant people practice mutual care and sharing, responsible use of power in society, honesty, and respect for the less powerful.

Well done!

You have completed the second participant guide, *Living the Covenant*. You studied daily from scripture about the importance of living out your covenant with God and others. In your Covenant group, you saw signs of faithful love and life that are always present among God's friends. Your relationships are deepening.

By now you have also developed a habit for reading the Bible daily. The stress of daily life can't outweigh the spiritual benefits of sharing your hopes, divine promises, and personal yearnings with your Covenant group.

Keep going! You are two-thirds of the way there. You can do it. The Bible is a big, ancient collection of books, and getting the "big picture" for the whole Bible is already helping you grow and become more faithful as a friend, parent, coworker, or leader. The loyal relationships cultivated in your Covenant group will produce fruit for the rest of your life.

Whether your group takes a break or continues right away, *Trusting the Covenant* is waiting for your input. You now understand how the biblical God relates to us through covenant and how we live out our faith in a community of friends who love God. In the third and last participant guide, you will learn how faithful and even faithless people somehow find a way to trust God in the face of overwhelming disappointment and devastating setbacks.

TRUSTING

the covenant

Participant Guide

Episodes 17–24

Contents

Trusting the Covenant

Other Covenant Modules

Creating the Covenant

Living the Covenant

Bible Readings at a Glance

Sign up with your group at CovenantBibleStudy.com to get daily readings by e-mail from your group leader.

Episode 17

Day 1	John 1:1-18; 3–4	God's children love the light.	❏
Day 2	John 5; 9; 11	From healing to discipleship	❏
Day 3	John 14–17	So that they will be made perfectly one	❏
Day 4	John 18–21	Resurrection community	❏
Day 5	1 John 2–4; 2 John; 3 John	Hospitality is Christian love in action.	❏
Day 6	Covenant Meditation on John 15:9-13	Living well for others	❏
Day 7	Group Meeting Experience with John 13:1-17	Foot washing	❏

Episode 18

Day 1	Psalms 1–2; 19; 119:1-42	God's expectations	❏
Day 2	Psalms 13; 22; 80; 90	Desperate prayer for help	❏
Day 3	Psalms 34; 107; 116; 138	Giving thanks	❏
Day 4	Psalms 8; 104; 148	Creation songs	❏
Day 5	Psalms 146–150	Hallelujah!	❏
Day 6	Covenant Meditation on Psalm 139:1-6	Lord, you know me.	❏
Day 7	Group Meeting Experience with Psalm 42	Like a deer that craves streams of water	❏

Episode 19

☐	Day 1	Job 1–2	Job's story
☐	Day 2	Job 3; 9; 19; 31	Job's response
☐	Day 3	Job 4–5; 8; 11	The friends' arguments
☐	Day 4	Job 38–41	God's speeches from the whirlwind
☐	Day 5	Job 42; reread Job 1–2	Job's response to God and the epilogue
☐	Day 6	Covenant Meditation on Job 2	What do you say to a friend in pain?
☐	Day 7	Group Meeting Experience with Job 42:7-17	Double for his trouble?

Episode 20

☐	Day 1	Jeremiah 1–4	Jeremiah's call and Judah's disregard of the covenant
☐	Day 2	Jeremiah 27–29	Living under Babylonian rule
☐	Day 3	Jeremiah 16; 18–20	Jeremiah's lament for himself and for his people
☐	Day 4	Lamentations 1–2; 5	The people's call for help
☐	Day 5	Ezekiel 34–37	Ezekiel's visions of transformation; a new covenant
☐	Day 6	Covenant Meditation on Lamentations 3:1-24	Living with crisis
☐	Day 7	Group Meeting Experience with Jeremiah 31:15-34	The new covenant

Episode 21

☐	Day 1	Isaiah 40–43	Creation
☐	Day 2	Isaiah 49:1–52:12	Comfort
☐	Day 3	Isaiah 52:13–55:13	Restoration
☐	Day 4	Isaiah 56:1-8; 58–61	Justice
☐	Day 5	Isaiah 63:7–66:24	Presence
☐	Day 6	Covenant Meditation on Isaiah 43:1-7	Hope comes from God.
☐	Day 7	Group Meeting Experience with Isaiah 40:12-31	God as creator of the world and of Israel

Episode 22

Day 1	1 Chronicles 10:1–11:9; 28–29	The temple at the center of the community	❑
Day 2	2 Chronicles 33–36	Return and restoration	❑
Day 3	Ezra 1; 2:68–6:22	Rebuilding	❑
Day 4	Ezra 7–10	Ezra continues the restoration.	❑
Day 5	Nehemiah 1–2; 4; 7:73b–8:18	Nehemiah rebuilds walls; Ezra renews the covenant.	❑
Day 6	Covenant Meditation on 2 Chronicles 15:12-15	Don't abandon each other!	❑
Day 7	Group Meeting Experience with 1 Chronicles 29:10-19	David's prayer	❑

Episode 23

Day 1	Daniel 1–2	The emperor's dream	❑
Day 2	Daniel 3–4	The emperor's madness	❑
Day 3	Daniel 6	Civil disobedience	❑
Day 4	Daniel 7	Fifth monarchy	❑
Day 5	Daniel 9	Daniel's prayer	❑
Day 6	Covenant Meditation on Daniel 9:4-19	Trusting the covenant	❑
Day 7	Group Meeting Experience with Daniel 11:27-35	What about apocalyptic visions?	❑

Episode 24

Day 1	Revelation 1–3	John is called.	❑
Day 2	Revelation 4:1–8:1	Opening the scroll	❑
Day 3	Revelation 12–14	Defeating evil	❑
Day 4	Revelation 15–17	Seven plagues	❑
Day 5	Revelation 19–22	Final destination	❑
Day 6	Covenant Meditation on Revelation 7:9-17	Making us new	❑
Day 7	Group Meeting Experience	Our covenant	❑

TRUSTING

the covenant

Covenant Creative Team

Video Cohosts

Christine Chakoian, Senior Pastor,
  First Presbyterian Church, Lake Forest, IL
Shane Stanford, Senior Pastor,
  Christ United Methodist Church, Memphis, TN

Writers: Trusting the Covenant

Episode 17 Jaime Clark-Soles, Associate Professor
            of New Testament, Perkins School of
            Theology, Dallas, TX

Episode 18 William P. Brown, William Marcellus
            McPheeters Professor of Old Testament,
            Columbia Theological Seminary,
            Decatur, GA

Episode 19 Amy Erickson, Assistant Professor of
            Hebrew Bible, Iliff School of Theology,
            Denver, CO

Episode 20 Linda M. Day, Assistant Professor of Old
            Testament and Chaplain, Hiram College,
            Hiram, OH

Episode 21 Patricia K. Tull, A. B. Rhodes Professor of
            Old Testament, Louisville Presbyterian
            Theological Seminary, Louisville, KY

Episode 22 Melody D. Knowles, Vice President of
            Academic Affairs and Associate Professor
            of Old Testament, Virginia Theological
            Seminary, Alexandria, VA

Episode 23 Daniel L. Smith-Christopher, Professor of
            Theological Studies, Loyola Marymount
            College, Los Angeles, CA

Episode 24 Thomas B. Slater, Professor of New
            Testament Language and Literature,
            McAfee School of Theology, Atlanta, GA

John; 1, 2, and 3 John

LIFE TOGETHER
Abundant, eternal life with others

Bible Readings

Day 1: John 1:1-18; 3–4

Day 2: John 5; 9; 11

Day 3: John 14–17

Day 4: John 18–21

Day 5: 1 John 2–4; 2 John; 3 John

Day 6: Covenant Meditation on John 15:9-13

Day 7: Group Meeting Experience with John 13:1-17

Covenant Prayer

For those who walk in darkness

The word was life, and the life was the light for all people. (John 1:4)

For those who flourish for others

This is the testimony: God gave eternal life to us, and this life is in his Son. (1 John 5:11)

OUR LONGING FOR RELATIONSHIP

We are created to be in relationship—with God and with God's creation. Our tendency to separate from God and others disrupts the rhythms of life and leaves us unsettled, undone, and unsure.

JOHN'S GOSPEL

John's Gospel points us to an authentic community characterized by trust, intimacy, love, and abundant, eternal life. The purpose of the Gospel is clearly stated in John 20:31: "These things are written so that you will believe that Jesus is the Christ, God's Son, and that believing, you will have life in his name." The fourth Gospel is a narrative, not a newspaper account. John writes not simply to convey information but to draw you into an encounter with the risen Christ, into a relationship that from then onward will shape every minute of your precious life—every thought, deed, habit, and desire.

John's Gospel was written in stages over decades, taking its final form in approximately 100 CE. This makes it the last Gospel of the four in our New Testament, and right away you'll notice that it's quite different from the other three Gospels (Matthew, Mark, and Luke), called Synoptic Gospels because they share many phrases and stories in common. (A good tool for comparing the phrases and stories in these books is the *CEB Gospel Parallels*.) We avoid trying to force John into the framework of the Synoptic Gospels. More than 90 percent of John's content doesn't appear in the Synoptics. Many of the dearly loved stories about individuals who encounter Jesus (Nicodemus, the Samaritan woman, Lazarus, Thomas) appear only in John. Sometimes we see characters who appear elsewhere, but the particular stories about them told in John are stunningly unique (Mary and Martha, Mary Magdalene, Peter, Thomas). Events sometimes even occur in a different order: In John, the "temple tantrum" occurs at the beginning, not the end, of Jesus' public ministry. Jesus also dies on a different day in John. Don't fret over the differences, but instead ask what John is trying to signify through his way of presenting the story.

John is obsessed with the power of words, so much so that he identifies Jesus as the Word (Greek *logos*). Words can surely lead to life. In John 6, Jesus speaks difficult words that cause him to lose many disciples. At that point he turns to his other disciples and asks them if they, too, would like to leave their committed community. Peter responds, "Lord, where would we go? You have the words of eternal life" (John 6:68).

But words can destroy, as well. That's why any responsible study of the fourth Gospel requires a word of warning about the role of "the Jews" in the narrative. Obviously, Jesus and all of the first disciples were Jewish, as was the early Johannine community. Before the destruction of the temple in 70 CE, Christianity was another form

John is obsessed with the power of words, so much so that he identifies Jesus as the Word (Greek logos*). Words can surely lead to life.*

10

of Judaism. But after the destruction of the temple, Christianity began the lengthy process of becoming a separate tradition. As that happened, sadly, this separation sometimes led to Christians using John's Gospel to insult or harm Jews because the original historical context of the Gospel's composition wasn't properly and intelligently tended. To avoid anti-Semitism, unintended or otherwise, the CEB translates the phrase *the Jews* as "Jewish leaders" or "religious leaders" to indicate that the debate was between the Jewish establishment and the Jewish reformers (for example, Jesus of Nazareth).

When the Gospel reached its final draft, the community that read John's story consisted of an amazingly diverse population in terms of culture, religion, race, and ethnicity: Jews, Samaritans, Gentiles, John the Baptist's former followers, Greeks, and Romans. Such diversity is always a gift and sometimes a challenge.

The fourth Gospel engages us with a masterful literary design:

Prologue—John 1:1-18: This rich text reveals much about who Jesus is and who we are in relation to God and each other. Think about how Genesis begins (covered in Episode 2). The prologue establishes all of the major themes that matter to John; everything after 1:18 fills in the details.

The Book of Signs—John 1:19–12:50: This section tells about Jesus' public ministry. He performs seven signs in John (as compared to approximately twenty signs in Mark), and they are never called miracles or deeds of power. They are signs, and signs point to something. In John, they point to the fact that Jesus is equal to God and, therefore, has power to grant life even in the face of death, especially in the face of death.

The Book of Glory—John 13:1–20:31: At this point in the narrative, Jesus turns inward to train his closest disciples as he prepares for his crucifixion, exaltation, and glorification on the cross. The words *glory* and *glorify* appear forty-two times in John, far more than in any other book of the New Testament, and they congregate in these later chapters. Jesus is not a victim—he knows what he has come to do and does it all with calm and peace.

Epilogue—John 21:1-25: John's Gospel has two endings. The first occurs at John 20:31. Chapter 21 was probably added later, perhaps by the same author or perhaps by a later editor. The last chapter is deeply poignant and speaks to our various diverse callings, including our tendency to get into competition with each other even as disciples; the importance of love in action; and the potential sacrifice and humility involved in answering Christ's call.

As you move forward in accordance with God's will, do you proceed deliberately with calm and peace? Jot down some thoughts about when you proceeded with confidence in helping others or standing up for the right thing.

11

1, 2, and 3 John: The letters of John reflect a later phase of the community that produced and read John's Gospel. We don't know whether all three letters were written by the same person (the elder) or whether that person had a hand in writing the fourth Gospel. Thematically speaking, the letters care about many of the same issues that we saw in the Gospel: testifying to truth, believing in Jesus as the incarnate Word, and unity among believers. Upon what should that unity be based? Doctrine, behavior, or love? How are those three related?

> **Optional:** *An additional video on incarnation and abundant love is available for download from* **CovenantBibleStudy.com**.

But most importantly, the letters announce God's love for us (1 John 4:19), the call to love each other (1 John 4:11), and the promise that fear is not our fate: "There is no fear in love, but perfect love drives out fear, because fear expects punishment. The person who is afraid has not been made perfect in love" (1 John 4:18).

Day 1: John 1:1-18; 3–4
God's children love the light.

When you read John 1:1-18 in the CEB, you will see that it's indented and presented in poetic form because it's a hymn. If you compare John's opening to those of the Synoptic Gospels (Matthew, Mark, and Luke), you will see that John goes back farther than anyone else, to the very beginning when God and Jesus created every single thing that exists. Jesus is presented in terms of Woman Wisdom, whom John would have known from Proverbs 8. She tries to teach wisdom through the Instruction (Torah), but people tend to prefer foolishness, even though that path never leads to life. But those who do listen to Wisdom, to God's Word, become enlightened by the light of the world and enjoy life as children in God's household.

> **Optional:** *Additional videos retelling the stories of Nicodemus, and Jesus and the Samaritan woman at the well, are available for download from* **CovenantBibleStudy.com**.

Not long after the prologue we meet Nicodemus, who comes to Jesus "by night" and hears about being born from above. He misunderstands and is stuck at the literal level, wondering how he might be born again, a second time. But Jesus is speaking metaphorically. He appears again in John 7:50 and John 19:39-42 (where he is once again identified as the one who came by night).

Does Nicodemus ever see the light? If not, what stands in his way? If so, how does it affect his life?

The next individual to encounter Jesus is the Samaritan woman in John 4. Unlike Nicodemus, she encounters Jesus in the brightest light of day, at noon. Notice that she engages Jesus in a theological debate and, as a result, receives a revelation that Jesus is God (John 4:26). She then immediately testifies to her neighbors and invites them to encounter Jesus for themselves.

Why is the time of these meetings, night or day, a crucial detail, given what has been said in John 3:17-21?

Day 2: John 5; 9; 11
From healing to discipleship

These chapters share the idea that Jesus provides healing, but the stories differ in certain ways. Compare the behavior of the man in John 5 to the behavior of the Samaritan woman one chapter earlier (John's placement of material isn't accidental) and the behavior of the blind man in John 9. Both the Samaritan woman and the blind man are models for the kind of discipleship that John has in mind. John 9 opens with the disciples revealing their assumption that illness is caused by sin. Throughout the chapter, Jesus reorients our vision to show us what true sin and true blindness are: the willful rejection of God and of abundant life, and resignation to existence in a dark, dank spiritual tomb where fear, death, and violence reign.

What makes the blind man an exemplary disciple? First, he is open to the creative power of Jesus: When Jesus spits and makes mud and wipes it on the man's eyes, we are supposed to remember the Genesis story where God uses the earth to create human beings. Second, the

13

man tells his truth as he knows it, and he never allows anyone—the neighbors, the educated or powerful religious authorities, not even his own family members—to deny his own experience. He keeps his integrity throughout, no matter what the cost. Third, he publicly testifies to his healing relationship with Jesus. Fourth, the more he encounters Jesus, the deeper his knowledge and faith become. He first calls Jesus just a man (John 9:11), then a prophet (John 9:17), and finally he proclaims, "Lord, I believe," and worships him (John 9:38).

Compare this story about the blind man with John 11.

Day 3: John 14–17
So that they will be made perfectly one

John 14–17 is known as the farewell speech. Here Jesus teaches the disciples everything they will need to know to be mature Christian leaders who can create spaces for healthy, authentic, and fruitful communities of dearly loved disciples. In John 14 he assures them that though he will no longer physically be with them, he is always present, as is the Companion. Against the notion that God, Jesus, and the Holy Spirit are "up there" some-where, and that we will all eventually get a room in God's heavenly resort, Jesus once again insists that the movement is always in the other direction. God has always come to us and is always coming to us. In John's Gospel, Jesus is described as "the one who is coming into the world" (John 11:27). There is no separation between heaven and earth (see John 1:51). As Jesus says of himself and God in John 14:23, "we will come to them and make our home with them."

In John 15, Jesus warns the disciples that their future won't be easy, but as long as they love each other and stay connected to him, they will experience peace and joy, even in the midst of the world's hatred. The discourse concludes with Jesus' prayer on behalf of his disciples, then and now, that we may all be one in Christ expressly for the sake of the world (John 17:20-21)—the very world that may hate them.

Think of a difficult time in your life. Did you experience peace and joy by loving someone else and staying connected in thought and prayer to Jesus?

Day 4: John 18–21
Resurrection community

In John 14:6, Jesus confidently declares himself to be the way, the truth, and the life. Yet by John 19:30, the truth is put on trial and killed at the hands of the same Pilate who had recently wondered aloud to Jesus, "What is truth?" After birthing the church at the foot of the cross (John 19:25-27), blood and water come out of Jesus' side—and one is reminded of all the language in John about birth and wombs (John 3:4; 7:38; 16:21). Then one thinks of our rituals for baptism and holy communion. All the makings of being in God's family are there, but Jesus' followers are too blinded by grief and fear to move forward into their future story. Only Mary Magdalene ventures to the tomb and finds it empty. Peter and the dearly loved disciple come to see for themselves, but they go back home. Mary remains, stays put, and, by doing so, she receives the first vision of the resurrected Christ and becomes the apostle to the apostles, proclaiming the good news to her community. The disciples fearfully lock themselves in a room, but nothing can separate us from Christ, so Jesus appears to grant them peace and the gift of the Holy Spirit that he had promised earlier. So what do the disciples do? They go back to living their pre-Jesus life. Again, Jesus comes to them. He frees Peter from his shame and infuses them with a sense of calling. They answered it, and the world hasn't been the same since.

If we acknowledge that each person can find a calling or purpose in life, what calling gives you purpose? What type of service or ministry is engaged through that calling?

Optional: *An additional video retelling the story of Mary Magdalene at the tomb is available for download from CovenantBibleStudy.com.*

Day 5: 1 John 2–4; 2 John; 3 John
Hospitality is Christian love in action.

The Johannine letters worry about Christians who deny the incarnation, the fleshly nature of Jesus, preferring to keep him an abstract doctrine. The author knows that the minute we deny the true humanity of Jesus and the scandal of that uncomfortable, messy truth, we are also likely to turn our eyes away from the true humanity of each other. Incarnation means that Jesus had flesh and blood like us and that we, too, live on this earth embodied and located in very specific circumstances, including our gender, sexuality, race, class, ethnicity, and levels of able-bodiedness.

Do we value certain bodies more than others in our society? In our church?

Surely these letters teach us about Christian hospitality, which is love in action. We see this in 1 John 3:17: "If a person has material possessions and sees a brother or sister in need and that person doesn't care—how can the love of God remain in him?" Compare 3 John 1:5: "Dear friend, you act faithfully in whatever you do for our brothers and sisters, even though they are strangers." Since there was no hotel system in the New Testament era and certainly no welfare system, Christians depended on each other for sustenance, and Christian travelers stayed with other Christians as they traveled.

But the letters display a real tension between hospitality and hatred, between orthodoxy and tolerance. For every verse that commands hospitality, one finds a verse that commands one to refuse hospitality to those who don't subscribe to proper belief (see 2 John 1:10-11). The letters reveal the tendency for disagreements to lead to schism. It is clear from 1 John 2:18-19 that this church has experienced the painful loss of some of its members. The author goes on the attack and declares those who left to be antichrists and deceivers.

Is it inevitable that Christians (or even human beings) consistently choose sides over issues so that the choice is either/or? Reflect on a situation where someone left a church or a group where you participated. What might have prevented that separation?

Instead we can rely upon the truth expressed, ironically, by the very same author just a few verses earlier: "The person loving a brother and sister stays in the light, and there is nothing in the light that causes a person to stumble. But the person who hates a brother or sister is in the darkness and lives in the darkness, and doesn't know where to go because the darkness blinds the eyes" (1 John 2:10-11).

Day 6: John 15:9-13
Covenant Meditation: Living well for others

Today's practice focuses on reading scripture in a structured, prayerful way in order to grow more attuned to God's presence in our daily lives. The classic name for this ancient pattern of praying the scriptures is *lectio divina*, which in Latin means "divine reading." Traditionally in *lectio divina*, there are four key movements through which we listen to a brief selection of scripture: reading, meditating, praying, and resting (contemplating) in God's word.

Our passage for today is John 15:9-13, in which Jesus addresses the essence of living well for others by experiencing God's love. Open your Bible to this scripture and mark its location. Get comfortable where you are seated, placing both feet on the ground and letting your breathing calm.

Read the passage slowly, aloud or silently, paying attention to the whole text—every sentence, phrase, and word. Approach the scripture as though it is new to you. When finished, wait in a minute of silence.

Read the passage again, now listening for one word or phrase that catches your attention. Try not to analyze why a specific word or phrase stands out to you, but receive it as something God invites you to hear. If desired, write this word or phrase in your participant guide. Take three minutes of silence to reflect on what has caught your attention. What does this word or phrase bring to mind for you? Let your mind engage with the word or phrase, and consider what it means to you right now. Resist editing your thoughts.

Read the scripture one last time. Now reflect on feelings or memories your word or phrase evokes. Does your word or phrase point to something that you or someone you know longs for or needs? In as much or as little silent time as you need, write down any reflections that come to your mind or heart.

When you are ready, offer back in prayer to God all that you have heard, thought, and felt in this spiritual reading practice. Entrust to God any insights, questions, worries, and longings that this scripture brings to light for you. Before you end this time of praying the scripture, ask yourself if you sense an invitation from God to act or respond in some way. There may be a small invitation (to check on a friend) or a broad one (to begin to recycle), or you may not yet sense an invitation. Stay open to the possibility that in the days ahead, an invitation may be revealed through this reading. Offer God thanks, and end the practice with "Amen."

Group Meeting Experience

John 13:1-17 | *Foot washing*

We noted in the introduction that John 1–12 can be called the book of signs. That's where Jesus performs his public ministry. Chapter 12 ends with the story about Mary, the sister of Martha and Lazarus (not Mary Magdalene and not the sinful woman from the other Gospels), anointing Jesus' feet as a foreshadowing of his burial, using her hair to wipe his feet. In John 13–14, Jesus wipes the feet of his disciples as he prepares them for his departure, calls them to become mature disciples who serve others in the name of Jesus, and equips them to do greater works than he himself did (John 14:12).

1. Compare the foot washing to John 12:1-6. What do you think about all of the physical touch present in these stories and many others in John's Gospel? Did you realize that the dearly loved disciple is reclining upon Jesus' chest, not next to Jesus (John 13:23-25)? Who is touching whom in each story? How would the same kinds of interactions go over in your community today? How does the Gospel's intimate touching relate to recognizing Jesus as a human being among us?

2. In biblical times, it was usually the job of a Gentile (not Jewish) slave or of a woman to wash the feet of her husband. Why does

Peter resist having his feet washed by a person considered to be his superior? What is Jesus trying to teach his disciples about power in this story? How does this relate to Jesus' proclamation in John 15:15: "I don't call you servants any longer. . . . Instead, I call you friends." Do you think of yourselves as a community of Jesus' friends or as servants submitting to a master? What difference does it make for relating to God and each other in covenant relationship?

3. In John 13:15 Jesus says, "I have given you an example: Just as I have done, you also must do." Have you ever participated in a foot washing? If so, what was it like? Does your community practice foot washing? If so, what effect does that practice have?

SIGNS OF FAITHFUL LOVE

The signs pointing to Jesus (who serves and lives for others, who brings about new birth) are visible through the intensity of personal actions, such as foot washing.

Psalms

PRAISE AND LAMENT
Bring everything to God in prayer.

Bible Readings

Day 1: Psalms 1–2; 19; 119:1-42

Day 2: Psalms 13; 22; 80; 90

Day 3: Psalms 34; 107; 116; 138

Day 4: Psalms 8; 104; 148

Day 5: Psalms 146–150

Day 6: Covenant Meditation on Psalm 139:1-6

Day 7: Group Meeting Experience with Psalm 42

Covenant Prayer

For the voiceless and oppressed

God! Hear my prayer; listen to the words of my mouth! (Psalm 54:2)

For truth-tellers and encouragers

You who are faithful to the LORD, sing praises to him; give thanks to his holy name! His anger lasts for only a second, but his favor lasts a lifetime. (Psalm 30:4-5a)

OUR LONGING FOR RELATIONSHIP

Whether life is going well or not well at all, we share our grateful praise and our desperate pleas for help with the one who loves us.

PSALMS

The Psalms mention our covenant with God at least twenty times. Psalm 25:10 assures us that "all the LORD's paths are loving and faithful for those who keep his covenant and laws." The covenant, which is confirmed in God's faithful love, allows us to bring everything to God in prayer, including prayers for help (laments), shouts of praise, and times for giving thanks concerning the things that God is doing.

Psalms is the longest book of the Bible and the most diverse in themes. Nowhere else in the scriptures is found such a varied collection of religious poetry: 150 psalms in the Hebrew canon; 151 in the ancient Greek translation (the Septuagint). The Psalter contains a remarkable array of literary forms: desperate prayers for help (or laments), ecstatic praises, songs giving thanks, songs declaring trust, and instructions for faithful living, not to overlook a wedding song and several psalms expressing regret for sin. The popular writer Anne Lamott identifies "three essential prayers" for the faithful life: Help, Thanks, and Wow (which is the title of her book). The Psalms have those covered, and much more.

Common to all the various forms of psalms is their focus on God. In the Psalms, the God who commands is also the God who sustains. The God of kings and the God of the poor, the God of judgment and the God of mercy, the God who creates and the God who redeems, God's hidden face and God's beaming countenance: All these opposites are represented in the Psalms (and elsewhere in the Bible). That's why Martin Luther regarded the Psalms as the "little Bible."

Yet, for all its variety, the Psalter consists primarily of human words directed to God or proclaimed about God in the context of worship. They are, in the broadest sense, liturgical. Many of them are used in temple worship but also in smaller, more intimate settings. Even as liturgy, the Psalms are unique for their personal tone: Some psalms are filled with anguish and despair, some burst with joy, and others exude gratitude.

Another common feature of the Psalms is their poetry. Psalmic poetry, like biblical poetry in general, has its own structure. It is filled with images and rhythms, inviting the reader to feel, sense, and imagine. As poetry, a psalm lends itself to recitation or singing, and only thereafter to interpretation. A poem must be sounded; otherwise, its oral quality is lost, its rhythm and rhyme with its repeated and pleasant combinations of sounds are missed. Such

A poem must be sounded; otherwise, its oral quality is lost, its rhythm and rhyme with its repeated and pleasant combinations of sounds are missed.

qualities have compelled many to compare poetry with music. It's no coincidence that many of the psalms include instructions for musical accompaniment (see, for example, the superscriptions for Pss 22; 45; 56; 60; 69; 80).

> **Optional:** *An additional video on the Psalms— which we speak aloud in worship and which tell our contemporary stories—is available for download from* **CovenantBibleStudy.com**.

As for the poetry of the Psalms, there are two defining features: parallelism and metaphor. One example illustrates both quite vividly:

> Just like a deer that craves streams of water,
>   my whole being craves you, God. (Ps 42:1)

Here the psalmist evokes the image of the deer and applies it to his (or her) whole being in the second line. The speaker's being is metaphorically identified with the thirsty deer. In the same way, streams of water are identified with God. The poet constructs this metaphor in parallel poetic lines: A deer bears a positive identification with the psalmist's whole being, as do streams with God. There is a positive, constructive relationship between the lines that advances the message, and this is called "synonymous parallelism."

The opposite of synonymous parallelism is also found frequently. Take, for example, the following two verses, each representing a two-line poetic unit:

> Some people trust in chariots, others in horses;
>   but we praise the LORD's name.
> They will collapse and fall,
>   but we will stand up straight and strong. (Ps 20:7-8)

The "but" in both verses sets up a contrast: Trust in military might is contrasted with praising "the LORD's name" in the first verse, and vanquished enemies are set apart from the victors ("we") in the second verse. The contrast reflected in each of these poetic verses is called "antithetical parallelism." Many verses in the Psalms, however, are neither "synonymous" nor "antithetical," as in Psalms 124:6 and 113:3, where the thought begun in the first line is completed in the second. However we regard the relationship between the lines of a poetic verse in Psalms, we can unlock the clue to its meaning when we understand that each poetic verse is constructed as a unit of two, and sometimes three (Ps 124:6), lines in parallel relationship to each other. In the Common English Bible, the first line of a verse unit begins at the left margin, and the second (and sometimes third) is slightly indented.

Like snowflakes, no two psalms are entirely alike. Yet many exhibit common forms or patterns. Various types of psalms can be identified, not unlike the way field biologists classify botanical species. The basic presupposition of studying the Psalms' forms or types is that any given psalm is best understood not in isolation, but in relation to psalms of similar language and structure. Among the 150 psalms of the Psalter, the following major types have been identified: complaint prayers or laments (which can be either individual or communal), hymns or praise songs, individual thanksgiving songs, songs of trust, and royal psalms. Several subtypes and mixed types have also been proposed.

The Psalter is a collection of collections of psalms. Several collections are determined by their superscriptions or titles, such as the Davidic collection (Pss 3–41; 51–71; 108–110; 138–145), the Korahite collection (Pss 42–49; 84–85; 87–88), and the Asaphite collection (Pss 50; 73–83). Each psalm within these collections bears a superscription or title that attributes the psalm to a person or people. Most prominent is David, whose name appears in nearly half of the Psalms: seventy-three, to be exact. The other "personal" collections include that of the Korahites, a guild of temple personnel; and that of Asaph, a temple singer appointed by David. These collections don't necessarily claim historical authorship. The Hebrew word for the preposition *of* in the title "A psalm of David" can also mean "for," "belonging to," or "about" David.

Other psalms bear no such attribution. Many are united by a common theme or literary distinction, such as the so-called enthronement hymns (Pss 47; 93; 95–99), pilgrimage songs (Pss 120–134), and hallelujah psalms (Pss 111–117; 146–150). The enthronement hymns celebrate God's kingship over Israel and the nations with the resounding proclamation "The Lord rules!" (Pss 93:1; 96:10; 97:1; 99:1). The pilgrimage songs (the Hebrew idiom is "songs for going up," sometimes translated "Songs of Ascents" in the NIV and NRSV) are a more diverse group and are distinguished by their unique superscription. They may have been sung by pilgrims going up to the Jerusalem temple to worship. The two groupings of hallelujah psalms include psalms for thanksgiving and praise, many of which open with the command to praise. Each of the last five psalms of the Psalter is bracketed by the command "Praise the LORD!" (*hallelujah* in Hebrew), providing a fitting conclusion to the Psalms as a whole. It is no coincidence that the Hebrew title to the book of Psalms is "Praises" (Hebrew *tehillim*).

Then there are those outlier psalms, such as Psalms 89 and 90, whose pedigree has no other precedent in the Psalter: Moses and Ethan. Psalms 72 and 127 are both ascribed to Solomon, but they are part of the Davidic collection and the pilgrimage songs, respectively. Several psalms lack superscriptions altogether; they are the "orphans" of the Psalter. They include Psalms 1–2; 10; 43; 71; 91; 104–107; 118–119; 136–137. Two, however, are simply untitled extensions of previous psalms, Psalms 10 and 43. Psalms 1 and 2, in addition, bear no superscription, perhaps because they serve as the introduction to the Psalter as a whole.

Day 1: Psalms 1–2; 19; 119:1-42
God's expectations

Although Psalms 1 and 2 are quite different in content from each other, they are linked together and placed strategically at the beginning of the Psalter. Psalm 1 has as its central focus the "LORD's Instruction" (Ps 1:2), sharing a common concern with Psalms 19 and 119, so-called Torah psalms because they, too, contain instructions. Read Psalms 19 and 119 (the longest psalm in the Psalter) to see their similarities and differences. How is God's "Instruction" portrayed in each psalm? Psalm 119 is an acrostic, in which each section begins with a subsequent letter of the Hebrew alphabet (which is illustrated in the CEB).

The second psalm, a royal psalm, features God's chosen king established on Zion (Ps 2:2b, 6-7). The first psalm features two antithetical characters: the wicked and the righteous. Note how both are vividly described, metaphorically and ethically, in contrasting ways. The second psalm also juxtaposes two contrasting characters: God's "anointed" king and the raging enemies that threaten him. God's decree of the king's sonship (Ps 2:7) ensures the king's victory. How are these two contrasting characters in Psalm 2 described?

Though widely divergent in content and style, these two psalms are linked together. Can you find any similarities between these psalms in terms of language and theme? For example, consider how Psalm 1 begins and how Psalm 2 ends.

What are the various contexts or situations for "happiness" according to these two psalms?

Day 2: Psalms 13; 22; 80; 90
Desperate prayer for help

The lament psalms (also called complaints, prayers for help, or petitions) constitute the majority of psalms in the Psalter, more than one-third. Indeed, they form the Psalter's "backbone." They are most frequently cast in the first-person singular voice ("I"), as in Psalms 13 and 22. Psalms 80 and 90 are examples of community laments in the plural voice ("we").

Most laments move from complaint to praise. A simple example is Psalm 13. Observe how this short psalm moves quickly from complaint (cast in the form of questions) to prayer, and from prayer to confession of trust and praise. Note also the reasons given by the speaker for why God should save him (Ps 13:3b-5).

Psalm 22, by contrast, is much more elaborate. No other psalm in the Psalter plumbs despair so deeply and scales the heights of praise so resolutely. It stretches the genre of lament as far as it can go, extending fully in both directions: complaint and praise. Read the psalm carefully, noting how it moves from complaint and despair to trust and prayer, frequently alternating back and forth, and finally leading to a glorious buildup of praise to God. Some of the images in this psalm may seem particularly familiar to you, since the authors of the Gospels knew this psalm well and used images from it to describe the suffering and death of Jesus.

Where precisely does Psalm 22 make the switch from prayer to testimony of salvation, resulting in the speaker's trust and praise? (Hint: It happens so quickly that it can easily be missed!)

Day 3: Psalms 34; 107; 116; 138
Giving thanks

Psalm 107 qualifies as the most elaborate thanksgiving psalm in the Bible. Compare it with the simpler Psalm 138. The defining mark of a thanksgiving psalm is the testimony to God's deliverance in response to prayer (see Ps 138:3, 7). Psalm 107 opens with a command to give thanks, followed by the reason or motivation for doing so, namely, God's "faithful love" (Ps 107:1b). The psalm then depicts four situations of distress.

How would you describe each of these situations? How is God's "faithful love" operative in each situation?

Each scene concludes with an exhortation, which serves as a refrain for the entire psalm: "Let them thank the LORD for his faithful love" (Ps 107:8, 15, 21, 31). In the Psalter, "faithful love" best summarizes God's nature with respect to the covenant between God and individual or community. To speak of God's "faithful love" is to acknowledge God's responsiveness to human need, particularly in times of distress (see Ps 103:8).

The final section of the psalm (Ps 107:33-43) is filled with summary statements illustrating God's grace and judgment.

Who receives God's judgment? God's grace?

The psalm appropriately concludes with the admonition to pay attention, "carefully considering the LORD's faithful love" (Ps 107:43). To consider God's love, the psalmist contends, leads naturally to thanksgiving. Psalms 34 and 116 are other excellent examples of thanksgiving psalms. Psalm 34 is also an acrostic, with each verse beginning with the next letter of the Hebrew alphabet (which is illustrated in the CEB).

Day 4: Psalms 8; 104; 148

Creation songs

Psalm 104 is a hymn that celebrates the sheer diversity of creation (Ps 104:24). It begins and ends with the command to "bless the LORD," that is, give God due praise (Ps 104:1, 35*b*). Most of the psalm describes God's acts in creation and God's provision of water, vegetation, food, and habitat for a variety of animals, from lions to Leviathan (elsewhere described as a monster of the deep; see Ps 74:12-14). God's "breath" (Ps 104:30) creates and renews life. For the beauty of the earth, the psalmist boldly attributes to God well-deserved joy ("rejoice . . . !") in creation (Ps 104:31*b*). The last verses cast the psalm as an offering of praise that God, it is hoped, will find "pleasing" (see also Ps 19:14).

One of the striking things about Psalm 104 is the place of humanity within this cosmic panorama. Compare the place of humanity in this psalm with humanity's place in Psalms 8 and 148. Are they different? In Psalm 104, human beings aren't mentioned until verse 15, and in verses 21 through 23 the only difference between humans and lions is that lions take the night shift!

How does Psalm 104:35a, with reference to the wicked, reveal the psalmist's view of humanity in creation?

Day 5: Psalms 146–150

Hallelujah!

The concluding songs of the Psalter (Pss 146–150) each open and conclude with the command "Praise the LORD!" (*hallelujah* in Hebrew). Note their differences and similarities, particularly with respect to how each psalm describes what God has done to warrant such praise. Psalm 147 may very well be the most elaborate praise psalm in the Psalter because it contains three separate hymns, each one with its own particular emphases. As is typical with songs of praise, each hymn within this psalm opens with a command to render praise to God.

The first mini-hymn (Ps 147:1-6) celebrates God's redemptive and healing activity on behalf of Israel amid the ravages of exile. In addition, the hymn celebrates God's work in numbering and naming the stars (Ps 147:4). The second hymn (Ps 145:7-11) includes God's acts of creation and provision for animals, but concludes with God's delight specifically in "the people who honor him" (Ps 147:11). The final hymn is the most intricate, given the specific focus on God's "word" and its wide range of functions (Ps 147:15-19), from controlling the seasons to delivering Israel's Instruction. Psalm 147 is a testimony to the variety of divine activities in the world and within the community.

What would cause you to say "hallelujah" today?

Day 6: Psalm 139:1-6

Covenant Meditation: Lord, you know me.

As we have learned through this week's readings, the Psalms contain many honest prayers about despair, depression, confession, doubt, anxiety, pride, humility, joy, and praise. Too often in the congregation we feel pressure to express positive, joyful, and uplifting thoughts when praying. And yet here in the Psalms, through these songs and laments, we are reminded that our covenant with God makes room for us to bring all we experience into prayer. If not to God, then to whom can we speak the fullness of the light and darkness, trust and doubt, praises and laments of our lives?

For this devotional reading, meditate on Psalm 139:1-6. We will practice prayerful listening for a verse or phrase in the text with special meaning for your life today. God wants you to listen.

Read the full text once slowly and with intention, attending to every phrase and verse. Then do this again, at the same pace. Select one verse or phrase that catches your attention in any way; don't analyze why this is. Now read this one verse or phrase slowly a few times. In an attitude of prayer ask God, "What do you want me to hear?" Try to be still for a few minutes with this question and listen.

You may hear a word from God in this quiet time—an instruction, a correction, an encouragement—and if so, receive this as a prayer for you. You might not hear anything particular from this reading now, but it may stay with you until another time of listening to God. Just sitting still and silent with these words is true prayer.

After your time of listening is complete, give God thanks for this time.

Group Meeting Experience

Psalm 42 | Like a deer that craves streams of water

During this week with the Psalms, we learned about parallelism in poetry and how thinking or communicating with images (metaphor) is helpful when expressing our deepest yearnings and frustrations to God.

1. In certain psalms, a single image bears a wealth of metaphorical associations. Discuss how the imagery of water is used metaphorically, particularly in the first seven verses of Psalm 42.

2. What is repeated that constitutes the psalm's refrain? Who is addressed in the refrain?

3. How would you describe the mood of the speaker? Can you detect shifts in the speaker's emotional disposition? What seems to cause such shifts?

4. What is the relationship between Psalms 42 and 43? Could they constitute one psalm together? Cite evidence one way or the other, taking into consideration repeated words and phrases, as well as the usual form of the lament.

SIGNS OF FAITHFUL LOVE

While Covenant people need to reach and touch the Lord,
there are moments when the Lord reaches for us in faithful love.
The Psalms shout our mutual, loyal love in deep and
trusted words that are spoken, sung, screamed, and cried.

Job

TRAGEDY
God's role in human suffering

Bible Readings

Day 1: Job 1–2

Day 2: Job 3; 9; 19; 31

Day 3: Job 4–5; 8; 11

Day 4: Job 38–41

Day 5: Job 42; reread Job 1–2

Day 6: Covenant Meditation on Job 2

Day 7: Group Meeting Experience with Job 42:7-17

Covenant Prayer

For those who feel abandoned by God

Come back to me, Lord! Deliver me! Save me for the sake of your faithful love! (Psalm 6:4)

For faith communities and faithful friends

Come back to us, Lord! Please, quick! Have some compassion for your servants! . . . Let the kindness of the Lord our God be over us. Make the work of our hands last. Make the work of our hands last! (Psalm 90:13, 17)

OUR LONGING FOR RELATIONSHIP

When life gets tough, and loss or suffering is all around, you ask, "Why?" You ask for help. You need comfort. You can't explain why, and your friends can't explain the loss.

JOB

The book of Job begins by presenting a single character's experience of personal tragedy. First, a narrator tells of the reversal of Job's circumstances and fortunes, which includes the loss of his family, his prosperity, and his health. Then a range of voices—including Job's friends, God, and the narrator's own voice—debate the connection between personal experience and religious tradition. Can one draw conclusions or formulate doctrine about who God is based on a single person's experience? How should humans respond to God based on Job's experience? In trying to understand why tragedy occurs, should you favor your immediate experience, or can you gain a mature peace with human suffering by looking at a long tradition of reflection about God's ways with the world?

The book of Proverbs is a book like Job that contains the wisdom of Israel's sages. Proverbs teaches that if one looks closely enough at the structures of creation, we will find God's deep commitment to order, which is embedded within the universe. By contrast with Proverbs, the book of Job raises the possibility that one will find no divine commitment to order or justice. Rather, if one looks at God through the experiences of the character Job, we seem to encounter a God who does what God pleases and who seems unconcerned with justice for Job. If we read with Job, we find the God of a nightmare who permits and imposes excruciating tests of righteousness on a good and righteous person. Job uses the lens of personal tragedy, rather than that of doctrine, tradition, or orthodoxy, to inspect God's intent for the world. When this lens is held up to God, as Virginia Woolf once said, "God does not come off well."

And yet, Job's perspective in the dialogue isn't the only one the reader encounters in the book. Job's view is rooted firmly, even stubbornly, in his own experience of terrible tragedy and in his own conviction that the faithful ("the righteous" in the language of the Old Testament) should be rewarded, rather than tested or afflicted. Job never mentions the great biblical covenants describing the responsibilities of God and people to each other, but his protests clearly assume the theology of rewards and punishments present in the biblical covenant at Mount Sinai. Alongside Job's view, the author(s) present other theological worldviews, including those represented by the prose story, Job's three friends, the wisdom poem (Job 28), Elihu the fourth friend (Job 32–37), as well as the literary character God (Job 38–41).

Through the voices of these different characters, the book raises and debates a stunningly wide range of questions, including the motivation for piety, the meaning of suffering, the nature of God, the place of justice in the world, and the relationship of order and chaos in God's design of creation.

Often, when readers engage the book, from start to finish they find it to be overwhelming, confusing, or even nonsensical at times. Jerome (a Christian scholar from the 300s CE) said that the book of Job is like an eel, "for if you close your hand to hold an eel, the more you squeeze it, the sooner it escapes." But the fact that the book doesn't speak with one voice may point to its purpose. The writer(s) is probably a skeptic, not only when it comes to tradition and orthodoxy, but also in the face of any single proposal of truth. The swirling perspectives and opposing views communicate that tragedy can't be explained easily or simply, and definitely not by one voice. When the innocent suffer, there are a variety of ways to make sense of that suffering, but each of the explanations we can give and perspectives we can offer ultimately fails to win the day. Though the book undermines theological certitude, the book also assumes that God hasn't completely abandoned the world to its own problems and evils and that God is in relationship with us, involved in our human suffering.

The book implicitly claims that humans are able to survive and endure suffering because they try to make sense of it. By trying to make sense of it, we engage in the process of bringing some order to the chaos of tragedy. Perhaps best of all, however, the book gives readers permission to *not* make sense of suffering. While we are encouraged to ask the questions and formulate ideas and arguments, the book's voices, sometimes a choir and sometimes a noisy crowd, ultimately assure us that while we may formulate answers to tough theological questions about pain and suffering, they won't ever be the final answers.

It is very difficult to identify the historical setting that produced Job. It contains only a handful of historical clues (for example, the Chaldeans in Job 1:17). The story is set in the far-off and non-Israelite land of Uz and features characters with non-Israelite names. The prose narrative, in particular, gives the impression that the story is one from ages past. For linguistic reasons, most scholars agree on a Persian-period date for the book (600–400 BCE), at some point after the Israelites were dispersed into exile. Since the book of Job deals with the universal experience of tragedy, its precise historical setting is less important than the broad issues it engages.

> *God hasn't completely abandoned the world to its own problems and evils, and God is in relationship with us, involved in our human suffering.*

Some scholars think that the prose tale (Job 1–2; 42:11-17) existed and circulated independently as a folktale. Later, a scribe (or scribes), a member of the learned elite in Jerusalem, possibly added the dialogue (Job 3–31), including the wisdom poem (Job 28) and the divine speeches (Job 38–41), as a way to articulate implicit questions raised by the prose tale. A third stage may have occurred when a still-later reader who found the friends' defense of traditional theological views lacking added the speeches of Elihu to the book in order to provide a more compelling, orthodox response to Job's suffering. But most readers of Job don't worry about how the book was edited and favor looking at the ways the various speakers interact, anticipate, contend with, or undermine each other in the book.

The dialogue between Job and his friends (Job 3–27) is often compared to a text from Mesopotamia, the "Babylonian Theodicy," which features a conversation between two friends— one who is experiencing suffering and one who offers traditional theological advice as a means to reflect on the meaning of suffering.

Day 1: Job 1–2
Job's story

The story in Job 1–2 is striking because it begins by depicting God as allowing, and even condoning, the imposition of tremendous suffering—emotional and physical—on an innocent individual. Job is described not merely as innocent but as "honest, a person of absolute integrity; he feared God and avoided evil" (Job 1:1, 8; 2:3). The question about Job's character is posed by the Adversary (Hebrew *satan*), who here is one of the divine beings in the heavenly court (but not the prince of evil from the New Testament). While the Adversary questions the motivation underlying Job's righteous behaviors, both God and the narrator affirm the perfection of Job's character. And yet, God allows his destruction as a means to test that character. In Job 1–2, Job's response to his suffering is quite different from what we will find in the dialogue that follows. In the prose story, Job is an example of traditional piety, accepting his suffering without complaint (Job 1:20-21; 2:10). According to the prologue, tragedy is the result of divine testing, and Job's submission to God's will is an example of the proper response.

And yet, when you read the story closely, attending to the details of this tale, you may find that the story begins to raise theological questions of a more skeptical nature for you.

Do you think that God tests us with suffering?

Day 2: Job 3; 9; 19; 31
Job's response

The accusations Job levels at God in the course of his speeches are among the most theologically daring statements in the Old Testament. His characterization of God as one who intentionally distorts justice and willfully attacks innocents is radical, and at times even horrifying (Job 6:4; 9:22-24; 16:9-14; 19:8-12).

While other texts in the Old Testament indict God for human suffering, they sometimes temper their accusations or justify divine anger by referring to human sin (Pss 32:5; 38:18; 41:4; Lam 3:40-42) and seek to pacify God's anger with pleas for mercy. But Job insists in the speeches that divine acts of violence and harassment against him are arbitrary and erratic, and he demands justice from God. Other Old Testament texts suggest that human suffering occurs because God is sleeping or not paying attention; therefore, human enemies are free to oppress innocent people (Ps 28:1-2). Job, by contrast, depicts God as one who pays particular attention to faithful people, watching them and waiting for them to sin so that God can torment them. Job begs God, not to see him and save him, but rather to look away from him and leave him alone (Job 7:16-21).

For Job in the speeches, the cause of his personal tragedy is God. Therefore, in contrast to the laments in the book of Psalms, which often complain about "the enemies" and their relentless harassment of the faithful, Job resists introducing a third party who might shoulder some of the blame for his suffering. In fact, Job's hope persists not in the possibility that God will intervene and redeem him, but in the desire that some third party (for example, "a mediator") might intercede on Job's behalf and restrain God from tormenting Job (Job 9:33-35).

Have you ever yelled at God? Or demanded an explanation for pain and suffering? What was the cause of your frustration?

Day 3: Job 4–5; 8; 11
The friends' arguments

Job's friends—Eliphaz, Bildad, and Zophar—maintain that God has reasons for imposing suffering on people that we can't always understand at first. They propose that God may be trying to draw Job closer into relationship with God. They urge Job to turn back to God by turning away from sin. In the face of Job's personal and theological world falling to pieces, they counsel Job to remember the tenets of their common faith, to lend order to the chaos of his suffering with the theological convictions of their common tradition. For the friends, tragedy happens for a reason: human sin and frailty (Job 4:7-8). We should accept suffering as an opportunity to reflect on our weaknesses. We should turn away from sin to draw nearer to God and to become more faithful.

Although the friends' views are rarely taken seriously when we sympathize with Job, and in spite of the friends' bluntness, they may have something theologically significant to offer to the dialogue when encountering the problem and causes of pain. The friends express views held by many people of faith, especially when thinking that the suffering person is at fault or when wondering whether a particular person deserves pain as a punishment.

Do you think that some pain and suffering is deserved?

Day 4: Job 38–41
God's speeches from the whirlwind

How do God's speeches answer the questions and issues Job raises in the dialogue? After the dialogue's focus on the expectation for justice and the reason for human suffering, God suddenly appears and speaks not about justice (at least on the surface), but about creation. A related question raised by God's speeches has to do with the speeches' tone. Some readers experience God as a bully, badgering the suffering Job and bragging about God's handiwork in creation. Therefore, they ask, "Is the creation theme a means to change the subject?" Do these speeches aim to distract readers from

God's behavior in the prologue? The two portrayals of God, in the prologue and in the divine speeches, are quite different. It is fruitful to explore the differences as well as the similarities between the two. Other readers, perhaps weary of Job's focus on his suffering, cheer the words from God, claiming that they rightly set Job straight and remind him that the world wasn't created solely with his comfort in mind. Either way, in the view presented by the voice of God, human tragedy isn't personal; it is the cost of living in a world in which order and chaos both have a place.

Are tragedy and suffering simply expected and inevitable in an imperfect universe?

Day 5: Job 42; reread Job 1–2
Job's response to God and the epilogue

Job's response to God in Job 42:1-6 is notable for its ambiguity. Issues with the Hebrew are often neatly cleaned up in English translations, but Job's final words in the book are open-ended. Job 42:6, the key to Job's response to God's speeches, has usually been translated in the tradition of the King James Version: "Therefore I despise myself, and repent in dust and ashes" (NRSV, NIV). This suggests that Job gives up his case against God because he finally recognizes his sin and the inaccuracy of his claims against God. But in the Hebrew text, the verb *despise* has no object (the word *myself* doesn't actually occur in Hebrew), and *despise* may also be translated "relent" or "reject." Furthermore, the verb rendered as *repent* may be translated "find comfort" or "be consoled." Thus Job's response may be translated as it is in the Common English Bible: "Therefore, I relent and find comfort on dust and ashes." Job stops arguing not because he has changed his heart and mind, but because he recognizes he is merely a limited human being—and he makes peace with that. Readers can't know for certain if Job's words indicate heartfelt satisfaction with what God has said or if they are uttered sarcastically or with resignation.

Whereas Job 42:1-6 is the conclusion to the conversation with God that precedes it, the epilogue in Job 42:7-17 returns to the naive style of the prologue. This ending to Job is one of the most difficult aspects of the book. In the wake of the book's complex presentation of the issues and questions related to innocent suffering, many readers express dissatisfaction with Job's ending because it negates what the book appears to teach—in Job's argument and in God's speeches—that there is no connection between tragedy and the pious avoidance of sin. The return of Job's possessions and the granting of a new family appear to be a reward for Job's speaking rightly about God (Job 42:7). Readers may feel as though they are back where they started with a theology of rewards and punishments that always works. And yet, if the book's aim is to frustrate attempts to provide a single explanation for innocent suffering, the epilogue succeeds by questioning the explanation for tragedy in the divine speeches. If readers accept the speeches from God (Job 38–41) about suffering, and if readers dismiss the prologue's view as overly simple or naive, the epilogue opens up the conversation again.

After something terrible happens to a person, what do you tell that person? What spiritual wisdom about God do you try to convey?

Day 6: Job 2

Covenant Meditation: What do you say to a friend in pain?

Without the details of Job's tragic loss, there is no story here for us. In the first two chapters of Job, everything of value to him—children, wealth, honor—is destroyed through tragedy until he has nothing to show for his life but sores and ashes. Our devotional meditation for this week invites you to become more attuned to Job's experience of tragedy, reading scripture with your imagination.

This week's theme, "Tragedy," is viewed through the complex and varied perspectives of the book of Job. In the first chapter we witness the orchestrated, tragic destruction of all that is valued by one righteous, God-fearing man. But what especially illumines Job's losses for us is that the God of the covenant not only refuses to prevent the pending tragedies, but also knowingly permits them to occur.

In the first chapter Job is presented as an "honest" man, "a person of absolute integrity" (Job 1:1) and endowed with sons and daughters, servants and livestock such that "he was greater than all the people of the east" (Job 1:3). We also read that Job is faithful to God before tragedy strikes and after losing everything he loves. Yet, even then, his trials are not over.

Read Job 2:1-13. As you do, try to imagine that you are Job's close friend, sitting with him as he grieves the news of his losses. Pay particular attention to verses 2 through 13. How do you feel as you imagine being there? From where you sit, what do you hear, see, taste, smell, or touch in this scene? What are you talking about with your friend? What does Job look like before the sores appear; how does his appearance change? How do you react when his skin suddenly breaks out with lesions all over his body? What do you want to do? How do you react to what Job's wife says to him? Imagine how she appears in her own grief as the other three friends show up to console Job. Pay attention to the feelings this reading brings up for you about your own experience of tragedy or that of a friend. Reflect on any insight or question that comes to you through this reading. Release all of this to God in prayer.

Group Meeting Experience

Job 42:7-17 | *Double for his trouble?*

In the final scene of Job, the author tries to tie up loose threads from the book and returns to the losses named in the opening prologue (Job 1–2). The epilogue returns the reader to the world of the prologue, and yet, as we have seen, there are differences. What is the significance of these differences? Are we back where we started? Or does the epilogue move the conversation about tragedy in a new direction?

1. God indicates in the epilogue that Job has spoken what is right about God (Job 42:7), which is not what God says in the poetic speech at Job 38:2; there Job speaks "words lacking knowledge." What has Job said that is "right"? And what have the friends said that is "wrong"?

2. Read Exodus 22:4-9 and then reflect on what it means if "the LORD doubled all Job's earlier possessions" (Job 42:10). Is God compensating Job out of regret for allowing the suffering? Or is God merely showing compassion for what Job has suffered? Also discuss the narrator's judgment that Job's family "comforted and consoled him concerning all the disaster the LORD had brought on him" (Job 42:11).

3. How do you explain God's role in the murder of Job's children in the prologue, along with the narrator's report in Job 42 that Job has ten new children (three daughters and seven sons, just as before in Job 1:2)?

4. The epilogue returns the reader to the world of the prologue, and yet the Adversary is absent from the scene. Why? And what does his absence in the epilogue tell us about his purpose in the prologue?

5. There are tensions between the "patient Job" in the narrative of the prologue/epilogue and the angry, "outspoken Job" in the poetic sections in between. Following a proliferation of words in the dialogue, Job doesn't speak in the epilogue. In what ways do the "Jobs" of the various portions of the book complement and contrast with each other? In the same way, there is tension between the depiction of God in the narrative and in the divine speeches. Compare and contrast these portrayals of God and discuss whether there are multiple views about God's role in the book.

6. Which of the voices in the book of Job, or combination of voices, provides for you the most satisfying response to the crisis of undeserved suffering? Why do you resonate with this voice in the book of Job?

SIGNS OF FAITHFUL LOVE

When suffering deep pain and loss, it is acceptable to tell God how you feel and why God's promises are broken. If you are yelling at God, at least you know God is present, and often that is enough.

Jeremiah, Lamentations, Ezekiel

CRISIS AND STARTING OVER

When one covenant seems to end, start over again.

Bible Readings

Day 1: Jeremiah 1–4

Day 2: Jeremiah 27–29

Day 3: Jeremiah 16; 18–20

Day 4: Lamentations 1–2; 5

Day 5: Ezekiel 34–37

Day 6: Covenant Meditation on Lamentations 3:1-24

Day 7: Group Meeting Experience with Jeremiah 31:15-34

Covenant Prayer

For children in foster care and orphanages; for youth who are incarcerated or banished from home; for all who are homeless for the first time in their lives

Why do you stand so far away, LORD, hiding yourself in troubling times? (Psalm 10:1)

For all who work in halfway houses, orphanages, and juvenile detention centers; for all who serve in shelters for refugees, domestic abuse victims, and runaway youth

I give you a new commandment: Love each other. Just as I have loved you, so you also must love each other. (John 13:34)

OUR LONGING FOR RELATIONSHIP

When things are going wrong in life (such as loss of income, loved ones, or status), relationships become fragile, and it seems like our covenant with God is broken beyond repair.

HISTORICAL CONTEXT

A crisis links the three biblical books that are the focus of this episode: Jeremiah, Ezekiel, and Lamentations. They are each a response to Babylon's attack and defeat of Judah in the early sixth century BCE.

Ever since the ninth century BCE, the northern kingdom (Israel) and the southern kingdom (Judah) had been strongly affected by international affairs. They, along with other small nations in the area of Syria-Palestine, were vulnerable to the much more powerful nations of Egypt, Assyria, and then Babylon. Their leaders always needed to decide whether to cooperate with these superpowers or to assert independence from them.

After dominating the area for several decades, Assyrian power was on the decline in the late seventh century BCE. Judah, under King Josiah, underwent religious reforms and tried to strengthen its territory. Soon afterward, Egypt and Babylon engaged in ongoing conflict, with Judah caught in the middle. While the Babylonian army was reorganizing, Judah decided to revolt. Babylon responded by mounting a military campaign against it. In 597 BCE, in what is called the first deportation, the Babylonians entered Jerusalem, raided the temple, and forced into exile the most important citizens in Jerusalem. The Babylonians installed a new king, Zedekiah, who submitted with humility for several years, but then he, too, decided to rebel. Babylon quickly responded by attacking again, destroying many of the cities in the land of Judah and putting Jerusalem under siege. Jerusalem withstood the siege for almost two years, but the city was finally captured and destroyed in 587 BCE. Much of the population that had survived was exiled to Babylon (the second deportation). A description of these events is found in 2 Kings 22–25.

The people were rocked by the violence and the trauma of these horrific events. They were left wondering why all of these things had happened. How could God let Judah—God's own nation—be destroyed? Hadn't God promised to always protect the temple and the city of Jerusalem? Didn't God care that the people were suffering so acutely? Did these events prove that their covenant with God had been broken beyond repair? The books of Jeremiah, Ezekiel, and Lamentations grapple with these sorts of questions.

JEREMIAH

Jeremiah was a member of a minor priestly family in Anathoth, a small village a few miles outside Jerusalem. His prophetic ministry was exceptionally long, beginning in 627 BCE and spanning some forty years. Throughout his career, Jeremiah preached in Jerusalem. After the fall of the city, he stayed there until he was forced to escape to Egypt. The organization of the book of Jeremiah is complex, and it includes several types of prophetic literature. In addition, the book appears to have undergone significant editing over time.

The book emphasizes the covenant relationship between God and the people. Jeremiah looks back to the covenant established by Moses, whose commandments make up the Torah, the Instruction for Israel (for example, Exod 19–31). This covenant is conditional: It is based on the people faithfully following its instructions. Jeremiah claims that the people are breaking it with their disobedience. Israel needs to turn away from their unfaithfulness in order to renew their relationship with God. Throughout the book we see the grief and anguish experienced by the prophet, the people, and even God. Jeremiah urges the people to find their security not in the temple, but in returning to their ancestral faith.

EZEKIEL

Ezekiel also prophesied during the time of the destruction, but he was most likely of a younger generation than Jeremiah, perhaps in his thirties. He was one of the prominent citizens who were taken in the first deportation to Babylon. He lived there for a few years before receiving the call to become a prophet in 593 BCE, and he continued preaching for roughly twenty more years. Like Jeremiah, Ezekiel was a priest, possibly a member of the powerful priestly family who served the temple in Jerusalem. Though he lived far away, he seemed to have a thorough knowledge of the situation there.

The book begins with a striking vision of God in a chariot. God is no longer tied down to Jerusalem but comes to be with the exiles! As we might expect from a priest, Ezekiel stresses God's holiness. The people's sinfulness shows their impurity and therefore separates them from God. The prophet is especially concerned for the temple, and his answer for the crisis of the temple's destruction is that God will build a new and better one. The book is a challenge to read, as it can seem rather strange.

The prophet describes odd visions and speaks of performing dramatic signs, being in trances, struck speechless, and carried away by a spirit. The book is well-organized, however, and the language is sophisticated. It seems that Ezekiel wrote rather than spoke many of his prophecies.

LAMENTATIONS

The book of Lamentations provides the perspective of the people who experienced the destruction and fall of Jerusalem. It's a firsthand witness to the hardship and pain that resulted from this event. The book is a series of five poems that present the viewpoints of various figures, including the community, an individual survivor, the poet, and the city itself. The poetry includes elements of biblical lament psalms, funeral songs, and city lamentations, all forms of speech that are known from ancient Near Eastern literature. The speakers tell of the horrors the city has experienced and the immense suffering of its inhabitants. They cry out for God to see their pain and to show mercy, but there is no response. God's silence is the book's main theological issue. The images in Lamentations are violent, haunting, tragic, and heartbreaking. It's hard not to turn our eyes away. Yet this biblical book helps us to imagine what it must have been like for the Israelites to experience the Babylonian attack, siege, and conquest.

These three biblical books react to the crisis of the destruction of Jerusalem from distinct perspectives:

1. a prophet in the city who is eventually exiled to Egypt (Jeremiah);

2. a prophet who has already been exiled to Babylon (Ezekiel); and

3. the city residents themselves (Lamentations).

They show us that there are many ways to respond to tragedy. Yet there are some common perspectives among them. Both Jeremiah and Ezekiel prophesy judgment as punishment for a sinful people before the fall of Jerusalem, but afterward they speak of hope and renewal. Though hope is hard to find in the midst of raw suffering, the speakers in Lamentations still continue to pray to God, to yearn for a relationship with God, and to anticipate an answer. The vantage points of these three books represent the geographical situation of diaspora that will emerge—many people in Babylon, some people in Egypt, and some people still in the land of Judah. In the diaspora, Israel will face the task of starting over and finding their new identity as the people of God. The writings of Jeremiah, Ezekiel, and Lamentations open the way to that new beginning.

Day 1: Jeremiah 1–4
Jeremiah's call and Judah's disregard of the covenant

Our first selection is the opening chapters of the book of Jeremiah. Many prophets and leaders in the Old Testament receive a call from God, and Jeremiah's call to prophesy is in the form of a dialogue (Jer 1). It was planned even before Jeremiah was born! God will transform the prophet's actual speech, putting words in his mouth. What God wants Jeremiah to say will be a message that's both difficult and hopeful, including both destruction and rebuilding. Jeremiah's call not only gives a beginning point to his ministry, but also proves that he is a true and authentic prophet.

What does Jeremiah's call and commissioning suggest about the challenge of being a prophet? In what ways does God promise to help and protect him?

Jeremiah 2–3 focuses on Israel's unfaithfulness, as do Hosea 1–3 and Ezekiel 16 and 23. Like Hosea and Ezekiel, Jeremiah uses the metaphor of a marriage to bring home his point. God's covenant with Israel is like a marriage covenant. The wife, Israel, however, has been unfaithful, has broken the covenant bond, and thus deserves punishment.

The crisis is at hand (Jer 4). In terrifying images, Jeremiah describes the disaster that's coming. An enemy who invades from the north, the direction from which Babylonian armies approach Jerusalem, is a common theme in the book. Jeremiah continues to call the people to see the very real danger of their wrong behavior, trying to convince them to return to God before it's too late.

In contemporary faith communities, whom would we say is "called"? Are there any similarities between their tasks and what Jeremiah is being charged to do?

How does the passage reflect historical marriage customs in which the husband had authority over the wife? Is it troubling to compare religious disobedience to a wife's marital infidelity?

Day 2: Jeremiah 27–29
Living under Babylonian rule

In this passage, Jeremiah speaks to two audiences: the people still in Jerusalem and the exiles who have already been taken to Babylon. In so doing, he clashes with two of the more popular prophets of the day, Hananiah and Shemaiah. Jeremiah's message in both situations is surely not what the listeners were expecting—or wanting—to hear.

Jeremiah wears a yoke to symbolize that Jerusalem's citizens are to submit to the rule, the "yoke," of Babylon (Jer 27–28). He tells the people it's God's will that Babylon, their powerful enemy, will defeat them. They aren't to resist, but are to surrender.

In a letter to the exiles in Babylon, Jeremiah's message is also that they accept their fate (Jer 29). Though God will eventually bring the people back home, it won't be in their lifetimes. The exiles need to start over and make new lives for themselves there—build houses, have families, and even pray for the good of their new neighbors.

Both of these messages confirm divine sovereignty, God's rule over creation. It is God who decides what is right in any given situation, even if it's the victory of a cruel tyrant. Jeremiah's message reminds us that we often need to take a broad view of what God might be doing in the world.

What do you think about Jeremiah's view that God takes the side of a violent empire to punish Jerusalem for its unfaithfulness? What do we do when God's word to us isn't what we want to hear? How can we get to a place of accepting it?

Day 3: Jeremiah 16; 18–20
Jeremiah's lament for himself and for his people

This reading gives insight into how difficult the prophet's life must have been. The book of Jeremiah is unique among the prophetic works in the degree to which it gives us glimpses into the interior emotional life of a prophet.

Jeremiah performs several signs during his ministry, and we see two of them in this passage. In both of them the prophet uses pottery to make his point about God's freedom to do as God chooses in this crisis situation. Just as people can break and remold pots, so God can do these things to Israel if God is displeased. These are images of a people with their covenant broken beyond repair.

In Jeremiah's cries for help, what is the prophet upset about? Does he have reason to accuse God of enticing and overpowering him?

Jeremiah sacrifices a great deal. He isn't allowed to marry or have a family in order to emphasize that destruction is coming. People plot against him and bring false charges. He's arrested and put in jail. Jeremiah's laments show the high emotional price of serving God and may be the most moving part of the entire book. These poems are much like the laments (cries for help) in the book of Psalms. Jeremiah protests his situation, accuses God, demands revenge, and at his lowest point, questions why he was even born. These details of his personal life show the struggle and the suffering required when preaching God's word.

How can we reconcile the severity of God's punishment in this passage with what we believe about God's love and mercy? Is it uncomfortable to think that God can break the people like a jug?

Day 4: Lamentations 1–2; 5
The people's call for help

The entire book of Lamentations shows the people in full crisis mode. This reading includes three of the five chapters of the book. These texts describe the collapse of society on many levels.

In Lamentations 1 and 2, the city of Jerusalem is imagined as a person, Daughter Zion. (Zion is another name for Jerusalem.) "Is there any suffering like the suffering inflicted on me?" she asks (Lam 1:12). Because it's presented as though it were happening to an actual woman, the destruction of the city seems more immediate and more emotional. These chapters include repeated images of violence and shame. All the inhabitants of the city alike are harmed—young and old, women and men.

Lamentations 5 describes the experience of the people living in their occupied land, under the control of the Babylonians. For those lucky enough to have survived, daily life is filled with numerous difficulties, and even dangers.

Again and again throughout this passage, the people call out to God to see what's happening to them. Surely their suffering is too great to bear! Yet the poet repeats that no help ever arrives, from God or from their neighbors. There's no one to comfort the people and no hopeful resolution to their wretched circumstances.

Think of cities or lands in recent years that have experienced widespread destruction. How are the experiences of their inhabitants similar to those of the inhabitants of Jerusalem?

Day 5: Ezekiel 34–37
Ezekiel's visions of transformation; a new covenant

Our single reading from the prophet Ezekiel is addressed to his contemporaries in exile in Babylon. The passage begins right after the news of Jerusalem's destruction reaches Ezekiel and the exiles (Ezek 33:21-22). This is a turning point in the book, where the prophet's message turns from warning to hope.

Ezekiel here uses images and metaphors to portray Israel's transformation. Several are contrasted with each other: for example, good sheep and bad sheep; the mountains of Israel and Mount Seir in the nation of Edom; and a new heart and a heart of stone. Two metaphors of transformation especially stand out. One is the image of God as Israel's shepherd (Ezek 34). We see the image of the good shepherd who lovingly cares for the sheep, God's people, elsewhere in the Old Testament (most famously in Ps 23) and in the New Testament (Jesus as the good shepherd; John 10:1-18). The image of dry bones is also especially powerful (Ezek 37). The people in exile felt as dead as old bones, picked clean by their predators and bleached dry in the desert sun.

The people in exile felt as dead as old bones, picked clean by their predators and bleached dry in the desert sun.

It's important to recognize that God is the one who brings about Israel's transformation. It's God who gathers the sheep (Ezek 34:11-16). It's God who breathes new life into their dead bones (Ezek 37:5-10). It's only because of God's honor, God's holiness, that Israel will be redeemed, and not because of any actions on Israel's part.

Ezekiel sees not an end to the people of Israel, but a new beginning. What seems impossible at this point can become possible. The prophet reports that the scattered people can come together once more, the temple can be rebuilt, and the land can become fertile again. The covenant between God and the people can be renewed (Ezek 34:25; 37:26).

How does Ezekiel imagine the natural world—animals, plants, land—in his vision for a new future? How is the healing and renewal of the people connected to the environment?

Day 6: Lamentations 3:1-24
Covenant Meditation: Living with crisis

Crisis, personal or communal, can strip us down to our most vulnerable, raw, and honest selves. Crisis can peel away any facade about being in control of our lives. Often our first response to crisis is to plant our feet more deeply into the ground in order to stay upright and then to get a stranglehold on what we think will save us. But no matter how strong our hold may seem, crisis by its very nature undoes something in and around us. Crisis peels life down to a layer of vulnerability that we thought we had skillfully covered up or, at the very least, managed well.

So when crisis strikes, we are rarely at ease speaking about our fear, despair, or hopelessness—not with each other, and not even with God. We seldom practice the language of despair and lament because, somewhere along faith's way, the message was clear that to do so shows a lack of faith. Yet our readings this week counter this message and instead provide us with some of the most raw, honest crisis language "spoken" and preserved by God's children. Therefore, our spiritual reading practice for this week invites us and asks us to rehearse, through prayer, the crisis language of lament. Today we will pray the scriptures by joining with a member of the community who is suffering, grieving, and feeling so hopeless that even God seems uninterested and removed.

To prepare for the reading, locate Lamentations 3:1-24. Before reading this text, try to set aside any judgment about the content of this prayer, about whether or not you would pray these words. This prayer may not name your beliefs about God or God's ways. Instead, approach this lament with anticipation of giving voice to a sister or brother who is living in the midst of life-wrenching crisis.

Now, silently or aloud, read the verses slowly, attending to the emotions that arise with each image and phrase. Resist judgment about the prayer, but receive it with compassion and acceptance for the one who first prayed these words.

When the reading is completed, offer a brief prayer for all who live in crisis and are calling out to God for help.

Group Meeting Experience

Jeremiah 31:15-34 | *The new covenant*

In this speech, Jeremiah describes God's new covenant with the people as the basis for a new start after their deepest crisis. As Ezekiel also does, Jeremiah focuses on the people's new heart, that is, the new direction of their lives (Jer 31:33; Ezek 36:26-27). (If time permits, read all of Jer 31. It contains a beautiful expression of God's faithful love for Israel.)

1. Who is Rachel, one of Israel's ancestors? Why was she so important? How is Rachel being used as a symbol in this passage? What group is suggested by the reference to "her children"?

2. What will healing and restoration look like? How is this a new creation? How will the people be different after the restoration?

3. What is God doing in this passage? What are God's emotions? Do they surprise you at all?

4. How does the language about building and planting echo that in Jeremiah's original call to prophesy (Jer 1:10)? Do the images of fertility enhance the prophet's message?

5. How do we understand the Instructions that are engraved on the people's hearts? How is the "new covenant" different from the previous covenant?

SIGNS OF FAITHFUL LOVE

Covenant people may seem abandoned and broken beyond repair, but they hope again when their trust in God is restored through new relationships and even through a new covenant.

Isaiah 40–66

EXILE AND RENEWAL
The risk of being in charge

Bible Readings

Day 1: Isaiah 40–43

Day 2: Isaiah 49:1–52:12

Day 3: Isaiah 52:13–55:13

Day 4: Isaiah 56:1-8; 58–61

Day 5: Isaiah 63:7–66:24

Day 6: Covenant Meditation on Isaiah 43:1-7

Day 7: Group Meeting Experience with Isaiah 40:12-31

Covenant Prayer

For those uprooted from their home for any reason

I know the plans I have in mind for you, declares the LORD; they are plans for peace, not disaster, to give you a future filled with hope. (Jeremiah 29:11)

For poets, artists, writers, and dancers who bear the beauty of God's hope to others

Don't fear, because I am with you; don't be afraid, for I am your God. I will strengthen you, I will surely help you; I will hold you with my righteous strong hand. (Isaiah 41:10)

OUR LONGING FOR RELATIONSHIP

When faith becomes acceptable to the majority, or when we are in charge and our experience of God becomes mainstream, our challenge is to avoid apathy.

ISAIAH 40–66

The readings this week come from the second half of the book of Isaiah. Most Prophetic Books in the Bible are collections of speeches, many from the prophet after whom the book is named, but many also from followers of this prophet who have appended their speeches to those of their revered predecessor. Most of the speeches in the first half of Isaiah, which were studied in Episode 16, were composed by Isaiah of Jerusalem, who was active around 735–700 BCE.

The speeches in the second half of the book, Isaiah 40–66, which are now attached to the prophecies of Isaiah of Jerusalem, come from a very different time. They were composed by followers of Isaiah during the exile and afterward, beginning around 540 BCE, a generation after Jeremiah and Ezekiel. No one knows exactly when or how these various prophecies were joined into a single book. The most important thread binding them is their shared concern for Jerusalem and its relationship to God.

Of the four eighth-century prophets (Amos, Hosea, Micah, and Isaiah), Isaiah was the only Jerusalem resident. During his time, the rest of Judah and Israel were destroyed by the Assyrian Empire, and Jerusalem itself was nearly destroyed. Isaiah 39 (compare 2 Kgs 20) anticipates Jerusalem's eventual invasion not by Assyria in the eighth century, but by the next great empire, Babylon, in the sixth century.

The destruction of Jerusalem and of Solomon's temple by Babylon in 587 BCE is described in 2 Kings 25. The tragedy is vividly remembered in Jeremiah, Ezekiel, Lamentations, and in several psalms. Some Judeans were exiled to Babylon, and some took refuge elsewhere, but most were left destitute in Judah. For this reason, some scholars call this period the "exile," while others think of it as the period without the temple, which seems appropriate for the majority of people who didn't leave after Jerusalem's fall.

Not much is known directly about conditions of any Judean group in this period. This silence may indicate the unspeakable extent of the trauma. Instead of dwelling on the present, writers during this time reconstructed the deep past from which Judah's identity had emerged and, it was hoped, would reemerge. A great deal of the Bible's formation comes from this time. Rather than being destroyed, scripture as we know it was preserved, shaped, and reborn in tragedy and suffering.

See Maps 8, 10, and 12 showing the Assyrian, Babylonian, and Persian Empires in the CEB Study Bible.

About a generation after Jerusalem's destruction, when Babylon's power was waning, Persia's King Cyrus began to claim dominance. When he captured and entered Babylon itself, he decreed leniency toward captive nations, including the Judean captives there. According to Ezra 1:1-4 and 2 Chronicles 36:22-23, Judeans in Babylon were encouraged by Cyrus to return home and rebuild their city and temple.

ISAIAH 40–55: PROPHET OF THE EXILE

Second Isaiah, the prophet responsible for Isaiah 40–55, promotes this return. The prophet's poetry conveys both physical and spiritual restoration. It is written exuberantly, brimming with announcements of divine comfort and of Israel's restored standing as God's chosen servant. Unlike earlier prophecies, this poetry isn't characterized by judgment or even by significant ethical instruction. Its rhetoric attempts to finesse a rejoined relationship between Judeans living inside and outside of the land of Judah and to restore confidence in God's favor.

Like other ancient people, Judeans had previously understood that gods inhabited their own respective lands and protected their subjects within those lands. Conventional theology would have taken for granted that Babylon's more powerful gods had defeated Judah's God when Jerusalem fell to the Babylonians. Indeed, Judeans living in exile in Babylon had doubtless become familiar with the magnificent temples and rituals of Marduk and other Babylonian gods who were worshipped in the form of images made of precious metals.

But Second Isaiah develops a new theological claim, one the Western world takes nearly for granted today. The prophet claims that the world isn't populated by multiple deities whose images are housed in temples. Rather, the prophet says, one God made all creation and all people, an invisible God who rejects idols. And this God directs the affairs of all the earth's nations. According to this theology, Israel's God was by no means defeated, but rather allowed Jerusalem's destruction as punishment for Israel's sin (Isa 40:1-2) and now reaches even to Babylon to initiate unfolding events. Israel's God caused the victorious Cyrus from Persia to release captives and to restore devastated habitats, cities, and peoples (Isa 45:1-7).

A new theological claim: The world isn't populated by multiple deities whose images are housed in temples. One God made all creation and all people, an invisible God who rejects idols.

55

We don't know how many people heeded Second Isaiah's call to return to Jerusalem or whether most people living in Babylon considered this idea attractive. The intensity of Second Isaiah's rhetoric suggests he may have had a challenge in convincing his contemporaries to return to reconstruct Jerusalem. In fact, Jews continued living in Babylon and other lands throughout the centuries. The movement of return began slowly and was conditioned by hardship.

ISAIAH 56–66: PROPHETS OF RENEWAL

Rule by David's descendants wasn't restored in Jerusalem after the Judean exiles returned to it. Rather, under direct Persian rule, the Judean community's leadership in Jerusalem arose from the temple priests and from governors appointed by Persia. Most of Third Isaiah, Isaiah 56–66, deals with life in Jerusalem during Persian times. Several different prophets contributed to this section. Some portions, such as Isaiah 60–62, echo Second Isaiah. Other portions, most vividly Isaiah 58–59 and Isaiah 65–66, echo teaching from First Isaiah. The chapters reflect social struggle and religious innovation. They offer prayers, ethical instruction, and visions for a restored future of peace.

Both Second and Third Isaiah show that there can be differences of opinion among the faithful, even among scriptural writers, especially as new realities challenge settled truths. Second Isaiah challenges previous Israelite self-understandings. Whereas before it had been Judah's own Davidic king who was called God's "anointed," Second Isaiah names the foreign King Cyrus as God's anointed (Isa 45:1). Second Isaiah also envisions the divine promises, previously claimed by Judah's royalty, for the people as a whole. Whereas some roles were previously assigned to select individuals such as Abraham (as God's "friend") and Jeremiah and other prophets (as God's "servants"), Second Isaiah extends the covenant to God's entire people.

Third Isaiah likewise challenges previous assumptions. These chapters continue to promote the social justice already expected in First Isaiah and elsewhere. But these disciples of Isaiah suggest that people once viewed as ineligible for temple service—particularly immigrants and eunuchs—are welcome. They also

There can be differences of opinion among the faithful, even among scriptural writers.

promote the idea that nations and communities will no longer be saved or condemned collectively. Rather, individuals who worship God faithfully, no matter who they are, will be welcomed into the covenant community. But rebels, no matter what their pedigree, will in effect exclude themselves.

A running commentary on "God's servants" begins in Isaiah 41. Throughout much of Second Isaiah, a portrait is drawn of God's servant Israel, who will establish justice, who listens carefully to God's instruction, and who even suffers on others' behalf. In Isaiah 54:17 the plural word *servants* first appears, and in Third Isaiah's final two chapters (Isa 65–66), God's servants are sharply distinguished from those who rebel.

Day 1: Isaiah 40–43
Creation

The first three readings this week come from the prophet of the exile, Second Isaiah, whose speeches in Isaiah 40–55 have been attached to the collection of speeches from the original Isaiah of Jerusalem in Isaiah 1–39. Beginning in Isaiah 40:12, God's role as creator is explored: The one who made everything, with whom none can compare, can and will restore Israel.

Second Isaiah was directed toward a very specific purpose long ago. Yet, as we overhear words addressed to ancient people, we remember with gratitude the prophets who inspired the community's rebuilding. Had this return not taken place, faith would not have developed as it did. There would have been no Judaism, no Bible, no Jewish savior of the Gentiles, and no Christianity.

As the author envisions divine compassion for ancient people, we may find ourselves envisioning a God who creates, re-creates, and rejuvenates, who does new things, who calls the faithful, who loves and comforts the refugee, who encourages the discouraged, and who heals the scarred earth.

Does God always give second chances? What example would you give?

Day 2: Isaiah 49:1–52:12
Comfort

Isaiah 44–48 continues to develop themes found in the reading for Day 1. A corner is turned at Isaiah 49. Here the servant from Isaiah 42 reappears, telling his own story now, echoing themes from throughout the previous poetry. The world's natural elements are again invited to rejoice, celebrating God's comfort for suffering people.

From this point through Isaiah 54, poetry about the servant will be interwoven with poetry concerning Daughter Zion, the personified city of Jerusalem, who speaks up for the first time in Isaiah 49:14. Like Israel the servant, who expressed hopelessness in Isaiah 40:27, here Zion likewise protests that she has been abandoned by God. Like Israel, she receives reassurance. God is portrayed as the city's mother who will never forget her child. The poet envisions Judeans returning in droves to repopulate Jerusalem.

In Isaiah 50, the servant Israel returns, speaking this time of his faithfulness to God even in the face of harassment. His self-description resembles that of the lamenter in Lamentations 3, who recommended faithfulness even in desolation.

The poetry reaches its high point in Isaiah 51–52. After a reminder of Israel's deep historical roots in Abraham and Sarah, God's powerful arm is invoked to act on the people's behalf, as in the exodus from Egypt. Reassurances of God's comfort for suffering Zion are offered repeatedly. The prophet envisions the lookouts, rejoicing as God and an exiled people return to Zion.

Although this poetry addressed a specific moment, the themes of divine comfort and human faithfulness transcend time and give reassurance to believers today of God's extraordinary perseverance with humans throughout history.

Can you think of an example in recent history or even in your community where God's comfort gave refuge to a group of people?

Day 3: Isaiah 52:13–55:13
Restoration

This section begins with a passage referring to a suffering servant, a passage most familiar to Christians in relation to Jesus' crucifixion (Isa 52:13–53:12). It originally referred not to Jesus but to suffering Israel, reassuring the troubled that faithful endurance on behalf of others can itself be redemptive. Early Christians naturally thought of this passage when they examined Jesus' story. It became a sign of hope for people following Jesus' example of patient suffering (see 1 Pet 2:21-25).

The poetry continues to alternate between Israel as God's servant and Daughter Zion. The subject turns abruptly in Isaiah 54 to Jerusalem. Again she is instructed to rejoice in expectation of her "children's" return, and she is reassured by God. Here God takes the role of her formerly angry but now remorseful spouse. As in Noah's covenant, God promises never to destroy again and assures the people that God's covenant of peace will endure (Isa 54:9-10).

The final chapter of Second Isaiah, Isaiah 55, begins with an invitation to enjoy free food and drink, contrasting sharply with realities in a drought-ridden world. The people are invited to seek God, whose forgiveness is generous, whose ways are higher than human ways, and whose covenant with them is everlasting. Rejoicing mountains and hand-clapping trees will welcome Judeans homeward.

Parts of Second Isaiah's poetry may ring familiar to contemporary Christians—not only the description of the servant who bears suffering for others' sake, but also the God whose ways are higher than human ways, who comforts those who mourn, who rescues us from our troubles.

Have you ever suffered in order to relieve suffering for someone else? Or think of a loss that you experienced and reflect on who helped you mourn.

Day 4: Isaiah 56:1-8; 58–61

Justice

The last two readings this week come from prophets in Jerusalem after the exile, whose speeches have been gathered in Isaiah 56–66 and are described collectively as Third Isaiah. First Isaiah (Isa 1–39) preached righteousness and justice in human dealings. Second Isaiah (Isa 40–55) announced that God would comfort and do the right thing on behalf of God's people. Third Isaiah (Isa 56–66) begins with a verse uniting both these themes. Isaiah 56 goes on to announce God's welcome of immigrants and eunuchs. The term "immigrant" here is our English idiom for the Hebrew expression "sons of foreigners," which is a designation for non-Israelites. *Eunuch* is a Greek word for an obscure Hebrew term that some think referred to sexually mutilated men. This claim to include the immigrant and the eunuch in the covenant community, contrary to Deuteronomy 23:1-3, shows how scripture contains more than one point of view about God's Instruction (Torah).

Isaiah 58 resumes the call to social justice, first introduced in Isaiah 1. This chapter promotes care for the needy as crucial to honest piety. In fact, the prophet claims, Jerusalem's physical restoration depends on the strength of its social fabric. The same social ills that plagued the city before its destruction still plague the generations that follow—yet the prophet still calls for justice and continues to hope in God's salvation.

Most of Third Isaiah follows this thread of moral teaching and judgment, underscoring the difficulties of building a faithful city. But in the very center, Isaiah 60–62 envisions a future much more glorious than past or present. This prophet, just as Second Isaiah, assures the people that God's covenant with them will endure (Isa 61:8), no matter what happens in their lives. Thus, in Third Isaiah, judgment and hope intertwine. Inaccessible dreams and unrelenting judgments can each lead to despair. But the two together, tempering each other, can keep us mindful both of frustrations and of hopes that goad us onward.

Do you dream of a world where justice always prevails? Is that possible?

Day 5: Isaiah 63:7–66:24
Presence

This final section of Third Isaiah opens with a cry for help in Isaiah 63:7–64:12. It clearly reflects the time in Jerusalem before the temple was rebuilt there, perhaps even before exiled Judeans had returned home. Petitioners recall God's ancient saving grace before asking that God look down, remember them again, and return to heal the city. In Isaiah 65, the prophet asserts that God is likewise eager for reconciliation. Yet rebellious behavior persists. A distinction is drawn between those who behave as God's servants and those who continue to rebel, who won't enjoy God's bounty.

In Isaiah 65:17-25, a renewed heaven and earth are described, echoing hopes from Isaiah 2:2-4 and Isaiah 11:1-9. An era of earthly prosperity is imagined, when all may live their natural lives in peace.

Isaiah 66 continues visions of prosperous security in Jerusalem, with all but the rebels enjoying worship together. In spite of these glorious visions of renewal, Isaiah's final verse underlies the description of "hell"—actually *Gehenna*—in Mark 9:48. It is so disturbing that, in Jewish traditional readings of Isaiah, verse 23 is repeated afterward, allowing the book's final word to describe all humanity worshipping God, rather than the horror awaiting rebels.

Second and Third Isaiah convey years of Judean experience and thought. They reflect tragedy and resilience, exile and renewal. They show faith being reshaped through suffering. They reflect the perennial struggles between generosity and purity, between self-seeking and self-giving. These prophets don't resolve all questions. But in entertaining these questions, they invite us to rethink and broaden our understanding of God's ways.

Do you have optimism for your community and the wider world you live in? If not, what would restore your hope?

Day 6: Isaiah 43:1-7

Covenant Meditation: Hope comes from God.

In this week's readings, we learned that in a period where "the unspeakable extent of the trauma" experienced by God's people could barely be spoken, the writers of the time ensured that "scripture as we know it was preserved, shaped, and reborn in tragedy and suffering." Since that time, God's people have turned to this poetry of scripture because hope comes from God, and God is always with us. When facing grief and tragedy of our own, we can lose sight of or take for granted God's promise of hope and salvation, but these words from the prophets are forever present to guide us back to God's covenant promises if we will take them to heart. Today we will examine our hearts through the reading practice of *lectio divina*.

Turn to and mark Isaiah 43:1-7. Now take the time you need to become comfortable, calming your breath and releasing into God's hands all the current distractions of the day. It may help to close your eyes until you feel still enough to receive this text. Once you are ready to read, open your Bible to the selected passage and read it aloud slowly for a first reading.

Wait for a minute before reading it a second time. When you are ready, read it slowly again, aloud or silently. This time, listen for a word or phrase from the text that catches your attention. As before, don't try to analyze or judge the word or phrase that you receive. Just note it; write it down or underline it if you would like. For the next two minutes, reflect on this word or phrase. What feelings, images, or memories come to mind from the word or phrase? Note these in your mind or on a piece of paper. Again, just try to receive these and notice them without judgment or analysis.

Read the text for a third time, and attend to any invitation that the reading may extend to you. Does your word or phrase prompt you to some action? Does the whole reading invite you to respond in some fresh way to a circumstance in your life or in God's world? Meditate on this invitation for three or four minutes. Then, in a brief prayer, place into God's hands all that you have received in this practice—your word, phrase, invitation, and response—so that you and God carry these forward together.

Group Meeting Experience

Isaiah 40:12-31 | God as creator of the world and of Israel

This passage argues for God's unique power as creator of the cosmos. It may have been composed around the same time as the first creation story in Genesis 1:1–2:4*a*. Indeed, Second Isaiah shares many ideas with that account. Isaiah 40:12-31 emphasizes God's incomparable greatness and power. It prepares for the argument that God can and will rebuild the nation of Judah.

1. Read Genesis 1:1–2:4*a* alongside this passage and note similarities and differences between them.

2. Count the rhetorical questions (questions that don't seek to obtain information but to make a point; for example, "Who has measured the waters in the palm of a hand?"). What are they? What are their implied answers?

3. What does the language of measuring and weighing in Isaiah 40:12 convey about God?

4. What purposes might the description of idol-making in Isaiah 40:19-20 serve?

5. In what various ways is God's superior greatness and power conveyed? To whom and what is God compared?

6. What relationship can you see between God's naming of the stars and the claim that God is not ignoring Israel?

7. How is God's incomparable creative power related to the assurance in Isaiah 40:31 that "those who hope in the LORD will renew their strength"?

8. Which images of God in this passage seem familiar to you? Which ones are new? Which linger with you?

SIGNS OF FAITHFUL LOVE

To thrive as hopeful Covenant people, we must keep our eyes on God's purpose, which can be disrupted as much by distraction and complacency as from battlefields and the effects of war.

1 and 2 Chronicles, Ezra, Nehemiah

RESTORATION
Rebuilding life together

Bible Readings

Day 1: 1 Chronicles 10:1–11:9; 28–29

Day 2: 2 Chronicles 33–36

Day 3: Ezra 1; 2:68–6:22

Day 4: Ezra 7–10

Day 5: Nehemiah 1–2; 4; 7:73b–8:18

Day 6: Covenant Meditation on 2 Chronicles 15:12-15

Day 7: Group Meeting Experience with 1 Chronicles 29:10-19

Covenant Prayer

For those who feel distant from God

You are a God ready to forgive, merciful and compassionate, very patient, and truly faithful. (Nehemiah 9:17c)

For those who teach children about God's faithful love

The LORD's faithful love is from forever ago to forever from now for those who honor him. And God's righteousness reaches to the grandchildren of those who keep his covenant and remember to keep his commands. (Psalm 103:17-18)

OUR LONGING FOR RELATIONSHIP

After a time of loss, tragedy, or shame is behind us, we're relieved but often frustrated by "the new normal." We've changed, and those around us have changed.

AFTER THE EXILE

The exile officially ended when Cyrus declared that the people from Judah (who were banished to Babylon) could return to their land and "build the house of the LORD" in Jerusalem (Ezra 1:3; 2 Chron 36:23). After the Persians conquered the Babylonian Empire in 539 BCE, the new rulers overturned earlier political policy and allowed all of those who had been deported by the Babylonians to return to their lands. According to Cyrus' edict, the exiles were given a change of residential address, and the people were allowed to return to rebuild the temple and worship together as God's people. In their distinct ways, the books of Chronicles, Ezra, and Nehemiah each configure the renewal of a community placing the worship of God in Jerusalem at the center of its life.

EZRA

The book of Ezra emphasizes this theme in its depiction of several waves of returnees who determine to worship God in their reconstructed temple. The various returns, led by Sheshbazzar in Ezra 1 and by Ezra in Ezra 6–7, seem almost like pilgrimages with their emphases on generous offerings, worship equipment, and God's guidance. These narratives repeat that the people aren't simply returning to the land. Their true destination is Jerusalem itself and the restoration of God's temple there (Ezra 1:3; 6:8; 7:7-8, 13; 8:31-32). Fittingly, upon their arrival, the groups present their offerings in the holy area where their temple once stood (Ezra 2:68-69; 8:33-35).

The first group of returnees meant to restore the temple and reestablish worship in Jerusalem. Ezra's initial chapters tell of the attempts to rebuild first the altar, then the foundation of the temple, and finally the temple itself. Again and again, however, detractors frustrate their efforts, including the neighboring peoples and Tattenai, governor of the province Beyond the River. Significantly, the returnees themselves turn away offers of help. One group, for example, asks to join in the construction because "we worship your God as you do, and we've been sacrificing to him ever since the days of Assyria's King Esarhaddon" (Ezra 4:2). These advances are rejected because the returnees consider this group as enemies rather than religious allies (Ezra 4:1).

Ezra's initial chapters tell of the attempts to rebuild first the altar, then the foundation of the temple, and finally the temple itself.

The narrative in Ezra evokes uneasy tension as it struggles to redefine community by setting rules for inclusion in the restored community and teaching how communal worship should be practiced in Jerusalem. In Ezra 6:21, participation in the Passover Festival is open to all who joined the community, yet the book concludes with the call to expel the foreign women who married into the community (Ezra 9–10). Clearly the stakes are high, as the returnees are understandably conservative in their decisions and cautious about provoking the divine ire and bringing about another exile. Restoration in Ezra thus means more than return to the land and rebuilding the temple. It involves the serious task of setting out the proper limits for the worshipping community.

NEHEMIAH

In the book of Nehemiah, these limits take on a physical dimension when Governor Nehemiah sets out to repair Jerusalem's protective walls. When he hears a report that the walls were broken down and that the gates had burned, Nehemiah sets out for Jerusalem (Neh 1:3; 2:5). Upon his arrival, he leads the community to repair the edifice section by section. As in the book of Ezra, the people face opposition and setbacks as they build, but they ultimately triumph. With the wall built, they are able to protect the restored community, whose members are trying to observe the covenant, follow God's Instruction, and worship according to divine teaching.

As they tell the story about the return to the land, the books of Ezra and Nehemiah incorporate official documents such as imperial edicts (Ezra 1:2-4), letters to the king (Ezra 5:6-17), and genealogical records (Ezra 2). The inclusion of these documents indicates that written records now have authority for the returning Israelite exiles. Given this special appreciation of official documents, some of the returnees themselves wrote down a version of their nation's earliest history. These documents articulate their ancient past and their distinct view of what true restoration might look like in the present. The author of this history used one of his people's own documents, which we call the Deuteronomistic History (see Episode 8), as the basis for this new version of Israelite history. And thus we have Chronicles, whose author, the Chronicler, tells the story of Israel from the time of Adam through the end of the exile.

1 AND 2 CHRONICLES

Although the books of Chronicles retell events *before* the time of Ezra and Nehemiah, they appear to have actually been written *later* in the period after the exile. The narratives in Chronicles reflect some of the same values as Ezra and Nehemiah, but they also take a unique view on some key issues. One of these distinctive views relates to the definition of *community*. The destruction of Jerusalem and the exile of its people began the diaspora, the dispersion of the Jews outside of Israel, not just to Babylon but to other countries throughout the Middle East. The Chronicler takes this larger context seriously and expands the limits of community beyond those assumed in Ezra and Nehemiah. Whereas the southern tribes of Benjamin and Judah are predominant in the earlier books, the Chronicler includes the northern tribes, united in worship with the southern tribes, as the ideal manifestation of the nation. The Chronicler also takes a much different attitude toward intermarriage. Instead of seeing all marriage outside the tribe as a threat that must be strictly opposed, the Chronicler includes notices of such intermarriage without censure (1 Chron 2:3; 3:2, and so on). Like the author of the book of Ruth, the Chronicler considers intermarriage as a way to grow and strengthen the people of Israel.

> **Optional:** *An additional video on exile and the return to worship in Jerusalem is available for download from* **CovenantBibleStudy.com**.

All of these books are united by the central place they give to Jerusalem in the people's lives and worship. In Chronicles, kings who support the temple are rewarded by God, and those who harm it or encourage worship elsewhere are punished. Indeed, there is a sense that Jerusalem's centrality is meant to become a way of life. This is underscored when 1 and 2 Chronicles are read in the context of the Jewish Bible, where they appear as the final books in the canon, making Cyrus' edict to rebuild the temple the final words of the Hebrew scriptures. In this literary setting, the end of Chronicles urges the faithful throughout the ages to claim their true identity, working to restore God's worship in Jerusalem: "Whoever among you belong to God's people, let them go up, and may the LORD their God be with them!" (2 Chron 36:23).

Day 1: 1 Chronicles 10:1–11:9; 28–29
The temple at the center of the community

The Chronicler abbreviates Saul's reign from twenty-three chapters (1 Sam 9–31) to a single chapter (1 Chron 10). Then he moves on to a more central interest: David and his preparations to build the temple. The account of David's rule extends for nineteen long chapters and is marked by a focused attention on Jerusalem and the temple. The importance of Jerusalem is demonstrated immediately by David's capture of the city in his first act as king (1 Chron 11). And when David's death looms in 1 Chronicles 28–29, his final words emphasize his extensive preparations for the temple that his son Solomon will build, the temple that will house the record of God's covenant with Israel (1 Chron 28:2). Thus the author emphasizes that David's rule extends far beyond the account of his reign: Future worship in the temple will be permanently marked by David's pioneering efforts, and future kings will be measured against his devotion to God's house in Jerusalem.

How important is it to have holy space, a place where people worship?

Day 2: 2 Chronicles 33–36
Return and restoration

Just as the Chronicler significantly revised the Deuteronomistic Historian's account of Saul, so the Chronicler takes the story of Manasseh from 2 Kings and reshapes it according to his specific emphases. In the book of Kings, Manasseh is Judah's worst ruler, committing serious sins regarding temple worship, leading the nation to do the same, and dying without changing his ways (2 Kgs 21). These deeds were so terrible that the Deuteronomistic Historian found in them the grounds for the exile of the nation years later (2 Kgs 24:3-4). Chronicles nuances this presentation in 2 Chronicles 33. To be sure, Manasseh commits many sins. But while being punished in exile, he seeks and receives God's forgiveness. After he is restored to the land, he spends the rest of his reign removing the foreign altars.

69

This version of Manasseh's reign stresses the immediacy of retribution, which is the same theology at the heart of the Deuteronomistic History: The king is punished for his sins, and the generation who went into exile are themselves to blame, rather than a long-dead king (2 Chron 36:6, 14-15). But the Chronicler's account also stresses the possibility of restoration: If even Manasseh can be forgiven and returned to the land, then anyone can certainly expect that they will be forgiven if they return to God. The Chronicler also highlights the significance of proper worship in Jerusalem. Second Chronicles ends, in fact, with Cyrus' edict directing the people of Judah and Jerusalem to reconstruct the temple at the center of their restored community.

When disasters occur in our country, is that a sign of God's punishment?

Day 3: Ezra 1; 2:68–6:22
Rebuilding

In response to Cyrus' edict allowing the Jews to return to Jerusalem around 539 BCE, the people set out under the leadership of Sheshbazzar (Ezra 1). He is succeeded by Jeshua (a priest) and Zerubbabel (an heir of David), who lead the people in rebuilding the altar (Ezra 3:1-6) and in laying the temple's foundation (Ezra 3:8-13). Local opposition to their work is described in Ezra 4:1-5, 24. As Zerubbabel and the community renew their attempt to rebuild the temple in Ezra 5, a report is sent by opposing forces to Darius, questioning the people's authority to undertake the reconstruction. After Darius does his own research of earlier edicts in Ezra 6, he allows the building to continue, and the people complete the temple around 520 BCE.

These chapters maintain a clear emphasis on the people's determination to rebuild the temple in Jerusalem as the focus of their new community and on the strength of the outside forces opposing this. With such a presentation, the author can highlight the temple's significance for the restored community while explaining the nearly forty-year delay in its completion.

When people are displaced by war, disaster, and famine, why are survivors so determined to rebuild?

Day 4: Ezra 7–10
Ezra continues the restoration.

About sixty years after the temple was completed, Ezra, a scribe with expert knowledge of the covenant, "the Instruction from Moses" (Ezra 7:6), obtained permission from King Artaxerxes to return with another group of Jews to Jerusalem to continue the efforts at restoration. Before setting out, Ezra received instructions from King Artaxerxes to "investigate Judah and Jerusalem according to the Instruction from your God, which is in your hand" (that is, a written record of the covenant), and to convey the empire's offering to the temple (Ezra 7:14-19). The very large donation of silver, gold, and temple equipment showcases the strong support of the Persian establishment for the temple (Ezra 8:26-27). Given the amount of opposition that the community faced, such support from the highest authorities must have been very welcome. The additional offerings from those who remained in Babylon highlight the temple's far-flung influence (Ezra 8:25).

Ezra's immediate task is to respond to the practice of intermarriage and to the larger issue of the definition and limits of the covenant community. Upon arrival, Ezra is immediately told that some have intermarried with the "peoples of the neighboring lands" (Ezra 9:1-2). Ezra's prayer judges the welfare of the people based entirely on whether they have observed the prohibition of intermarriage with the neighboring peoples. The focus on this particular covenantal responsibility alone, and the call for the expulsion of the foreign women, is disturbing. It points to the great threat that the small and vulnerable community believed they faced and to their struggle to preserve their community in the face of serious threats to its survival. Although the community acted quickly and in solidarity here, there are indications that not all members of the community supported the expulsion. Curiously, the book of Ezra never actually explicitly reports that the women were sent away. Intermarriage continues to be practiced in the time of Nehemiah (Neh 13:23), and other contemporaneous texts, such as Chronicles and Ruth, emphasize the beneficial effects that marriages with foreigners can have upon the nation. It appears that a lively debate continued in the community after the exile about how exclusive or inclusive their community should be.

Why do some groups oppose intermarriage? In addition to marriage across racial groups, what other kinds of intermarriage are often opposed by some members of a group?

Day 5: Nehemiah 1–2; 4; 7:73*b*–8:18

Nehemiah rebuilds walls; Ezra renews the covenant.

When he hears that the walls of Jerusalem were broken down, Nehemiah sets out to lead the community in making repairs (Neh 1–2; 4). As in the book of Ezra, the people face many difficulties in their efforts to rebuild Jerusalem, but they finally succeed. And when they do, they mark their success by joining together to renew the covenant under Ezra's leadership (Neh 7:73*b*–8:18). Ezra reads from the scroll that contained the covenant and God's Instruction, the Levites interpret Ezra's words to the people, and the people commit themselves to keeping the covenant (Neh 8:1-8; 10:28-29). One of their first acts is to reinstate the religious calendar of ancient Israel. The "seventh month" is the month of Tishrei (our September–October). During this month, the people gather the harvest and celebrate several religious festivals. The booths they construct commemorate the small huts of branches they made in order to stay in the fields during the harvest.

We know from other biblical books that the first day of Tishrei later became known as the New Year Festival, celebrated by the people resting from their labor, joining together, and offering sacrifices (Lev 23:33-43; Num 29:1). This feast was followed by the Day of Reconciliation (or Atonement) on the tenth day of the month, then the weeklong Festival of Booths, which began on the fifteenth day. According to Deuteronomy 31:10-13, contained in the Instruction scroll Ezra read, Moses commanded that every seventh year the Instruction be read to the people gathered for the Festival of Booths. It is probably this instruction that gave rise to the people's request that Ezra read them the teachings from God.

As they gather in the city made secure by the repaired walls, the people celebrate their ancient festivals. In so doing, the community joins with their ancestors, who marked their allegiance to God and to each other by implementing the teachings from Moses.

What festivals do you celebrate in your congregation or home, and how is scripture used in those celebrations? Which one is your favorite festival?

Day 6: 2 Chronicles 15:12-15

Covenant Meditation: Don't abandon each other!

The texts we studied this week from 1 and 2 Chronicles, Ezra, and Nehemiah are rich with details about significant individuals and events in the story of God's covenant people. As we wade into the depths and intricacies of the relationships and transitions revealed in these sacred texts, our inclination is often to retain in memory as much detail as possible to better understand what comes next in the scriptures. This is one of the many lifelong benefits of a comprehensive Bible study. We come to know more of scripture.

But as much as this week's readings instruct and inform our minds and memories, they also offer a way for God to form our hearts as people of faith. Through these readings, we also come to be more known by God. The spiritual reading practice of *lectio divina* will again serve to guide us.

First, go to a space in which you can be fully present to this reading with as few distractions as possible. Locate 2 Chronicles 15:12-15 and mark its place so that you can easily return there. Now take a few moments of quiet time to prepare your heart and life to receive this text freshly. If it helps to close your eyes and focus on your breathing, do so.

When ready, slowly read the whole text (aloud or silently). Then read it a second time, noticing the word or phrase that catches your attention or draws your energy, whether for a positive or a negative reaction. After completing the reading, return to that word or phrase and silently or quietly, perhaps with eyes closed, repeat it slowly several times.

Now read the passage a third time, with your word or phrase in mind. This time, let your thoughts engage the word or phrase. What feelings come to mind as you do so? What reactions do you have? What does your word or phrase bring to mind or spark in your imagination as you think about the whole reading? Take as much time as you need for this and for any questions that form for you. Write these down if you would like. When your thoughts begin to feel repetitive or complete, move on.

Read the passage one last time, and then offer to God all that you have thought about and wondered during this practice of sacred reading. Give God thanks for allowing the word to intersect your life today. Go in peace.

Group Meeting Experience

1 Chronicles 29:10-19 | *David's prayer*

This passage contains the Chronicler's version of David's final prayer—set before the first temple was built, but written after the exile. Knowing that the prayer was read after the exile, we will pay attention to how new concerns shape the covenant relationship between God and the people. By keeping the period of return and restoration in mind, try to answer the following questions:

1. What kind of God does David portray in his prayer? How is God's power manifested?

2. Where is God portrayed as just? Where is God portrayed as free?

3. How are human beings portrayed in this prayer? What is the role of the community?

4. Where do you see the prayer looking ahead toward the exile? Where does the author locate hope?

5. What does true restoration look like in this prayer?

6. What is the function of the temple in Jerusalem and within the restored community?

SIGNS OF FAITHFUL LOVE

After a time of loss or suffering, Covenant people
are restored to life and to our true selves when
we worship God as the center of our lives.

Apocalyptic: Daniel

HOPE
Trusting God in times of crisis

Bible Readings

Day 1: Daniel 1–2

Day 2: Daniel 3–4

Day 3: Daniel 6

Day 4: Daniel 7

Day 5: Daniel 9

Day 6: Covenant Meditation on Daniel 9:4-19

Day 7: Group Meeting Experience with Daniel 11:27-35

Covenant Prayer

For those who are harassed or imprisoned for belief in God

Turn to me, God, and have mercy on me because I'm alone and suffering. . . . Look at how many enemies I have and how violently they hate me! Please protect my life! (Psalm 25:16, 19-20a)

For liberators and peacemakers who offer hope where there is no hope

Hope in the LORD! Be strong! Let your heart take courage! Hope in the LORD! (Psalm 27:14)

OUR LONGING FOR RELATIONSHIP

We remain firm in faith, with confidence, during times when our covenant way of life is challenged or when our personal circumstances make us feel anxious, frustrated, and insecure.

APOCALYPTIC LITERATURE

The word *apocalyptic* describes a specific form of religious literature common in Jewish and Christian communities from the third century BCE through the fourth and fifth centuries CE. Although dozens of apocalyptic writings have survived from this period, only two examples are contained in the Christian Bible, namely, the books of Daniel and Revelation. Other parts of the Bible, however, are influenced by apocalyptic thought, including Isaiah 24–27, Zechariah 1–6, 12–14, and notably also the preaching of Jesus (Matt 25; Mark 13:14-36).

The apocalyptic literature in the books of Daniel and Revelation comes from communities living under the duress of foreign colonial powers, whose policies restrict their religious freedoms and even harass them for living out their covenant obligations. These books advocate faithfulness to God's covenant and resistance to the political policies that prohibit observing it. They also express fervent hope for the end of imperial control and the imminent establishment of God's kingdom. Their visions of the end of the empire oppressing them are cloaked in symbolic images that are strange and bizarre, but intended to protect the authors from the consequences of leveling such a direct critique against the ruling authorities.

These strange, symbolic visions of the end of imperial oppression in Daniel and Revelation are often misunderstood by readers today as aimed at some distant future, a future we can figure out if we try to decode these images by connecting them with nations today. In fact, the symbolic images of Daniel and Revelation were directed to the empires of the authors' own times. The divine intervention they expected was imminent, and they hoped it would radically change their own circumstances. What we can learn from these books is not a political map of our own century, but how covenant communities living in very difficult times were able to persevere and not give up hope for a better future.

DANIEL

The presence of two very different literary forms makes the book of Daniel among the most unusual books in the Old Testament. The first half of the book, Daniel 1–6, contains a series of hero stories or resistance stories in which Daniel and his friends provide models of covenant faithfulness and successful resistance to oppressive

The symbolic images of Daniel and Revelation were directed to the empires of the authors' own times.

imperial policies, even at great risk to themselves. The second half of the book, Daniel 7–12, contains three apocalyptic visions predicting the end of oppressive and ruthless human empires and the establishment of God's kingdom on earth.

On top of its two distinct literary forms, the book of Daniel has come to us in two different languages. But the language changes don't coincide with the literary changes. Daniel 1:1–2:4a and Daniel 8–12 are written in Hebrew, while Daniel 2:4b through Daniel 7 is written in Aramaic, a language closely related to Hebrew that was used for international communication at the time of Daniel, and which eventually replaced Hebrew as the common language of Palestine under Roman rule. The Apocrypha, a collection of books included in Roman Catholic, Greek, and Slavonic Bibles but not found in the Protestant Bible, contains additional material about Daniel: the stories of Susanna and of Bel and the Snake, and the Hymn of the Three Young Men. Our present book of Daniel therefore contains a selection of the "Daniel stories" that were in circulation among Jewish communities in the second century BCE.

The setting for the stories and visions in the book of Daniel is the Babylonian exile (Dan 1:1-2). Daniel is pictured as a hero resisting the Babylonian policies that threatened his covenant loyalties. But evidence in the book indicates that while these stories are set during the Babylonian exile, they were actually written for a later community during its own crisis over its life of faith. The author's memory of the Babylonian period is inexact. Neither the books of 1 and 2 Kings nor Babylonian annals record Nebuchadnezzar's attack on Jerusalem in Jehoiakim's third year (Dan 1:1). Belshazzar wasn't Nebuchadnezzar's son (Dan 5:2), and Babylon fell to Persia's King Cyrus, not to Darius the Mede (Dan 5:30-31), a figure not mentioned in the Bible or other ancient Near Eastern texts. By contrast, Daniel's author knows the history of the later Hellenistic (Greek) period very well. In Daniel 11 he recounts in detail the rise of Alexander the Great (Dan 11:3) and of the Ptolemaic kings of Egypt (Dan 11:5-8) and the Seleucid kings of Syria (Dan 11:9-20) that followed him, focusing in particular on the Seleucid king Antiochus IV (175–164 BCE; Dan 11:21-45), who was responsible for a fierce repression of the Jewish community in and around Jerusalem. This is the crisis during which Daniel was written and for which it was intended. Thus Daniel's experiences and visions of an earlier time were told by a member of the second-century Jewish community to inspire resistance and hope during their own period of oppression. Of course, the truths learned in any such crisis have a broader, universal value.

Court stories of Daniel 1–6: The intention of the stories in Daniel 1–6 is debated. If the stories are read as instructions to exiles for successful living while in exile (sometimes called the diaspora) outside of Judah and Jerusalem, then they are considered more hopeful. In fact, the stories of Daniel and his friends in the courts of kings in Daniel 1–6 seem friendlier to an empire than the visions of Daniel 7–12, which predict their violent demise. If, on the other hand, one notes the threats of horrific forms of punishment in these stories and the context of danger for the exiles practicing their covenant faith, then the stories take on a much darker tone, and they could be seen as encouraging resistance in the diaspora communities experiencing serious harassment and punishment. Recent readings of the Daniel stories are more attuned to the social and political resistance by minorities in circumstances of subordination. These readings are inspiring to the communities that suffered under the powerful colonial empires of the nineteenth and twentieth centuries CE.

> **Optional:** *An additional video on how contemporary communities identify with stories about Daniel is available for download from* **CovenantBibleStudy.com**.

Apocalyptic visions of Daniel 7–12: The symbolic visions in Daniel 7–12 are deeply concerned about making sense of the violent events of the second century during the reign of Antiochus IV (175–164 BCE). The visions express hope for a restoration of the Jewish people experiencing severe harassment (Dan 12:11-13). There are three distinct visions: Daniel 7, Daniel 8, and an extended vision in Daniel 10–12. The visions are interrupted in Daniel 9 by a prayer in which Daniel asks for God's help in the midst of a confession of sin that reviews the mistakes of Israel's past.

The Hellenistic ruler in Mesopotamia and Palestine, Antiochus IV, tried to expand his rule into Egypt but was forced to stop by Rome. In Jerusalem there was open revolt, initiated by a group within the Jewish community known as the Maccabees who thought Antiochus was in a weakened position. Antiochus IV's response was violent. Many Jews were killed or sold into slavery, and the Jerusalem temple was violated. Furthermore, the apocryphal book of 1 Maccabees indicates that there were Jews on many sides of this conflict and that they were divided into factions. The author of Daniel may well have been a member of one of these groups that self-identified as the "Maskilim," the "teachers" (or "wise ones"), who appear to be addressed in a "call to action" in Daniel 11:33-35. Their resistance was religious rather than military—and their visions were expressions of their deepest hopes for God's intervention in the conflicts.

Day 1: Daniel 1–2
The emperor's dream

Daniel 1 identifies Daniel and his three friends as members of Jerusalem's ruling class whom King Nebuchadnezzar deported to Babylon after attacking Jerusalem, and it explains how these young Judean exiles became important figures in the royal court of Babylon. This story describes Daniel and his friends' first act of civil disobedience (see Day 3): They refused to obey laws they believed would compromise their covenant obligations.

Daniel 2 describes their second great crisis. The conqueror of Jerusalem is having trouble sleeping. It isn't, apparently, out of regret for the thousands he had killed by his imperial conquests—rather, it is the result of a terrifying dream. He knows what he saw, but he doesn't know what it means. Dreams were believed to have power—even power over an emperor—and we know from ancient sources that they believed the way to break the power of a mysterious and threatening dream was to have it interpreted. Daniel, by God's inspiration, is able to advise the conqueror. And his advice? Effectively, it is to tell the king that his mighty kingdom won't be around much longer!

Each part of the great statue in this dream represents an ancient kingdom referred to elsewhere in the book of Daniel: Babylon's King Nebuchadnezzar is the head of gold (Dan 2:38), Darius the Mede is the chest of silver (Dan 5:30-31), Persia's King Cyrus is the torso of bronze (Dan 6:28), Greece's Alexander the Great is represented by the legs of iron (Dan 8:20-21), and the Ptolemies and Seleucids who followed Alexander and ruled in the author's own day are the feet of iron and clay (Dan 11). The dream predicts the demise of them all, including the Seleucids who were brutally harassing the Jews at the time that the book of Daniel was written. Daniel's message to the tyrant is our message to all conquerors, ancient and modern: Your kingdom of death can only be short-lived. God's reign of life and justice approaches!

How do you define tyrant? Who are the tyrants today?

Day 2: Daniel 3–4
The emperor's madness

Daniel 3–4 follows the same sequence as the stories in Daniel 1–2: An account of civil disobedience is followed by the king's dream symbolizing God's punishment of the empire. In Daniel 3, Daniel's three friends refuse to bow before the image of the king and his power, and they are thrown into the furnace, only to be miraculously protected by God. As in Daniel 1, they refuse to compromise their covenant obligations even when threatened by death.

> **Optional:** *An additional video retelling the story of Shadrach, Meshach, and Abednego is available for download from* **CovenantBibleStudy.com**.

The two stories in Daniel 4 must be read as interlaced. The tree hovers over the animals (the Babylonian Empire hovering over the conquered peoples) until God "frees" the animals by chopping down the tree. The story of Nebuchadnezzar's madness (he eats grass like a cow) makes sense in the context of the other story. In a classic reversal of fortune, Nebuchadnezzar must experience what it's like to be an "animal," that is, a conquered person. The resistant "humor" of oppressed peoples is often contained in such stories that change circumstances for the better. Daniel's author views the empire and its power ambiguously. It can feed and protect its people (Dan 4:10-12), but it can also become proud and abuse them (Dan 4:26-27).

What covenant obligation(s) would you refuse to compromise?

Gandhi has said that in Daniel 6 we see the greatest "passive resister" in history.

Day 3: Daniel 6
Civil disobedience

Generations of readers of Daniel have read the famous "Lion's Den" story as a story about the importance of standing firm for one's faith and about the importance of prayer. These convictions are important, but there is more to this story. When he came out of one of his first imprisonments in South Africa, Gandhi announced that in Daniel 6 we see the greatest "passive resister" (his term for nonviolent action) in history. Gandhi calls our attention to Daniel 6:10 and suggests that Daniel intentionally broke an unjust law. In fact, we can read this passage actively—that Daniel *himself* threw open the windows in order to make his prayers public! When is it important, in the words of Peter, to obey God rather than humans (Acts 5:29)?

In our culture, what are the options for disobeying the will of the majority? Are any of your faith or covenant practices considered illegal?

Day 4: Daniel 7
Fifth monarchy

The first vision of the second half of the book of Daniel picks up the "series of four" theme of Daniel 2, where four kingdoms—Babylon, Media, Persia, and Greece—follow one after the other in world history. Here, alluding to a primordial "battle" with beings from the sea, four beasts (or kingdoms), arise. They are composite creatures, mixing ferocious beasts. (The image of the fourth beast may be drawn from battle elephants; see also Dan 7:19.) The fact that they are mixed adds to the horror—especially in a context where Jews were being pressured to conform and give up their distinctive religious traditions (and thus become "mixed")! The final extraordinary beast is Antiochus IV, who attacks the Jewish community and outlaws its covenant obligations (Dan 7:25).

Optional: *An additional video on the "one like a human being" (or "Son of Man") and Jesus is available for download from* **CovenantBibleStudy.com**.

The beasts as world kingdoms leave little doubt about the political sympathies of the visionary. When God, "the ancient one" (Dan 7:9), arrives for judgment, power and authority are given over to the "one like a human being" (Dan 7:13), who descends from the clouds (as opposed to the beasts who arise from the sea). This descending figure likely represents Michael, the angelic protector of Israel and God's warrior—symbolizing God's kingdom and its ultimate victory. Christians later saw in this human figure an image of Jesus inaugurating God's kingdom. For early Christians to see Jesus in this role would have been courageous, contrasting Jesus against the violence and depravity of worldly kingdoms, in particular the Roman Empire under which they lived.

As you look at the state of the world, with one war after another between nations and empires, what role do you think Jesus plays now and in the future?

Day 5: Daniel 9
Daniel's prayer

Daniel 9 is an interesting interlude in a series of bizarre visions, and it is an example of prayer that became standard in Jewish communities after the exile. It is known as the "Penitential Prayer" (compare Ezra 9 and Neh 9). At the heart of this type of prayer was a confession that the events of the exile—and the continued life of diaspora outside Judah and occupation within Judah—was "our fault" because their ancestors had listened to the kings rather than the prophets and had disobeyed the covenant commandments (presumably alluding to the warnings in Deut 28 to cast them out of the land). This type of prayer appears in books separated by hundreds of years (including the very late apocryphal book of Baruch), and thus it was practiced for a long time. The prayer is not only a summary of history, but also a warning to observe covenant obligations and not to take chances with ignoring God's instructions in the future! These prayers remind us of the proper way forward by not repeating the mistakes of the past.

Should our prayers confess historical mistakes by a whole group of people more often?

Day 6: Daniel 9:4-19
Covenant Meditation: Trusting the covenant

Our devotional practice today will return us to one of the most essential and life-giving means by which to engage God's word. We will pray the scripture, or, more precisely, we will invite the scripture to become a prayer in us. With our week's theme of "Hope," especially when confronted by destructive political or institutional powers, prayer that arises from God's word is prayer grounded in God's hope.

Find a place in which you can be as undisturbed and quiet as possible for this reading time. Turn to Daniel 9:4-19, and mark this reading so that you can easily find it after a minute or two of silent prayer. In this silent prayer time, ask God to help you to be open to this reading in new ways and to remove any distractions from your thoughts that might interfere with your encounter and response to this text. After your silent prayer, slowly read Daniel 9:4-19, attending to each word and phrase.

When you have finished the reading, return to the text and choose one phrase or verse from the prayer that catches your attention for any reason. As best you can, resist analyzing your selection, but try instead to receive the phrase as a prayer for you. Use the phrase or verse to create your own one-sentence prayer. This selection can be exactly as it is translated in your reading, or you may want to develop your own short prayer. For example, if Daniel 9:9 is what catches your attention, your prayer might be: "Thank you, God, for your compassion and deep forgiveness." Take a few minutes to find and create your prayer out of this scripture. Write it down, and then, in silence or aloud, repeat your prayer a few times now and, if possible, off and on throughout the day. This is a prayer for your life arising from your encounter with God's word. Through this practice, we are trusting God's covenant of hope through our prayers.

Group Meeting Experience

Daniel 11:27-35 | *What about apocalyptic visions?*

While many Christians have read the apocalyptic books of Daniel and Revelation as political maps of the contemporary world and as codes to unlock the secrets of the end time, these books actually describe attempts by ancient covenant communities to live faithfully under government regimes that forced them to compromise their values and loyalty to their faith.

1. How does this text about the policies and exploits of the Seleucid king Antiochus IV describe the exercise of political power? Compare this portrait of him with the one you read in Daniel 7 (Day 4).

2. How does the portrait of political power in these visions compare or contrast with the way royal power is exercised in the stories you read in Daniel 1–6 (Days 1–3)? Do the portraits of power in Daniel teach us anything about the exercise of power in today's world? In what ways do governments today ask occupied peoples or their own citizens to compromise their religious values?

3. The "people's teachers" in this text (Dan 11:33, 35) may represent a group of faithful Jews of which the author of Daniel was a member. How do they appear to respond to political oppression?

4. Compare the "teachers'" response to political repression with the response of Daniel and his friends in the stories of Daniel 1–6. How does the author of Daniel view civil disobedience? What are the merits of this approach over the armed resistance of the Maccabees (described in the Old Testament Apocrypha books of 1 and 2 Maccabees)? How do we respond to political power today that we believe compromises our religious values?

5. The visions of Daniel about the end of an empire and its repressive policies are meant to provide hope for a covenant community in distress. How do visions about the just rule of God provide power to endure suffering and to remain faithful to God's covenant?

SIGNS OF FAITHFUL LOVE

We show loyal love and compassion to anyone who is
harassed or oppressed, just as we remain faithful in our relationship
with God when our commitments are unpopular or inconvenient.

Revelation

NEW CREATION
Trusting God, who makes all things new

Bible Readings

Day 1: Revelation 1–3

Day 2: Revelation 4:1–8:1

Day 3: Revelation 12–14

Day 4: Revelation 15–17

Day 5: Revelation 19–22

Day 6: Covenant Meditation on Revelation 7:9-17

Day 7: Group Meeting Experience: Our covenant

Covenant Prayer

For all who are endangered and harassed because of their faith

Because you kept my command to endure, I will keep you safe through the time of testing that is about to come. (Revelation 3:10)

For all who teach nonviolence and live for peace in the world

You have heard that it was said, You must love your neighbor and hate your enemy. But I say to you, love your enemies and pray for those who harass you so that you will be acting as children of your Father who is in heaven. (Matthew 5:43-45)

OUR LONGING FOR RELATIONSHIP

The world seems full of enemies and hostility. Evil acts in our communities make us fearful and challenge our courage to endure as Christ's followers.

85

BOOK OF REVELATION

The book of Revelation can be a very confusing book. So it's not surprising that many readers have misunderstood its imagery and warnings, which can result in bizarre predictions as well as disastrous consequences for gullible believers who followed a false leader. We proceed then with a sense of humility and awe as we examine an imaginative call to be faithful witnesses. We are urged through this book to inhabit a renewed heaven and earth and to become citizens of the New Jerusalem (Rev 21:1-2).

Revelation is written by a seer named John (Rev 1:1). For a variety of reasons, it's unlikely that this is the same author who wrote John's Gospel or 1, 2, and 3 John. The author identifies himself as a prophet. He assumes pastoral authority over churches in seven particular cities, and he is the recipient of a mystical vision of Jesus. Revelation was written during the reign of either Emperor Nero (54–68 CE) or Domitian (81–96 CE). When Revelation was written, there was little historical evidence that the entire Roman Empire was engaged in the systematic harassment and killing of early Christians. However, a regional repression probably did occur.

The residents of Roman Asia viewed their rulers as worthy recipients of religious honors. The rulers assumed or were granted the status of divine or semi-divine beings. This kind of emperor worship caused regional and local officials, as well as neighbors, to put pressure on Christians to conform to intolerable religious customs. Additionally, all seven cities in Revelation 2–3 were official sites recognized for emperor worship between 30 BCE and 130 CE. This tradition of granting allegiance to the emperor, to Caesar, would have seemed normal to most people. Anyone who refused to take part would have been seen as rebellious. Christian monotheism prohibited Christians from easily participating in worship of the ruler, making Christians open to ridicule and harassment.

In 1 Corinthians, the apostle Paul gives advice to Christians about whether it is acceptable to eat meat that was, before it was purchased, offered to idols. This raises issues of accommodation, especially when Christians need a meal. Compare Paul's advice about dealing with religious customs in 1 Corinthians 8–10 to John's dilemma over accepting the authority of local leaders who obey the emperor.

Apocalypse: The book of Revelation has actually become the name of an entire type of literature. The first word of the book is *apokalupsis*, a revelation or disclosure of hidden heavenly truths. An apocalypse often includes: (1) a vision of a new world order; (2) a heavenly mediator; (3) a human seer of high repute; (4) writing offered under the name or byline of a hero from the past (meaning that the author is "pseudonymous"); (5) a reimagination of traditions; (6) "prophecy-after-the-fact"; (7) history as predetermined and human society as dualistic; (8) holy numbers to convey meaning; and (9) origins in a marginalized or disenfranchised group. Other apocalyptic writings from this era include Daniel 7–12 in the Old Testament (see Episode 23) and several books from the Old Testament Apocrypha, including 2 Esdras (also called 4 Ezra), 2 Baruch, and 1 Enoch.

Revelation varies from the pattern because it wasn't written under a pseudonym. The writer describes it as a prophecy (not an apocalypse), and it has the features of a letter, which aren't found in other apocalypses. So Revelation is a mix of three genres: apocalypse, letter, and prophecy.

Revelation is meant to be heard. It's a very noisy book. Thus many hymns and poems are based on it. It's also visually powerful. Revelation has inspired the world's most admired visual artists (and some of that art scrolls across the Covenant table for this video episode). Much of the imagery is bizarre and fantastic, but it's meant to excite all the senses and stoke the imagination. Sometimes imagination is the gift God expects us to rely upon most heavily when we find ourselves in territory that is unsafe and uncomfortable.

Purpose: The purpose of the book of Revelation is to lead God's people on a final spiritual exodus to the New Jerusalem. Along the way, Christians must remain firm in their practices and fight evil with a faithful witness. Christians must never lose hope, no matter how bleak the trouble and social circumstances.

Christians never give up because God Almighty is the creator and Lord of the universe. God shares divine authority with Christ (Rev 2:28). God and Christ control history (Rev 1:4, 8, 17). Both are worshipped (Rev 5:13). Both protect the saints (Rev 7:14-17). Both reign in the New Jerusalem (Rev 21:22-27). Both are trustworthy and true (Rev 19:11; 21:5). God Almighty will dwell with the saints who reach the New Jerusalem (Rev 21).

Revelation offers a distinctive understanding of the Messiah, who is defined by the crucifixion. Christ is the slain Lamb. In Revelation 5, John weeps when no one is found worthy to open the scroll. Unless someone opens the scroll, God's plan can't come to fruition. An angel tells John that the Lion of the tribe of Judah is worthy to

The purpose of the book of Revelation is to lead God's people on a final spiritual exodus to the New Jerusalem.

open the scroll. The "Lion of Judah" is a metaphor for the Davidic messiah. However, when John turns he sees not a lion but a lamb. Additionally, the lamb isn't an adult, and the lamb appears to have been slain. This description of the slain Lamb upends Jewish messianic expectations, found in the apocalypses outside the New Testament. For example, 4 Ezra 11–12 presents the messiah as a conqueror, symbolized by a lion. The lion defeats God's enemies and establishes God's kingdom in 4 Ezra. The lamb in Revelation also conquers, but he conquers by dying.

The transformation of the lion into a slain lamb gave Asian Christians a way to understand and withstand their suffering—by following Christ's example. Revelation 1:2; 6:9; 12:11; and 20:4 should be read with this understanding, because victims are transformed into victors (for example, Rev 1:5-6; 5:9-10; 12:11; 19:13; 20:4).

Christ's primary function is to lead the Christian community on a spiritual exodus to the New Jerusalem (for example, Rev 2–3; 7:9-17; 14:1-5; 21:9–22:5). Christ provides benefits for the Christian community. Christ's death brings salvation to the faithful and gathers persons from every ethnic group (compare Eph 2:11-22). While the gathered community is often depicted as a holy army (Rev 14:1-5; 19:14), there is no narrative of a battle. This military imagery symbolizes the difficulty of maintaining Christian practices in an environment hostile to Christian commitments (compare Eph 6:10-20; Matt 10:16-23; Heb 4:12). The true peace of God will remain in the New Jerusalem, devoid of death, sorrow, disease, and pain. It will be perfect forever.

Day 1: Revelation 1–3

John is called.

Revelation 1–3 opens the apocalypse in a unique manner. The presentation of the prophet's visionary call is typical, but the instruction to write to specific contemporary churches (actually delivered by angels to those churches) is unique. These seven messages convey to those particular seven churches what each must do in order to reach the final destination, the New Jerusalem.

The vision described in Revelation 1:12-20 relates directly to the churches. The vision isn't an abstract, otherworldly idea that has little relevance to everyday life. The vision has no meaning apart from the life of the gathered Christian community, then and now. The letters are written to churches, not individuals. To persevere through tough social and political chaos, we do it together, gathered as the church.

As you read each of the seven letters, you will notice a pattern:

1. Jesus affirms praiseworthy strengths of the congregation;

2. Jesus points to areas of weakness in the church;

3. Jesus tells them how to get back on track;

4. and Jesus, like the biblical prophets, describes the negative consequences if they fail and the rewards if they succeed.

Fill out the chart, showing this pattern for each of the seven churches. Ephesus is filled in as an example.

	Praise	Weakness	Remedy	Reward
Ephesus	endurance	lost first love	change heart and life	paradise
Smyrna				
Pergamum				
Thyatira				
Sardis				
Philadelphia				
Laodicea				
My church				

Can you fill in the chart for your own church? Which church of Revelation, if any, is most like your own?

Day 2: Revelation 4:1–8:1
Opening the scroll

Revelation 4 contains a vision of God Almighty being worshipped in the heavenly court. The next chapter introduces a scroll (books with pages appeared after the Bible was written) that must be opened in order to put God's plan for the end of human history in motion. Only the slain Lamb is deemed worthy to open the scroll. The worthiness of the Lamb has come from his sacrificial death, not through military or political power. The Lamb's faithfulness provides a model for Christians to follow (compare Rev 20:4).

The opening of the seven seals launches the divine plan. The apocalyptic visions of Revelation 4–20 represent different versions of a single narrative. This is typical of an apocalypse. However, the repetition gives a novice reader the impression that there are multiple revelations. It's all one revelation. You will often hear people refer to "Revelations" as if it were plural, but that's incorrect. For example, the numbered visions of seals, trumpets, and bowls demonstrate how the intensity of the judgment is growing with each judgment. As another example of emphasis, in Revelation 7:17 and 21:4, God wipes the tears from the faces of the saints.

How is the transformation of the Lion into a Lamb a reversal of human expectations? Are there current or recent Christian movements with militaristic emphases that disagree with this example of the Lamb? Are there contemporary instances in our world where lambs have a more powerful effect than lions?

Day 3: Revelation 12–14
Defeating evil

Revelation 12 presents three visions about the struggle between good and evil. The first vision, Revelation 12:1-6, presents a pregnant woman. In this vision she symbolizes the Virgin Mary and the child Jesus. Satan's harassment of the woman and her child parallels the duress that Asian Christians experienced on earth at that time. The visions in Revelation 7–12 and 13–17 express in different ways this same hatred between Satan and the Christian community. Christians are not only assured of victory, but they are told how to achieve it through a faithful witness, even if it means dying for the faith (Rev 12:11). In fact, Revelation houses the earliest evidence of the use of the word *martyr* in the practical sense of dying for the faith. The Greek word *martyr* means "a witness" or "one who testifies."

While the two beasts of Revelation 13 represent Roman control on land and sea, Revelation 14 presents the Lamb and his heavenly military forces as celibate soldiers purified for battle (compare purity before battle in 1 Sam 21:4-5). However, in chapters 12 and 14, the saints don't engage in a military battle to defeat Satan. Rather, they conquer by means of their witness and their purity (see Rev 12:11; 14:5, 12-13).

You may have heard references to "the one hundred forty-four thousand." This text (Rev 14:3) understandably raises questions for readers. No women are included in the 144,000. In fact, women appear only as agents of defilement in chapter 14, and women are not portrayed in positive terms throughout the whole book of Revelation (compare Rev 17).

Though Revelation contains violent images, and certain interpreters have popularized military implications for the scroll, the message never calls Christians to violence. The slain Lamb calls Christians to nonviolent resistance against an oppressive society or ruler. Revelation teaches us that we are called to faithfully testify and persevere despite the costs. We may not always have the power to change our circumstances or the ability to prevent violence toward us and others, but even then we can choose to act faithfully.

How does Jesus defeat evil today? What particular form of evil concerns you? How do you partner with God in relieving pain and suffering?

Day 4: Revelation 15–17
Seven plagues

While Revelation 15 announces the final numbered series, the series itself begins in chapter 16. This series depicts total destruction of the haughty, power-drunk Roman Empire (symbolized as Babylon, the empire that was the oppressor of the Israelites in the sixth century BCE). Revelation 17 uses the imagery of a prostitute (compare Hos 1–3) as code language for those who know the traditions about the coming end of an oppressive empire.

The woman in Revelation 17 represents the city of Rome as a diabolical power. Rome was and is still known as "the city of seven hills" (see Rev 17:9). Here the heads, mountains, and horns represent Roman rulers. In Episode 23, we noted that a similar imagination is tapped in Daniel 7–11 to describe the empires that oppressed and devastated Israel with exile in the sixth through second centuries BCE. In Revelation, those who cooperate with the empire politically and economically are depicted as irredeemable and are described by means of disturbing violent and sexual metaphors. The author has no sympathy for those who benefit from their relationship with Rome.

The book of Revelation reflects the practice of civil disobedience by resisting the government and the surrounding culture, by naming its injustices and refusing to cooperate and perpetuate the injustice. Revelation assured late first-century Christians that suffering wasn't a result of their unfaithfulness, but rather of their witness and faithfulness. Firm, faithful endurance through suffering results from following the example of Jesus, and that eventually leads to the community's ultimate victory. The crucifixion and the resurrection of Jesus redefined victory for the Christian community and showed God's methods to be opposed to those of Caesar and his empire.

Compare the instruction given in Revelation regarding the relationship between the church and government with the advice given by Paul in Romans 13 or 1 Peter. How does your church bear witness, remain faithful, and help Christ to defeat evil?

Day 5: Revelation 19–22
Final destination

Evil is defeated three times in Revelation 19–20. In the first instance, Christ vanquishes the beast and imprisons him in "the fiery lake that burns with sulfur" (Rev 19:20). In the second, an angel binds Satan for a thousand years (Rev 20:1-4). Finally, Christ defeats Satan and throws him "into the lake of fire and sulfur . . . forever and always" (Rev 20:10).

Now that evil has been defeated permanently, it is time for the New Jerusalem, the final destination of the faithful, to descend to earth. Death, mourning, pain, or anything that prevents abundant life has no place there (Rev 21:4). Moreover, the faithful will be in direct communication with God. An intermediary is no longer necessary. Finally, God will personally console God's people: God "will wipe away every tear from their eyes" (Rev 21:4).

What aspect of your life would you hope to see restored in the New Jerusalem?

Look! I'm making all things new. (Rev 21:5)

Day 6: Revelation 7:9-17

Covenant Meditation: Making us new

As we conclude the Covenant episodes, the theme "New Creation" guides us back to the spiritual reading practice of engaging our imaginations. Revelation presents to us a vision of God's renewed creation. It transforms our hearts and lives, and by God's grace we are equipped through faithful witness in Jesus Christ to help fulfill God's covenantal promises.

But this future, this new creation, is not yet complete. We can't see or experience all that God intends for us and future generations. God continues to make "all things new" in our midst (Rev 21:5). Christ "was and is and is coming" (Rev 4:8*b*). We are still growing and changing in faith, witness, and trust as Christians of the current age who are committed to help the world be transformed by God's love. By using our God-given gift of imagination, we can draw more deeply from the word, testifying to the future that God intends and in which we are called to participate.

For today's reading practice, first move to a place that is quiet, with as few distractions as possible. Before reading, take a moment to prayerfully prepare so that you can approach the scripture as though you have never read it before. Now turn to Revelation 7:9-17.

Read these verses slowly, aloud or silently. Try to put yourself in the scene as the elder who asks the question in Revelation 7:13. Imagine what you see when the great crowd first appears. What do the people look like? What do the languages sound like? What is your first reaction to the crowd that is gathering in front of you? Why do you ask John this particular question? How do you feel when John's response to you is that "you know" (Rev 7:14) who the people are?

Imagine how you feel as you speak about the hardship these people have experienced. What hardships have you witnessed that come to mind as you read this text? Where have you witnessed the need of God's people for shelter and protection that is promised here? Who needs the "springs of life-giving water" (Rev 7:17) today, and what is this water? Whose tears do you pray that God will wipe away? How do you imagine God wiping away these tears? As you close this reading time, offer a prayer of gratitude for God's covenant promise in which you have a part.

Group Meeting Experience

Our covenant

Your group will share a meal and something each person has learned that will help you live together as Covenant people. What did *covenant* mean to you when you started? What does it mean now?

Your leader will also facilitate a time of commitment and prayer. Come prepared to share a story or memory of your time together and what steps you can take to help each other continue on the path of faithful life in Jesus. More concretely, think of the gifts and graces you see in the people in your group. How have they blessed your life? How have they challenged you? What will you do to stay connected to them?

SIGNS OF FAITHFUL LOVE

We put our hope and trust in Christ's ultimate victory over evil. We go into our communities to alleviate suffering and do all the good that we can.

Well done!

You have completed the third and final participant guide, *Trusting the Covenant*. You studied daily from scripture about the importance of trusting God even when the world comes apart. And in your Covenant group, you discovered the gifts and graces of friends for life. You will not be the same!

Your daily habit for reading scripture will continue to shape your life in powerful ways. The relationships you have formed will last into eternity. And you are empowered to share some of what you have learned through service to your church, community, and world.

The Bible is a conversation partner for life. While you can never plumb all of its depths, you have found a way to make sense of the big ideas that create a pattern for a living response to God's faithful love. God's call and promise—that you belong to a place and people who share your mission to help the hurting and the lost—has never been more clear in your life. Now is the time to discover how God's unique design of your gifts and passions will help you live as a committed disciple of Jesus Christ.

You will want to visit CovenantBibleStudy.com and explore some of the tools for plotting your part in God's ongoing salvation story. God's plan for restoring the world has you cast in a leading role!